Roger Miller

by Don Cusic

Roger Miller

Dang Him!

A Biography

by Don Cusic

Cover Design & Layout:

Wendy Mazur, Oddball Group

Production Coordinator:

Jim Sharp, Sharpmanagement

Table of Contents

Acknowledgements

Roger Miller left a lot of great stories and memories with those who knew him and, in doing this book, I have benefitted from them. First, I must thank his widow, Mary Miller, who gave me the go-ahead and invaluable help. I owe a huge thanks to Roger's son, Dean Miller, who told me great stories about growing up with his Dad. The Roger Miller Museum in Erick, Oklahoma, hosts Roger Miller Days and I attended several. Martha Holt Nichols is the "family historian" and she gave me valuable help with the Miller and Holt family trees.

I would also like to thank the following people who spoke with me about Roger Miller: Barry Coburn, Bayron Binkley, Bill Anderson, Bill Ivey, Billy Burnett, Billy Strange, Billy Swan, Bob Moore, Bobby Bare, Bobby Braddock, Taylor Strong, Bud Keathley, Buddy Killen, Buzz Cason, Charlie Dick, Charlie Fach, Chuck Blore, Curly Putnam, Dennis Morgan, Don Lago, Don Williams, Doug Gilmore, Eldon Hendrix, Fred Foster, Gail Davies, George Hamilton IV, George "Goober" Lindsay, Harold Bradley, Hugh Prather, James Best, James Crow, Jan Howard, Jerry Kennedy, Jimmy Bowen, Jimmy Dean, Jimmy Key, Joe Allison, John D. Loudermilk, Joy Brookshire, Vince Gill, Kris Kristofferson, Lou Dennis, Marijohn Wilkins, Marshall Chapman, Martha Holt Nichols, Mel Tillis, Micheal Smotherman, Mickey Raphael, Millie Kirkham, John Thomas, Otto Kittsinger, Pat Henry, Phyllis Forsythe, Ralph Emery, Randy Hart, Ray Price, Ray Stevens, Robert Oermann, Rocco Landesman, Roger "Captain Midnight" Schutt, Shari Miller Standridge, Shawn Camp, Shelby Singleton, Stan Moress, Tony Conway, Glenda West and Wendall Miller. A special thanks to Jim Sharp for layout and Wendy Mazur for the cover of this book.

I did research at the following archives: The Frist Library and Archive at the Country Music Hall of Fame, the Nashville Room at the Nashville Public Library, the Margaret Herrick Library at the Academy of Motion Picture Arts and Sciences Fairbanks, Center for Motion Picture Studio in Los Angeles, the Paley Center for Media in Los Angeles and the British Library in London, England.

Introduction

"Dang me, they oughta take a rope and hang me"
                                                    Roger Miller

Roger Miller was an American Genius. He proved it as a songwriter, writing hit songs, a standard ("King of the Road") and winning Grammys and Tonys. He also proved his genius with his wit and humor.

Part of Roger's humor came from the way he said things; his humor snuck up on you. It came out of left field and was a humor that bounced off what someone else said or did. It wasn't just a joke, it was a reaction. And part of Roger's humor was Roger himself; he loved to laugh and had as much fun saying funny things as the listener did hearing funny things.

On October 4, 1995 at the Twenty-ninth Annual Country Music Association Awards, Roger Miller was inducted into the Country Music Hall of Fame. Sadly, he did not make the Hall of Fame during his lifetime; he died three years before, almost to the day.

The show was hosted by Vince Gill, who won his fifth consecutive "Male Vocalist" honor that evening. Alan Jackson was named "Entertainer of the Year" and Alison Krauss took home three awards. There were performances by Shania Twain, Alan Jackson, Patty Loveless, Dwight Yoakam, Trisha Yearwood, John Michael Montgomery, George Strait, Reba McEntire, Martina McBride, Linda Davis, The Mavericks, Mary Chapin Carpenter, George Jones and Tammy Wynette, John Berry, Alison Krauss and Union Station, Russ Taff, David Ball, Faith Hill, Vince Gill, Pam Tillis, and Dolly Parton before it was Roger's turn.

After Vince Gill and Dolly performed "I Will Always Love You," Dolly began Roger's induction into the Hall of Fame. She noted she met Roger when he did a guest appearance on "The Porter Wagoner Show," then introduced Willie Nelson, who had been inducted into the Hall of Fame in 1993. Willie, with long, flowing hair, sang a verse of "Old Friends," a song Roger recorded with him and Ray Price, then noted that

"Roger used to say about my phrasing that I flushed to a different plumber." There was a clip of Roger singing "In the Summertime," then Dolly told the story of Roger and Norro Wilson back in 1958 selling Bibles door to door for two days. When asked why they quit, Roger said, "The Lord called us out of it."

Dwight Yoakam performed a verse and chorus of "It Only Hurts When I Cry," a song he and Roger wrote, and stated that on the recording session for that song he told Roger that it looked like he was on a diet. Roger replied, "I'm trying to get back to my original weight—seven pounds and ten ounces." Roger told Dwight and the crew that he was from Erick, Oklahoma and when Dwight asked, "What's that near?" Roger replied, "It's close to extinction. The population is 1500 and that includes rakes and tractors." Also during that session Roger was asked for his driver's license for the Musicians Union time card; Roger replied, "How fast was I singing?"

There was a clip of Roger fiddling before Marty Stuart took the stage and sang a verse of "You Can't Roller Skate in a Buffalo Herd." Roger loved scat singing—and making weird noises with his mouth like a jazz instrumentalist doing improvisational riffs. There was a video clip of Roger scat singing before Marty said "I had recorded my first album and was starving waiting for it to come out and Roger said, 'I've been noticing the buzzards circling your career—you might need a job'" and then invited Marty to join his band. Roger also said to Marty, "I can see your career is gaining momentum, as everything does when its going downhill" but Marty's "favorite Roger witticism was when he walked up to blind singer Ronnie Milsap, put his hands over his ears and said 'Guess who?'"

There were clips from Roger's Memorial Service, held just after he died in 1992, of Chet Atkins, Kris Kristofferson, Mel Tillis and Waylon Jennings, then a clip of Roger singing "Muddy Water" from the Big River score.

Dolly introduced a video clip of actor John Goodman, who played "Pap" on the Broadway run of the musical *Big River*, who said he asked Roger how a country songwriter could get involved in a Broadway musical. Roger replied "I'd never even read *Huckleberry Finn* but Rocco made me an offer I couldn't understand." This was followed by a clip of Roger singing "Guv-ment," the song he wrote for *Big River* that John Goodman originally sang. (Roger played the role of "Pap" after Goodman left the cast.)

Dolly stated that Roger, "like all of us" was vain and once said "Did you ever notice a chicken can gain weight and it never shows in their face?"

Merle Haggard came on and sang a verse of "Engine, Engine Number 9," followed by a series of clips showing Roger singing "Dang Me," "Husbands and Wives," "Chug-a-Lug" and "Do Wacka Do."

Dolly then introduced "the song that made Roger Miller a country music icon." As Roger performed "King of the Road" on a rear screen, Merle Haggard, Dwight Yoakam, Marty Stuart, Willie Nelson and Dolly Parton all came on stage and joined in singing "King of the Road" with him.

Dolly invited Merle Haggard to present Roger's Hall of Fame plaque and Merle introduced "former First Edition artist and the love of his life, his beautiful wife, Mary Miller."

Mary held Roger's plaque close and told the audience, "Roger was a dreamer and this would have been his wildest dream come true, the ultimate recognition of his songwriting and musical artistry. If he were here tonight I know he'd want to thank his children, Alan and Rhonda, Shari and Shannon and our son, Dean for carrying on the Miller musical tradition and our son Adam and our daughter Taylor for their unconditional love and hugs and kisses. And I know he'd want to thank his mother, Laudene Burdine for passing her funny bone along to him. And all his fans and friends who stuck with him even though he was eccentric and unorthodox and, as he said '20 minutes ahead of his time.' And I'd like to thank him for a wonderful life together. His genius will live on with many of us for a long time, so thank you CMA for this wonderful moment. Our family will never forget it."

After this, Jo Walker-Meador, the former Executive Director of the Country Music Association, received her induction into the Hall of Fame.

No one could ever doubt that Roger Miller was funny. No, wait, he was more than that. Roger Miller was incredibly laugh out loud until your face hurt and your sides ached funny. Those who knew Roger remember his wit, his humor, his snappy come-backs and one liners that made you laugh so long and so hard that you could hardly catch your breath.

This book could be filled with Roger's funny sayings although, oddly enough, a lot of people remember that Roger was funny but can't remember exactly what it was he said that was so funny. Or they can only remember a line or two.

*Roger walked into a room and up to the wall thermostat and exclaimed, "I've lost 80 pounds!'"

*Roger watching the sun come up: "Here comes God with his brights on."

*Roger looking at the Grand Canyon: "Just think what God could do if he had money."

*Roger asked a young child "How old are you?" The child replied, "Six." Roger, looking directly at the child, said "When I was your age I was nine."

*Roger to an audience: "I'd like to do something from my younger days. I'd like to starve to death for you."

*Roger on his home town: "Our town was so small we didn't have a town drunk. We had to take turns."

*Talking about the flat, nearly treeless area in Oklahoma where he grew up, Roger said "Where I come from was back-woodsy, but there wasn't no woodsy."

*To Johnny Carson on "The Tonight Show": "I do a lot of different things. Someday I'll come on your show and drive a tractor."

*After he got into a van where the air conditioning wasn't working, "Is it hot in here or is my career taking off again?"

*"The town where I grew up was so small that we held a parade and there was nobody to watch."

*"My mother's cooking was so bad that the flies took up a collection to fix the screen."

*(About his mother's cooking). "Every year the natives from South

America would come up and dip their arrows in her gravy."

*"There was a Japanese Jewish gardener and every December seventh he bombed Pearl Schwartz."

*Someone asked Roger, "Did you ever pick cotton?" Roger replied, "I'd pick my nose for a dollar."

*At a fancy party, Roger put a can of Coke to his forehead and the soft drink ran down his face as everyone turned to watch. When the can was empty, Roger took it down and said, "I thought I was taller than that."

*Roger told friends he had a pet parrott "and taught him how to 'soft-claw'"

*Roger, showing why a crab swam sideways, said with his elbows out imitating old time song and dance men "so they can sing 'There's no business like show business'"

*"Old songwriters never die. They just decompose."

*Speaking of someone that everyone wanted to avoid, "He'd turn a funeral up an alley."

Roger Miller was filled with nervous energy and could go for hours entertaining a crowd, making funny off the cuff comments and playing songs. Roger loved to be the center of attention, loved to be surrounded by people who laughed at his jokes and loved his songs. One of the things that made him so funny and entertaining was that he was entertained too; he laughed at his own jokes and funny lines. Roger Miller loved to laugh, loved to have fun and wanted to make other people laugh and have fun.

In his book *The Outliers*, author Malcolm Gladwell states that it takes 10,000 hours of practice for someone to become an expert. Well, Roger spent 10,000 hours and then some practicing being funny. His mind was constantly playing with words, turning phrases, laughing at himself. His mind was constantly active, constantly busy, always "on" to find a new way of looking at something, a new phrase to say, a new way to get a laugh, a new idea for a song, another angle to view life. Roger thrived on being different, on being unique. He worked at being different, although he never thought of it as work. Roger hated work; he wanted to have fun and spending hours making up funny things and playing with words was his idea of fun.

But there was more to Roger than just being funny; he had depth and he had hurts. That was a side of Roger that most people never saw. Roger was moody, could be obstinate and difficult, but for most of his life, he entertained the people who were around him.

One thing that everyone agrees on: Roger Miller was a genius. Knowledge can be acquired by anyone but genius is for the chosen few. Genius is an inborn talent; geniuses absorb their influences. Roger Miller never went to college—he did not even finish high school—and was never known to read books or study a subject but his genius was evident to those who knew his songs and those who enjoyed his witticisms and observations on life. Genius is not bound by precedent, direction or fences; it is original and all its own. If there is a consensus about Roger Miller it is that he was a one of a kind, unique, original individual. There was no one else like him.

Chapter 1
The Millers and the Holts

It was like a fist slammed hard into your belly. The Great Depression and the Dust Storms took the wind out of folks in Oklahoma and Texas during the 1930s. In Erick, Oklahoma the worst was Black Sunday, April 14, 1935 when a dust storm turned the bright day dark as night and filled the sky full of blowing sand. There was sand everywhere and into every-thing—cracks in houses and barns—and if you were outside in the wind that sand felt like millions of sharp pins being driven into you.

Jean Miller was born March 22, 1909 in Cauthron, Arkansas, on the western side of the state, close to the Oklahoma state line. He fell in love with Laudene Holt, born September 5, 1913 in Pecan Gap, Texas and used to walk her home from school. He told her "one day we're going to marry" and she said, "O.K." Both had eighth grade educations "because nobody went beyond the eighth grade back then."

In 1929 Jean Miller moved to Fort Worth, Texas where he obtained a job driving a truck for the Swift Meat Company; he was also a catcher on the Fort Worth Cats baseball team, a minor league team affiliated with the Brooklyn Dodgers. After he landed his job with the Swift Meat Company, Jean sent a letter to Laudene stating "I aim to come get you to marry you." Jean kept his word; on October 5, 1929 Jean and Laudene Miller were married in Cauthron. Jean was 19; Laudene had turned 16 a month before their wedding. Later, Laudene told relatives that she agreed to marry Jean because "I wasn't doing anything else at the time" and "I'd never seen the other side of Poteau Mountain, so I thought going to Texas was exciting." [1]

By the end of 1935, Jean and Laudene Miller had two young sons, Dwayne and Wendall and Laudene was pregnant again. On January 2, 1936, their third son, Roger Dean Miller was born in Fort Worth. They named him after two great St. Louis baseball players. Rogers Hornsby and Dizzy Dean both played for the St. Louis Cardinals during their heyday, but Hornsby was a player manager for the St. Louis Browns while Dizzy Dean still pitched for the Cardinals when Roger was born. Times were tough but Jean had a pretty good job with Swift in addition to his baseball career so they were doing O.K. But things took a turn for the worse early the following year when Jean Miller came home from work one day and told Laudene, "My head hurts so bad I don't think I can stand it." Laudene gave him some aspirin but, a little later, Jean said "I just can't stand it anymore." He was taken to the hospital where he died of spinal meningitis on March 2, 1937; he was 26 years old. He was buried in Mount Olivet Cemetery in Fort Worth.

Jean left behind a 23-year old widow who was six months pregnant with their fourth child, a daughter, but Laudene miscarried after his death. Laudene had never worked outside the home and had three young boys. Laudene did not know the ways of the world and wondered how in the world she would be able to raise her three boys; there was even the thought of putting them all in an orphanage until she could get on her feet. For a while she sold flowers in downtown Fort Worth, after she found a boarding house that would keep the children while she worked.

Jean Miller had five brothers; Elmer, Luther, Rowe, Emmett, Omer and one sister, Margie May. (Another brother, Lou, died as an infant.) Shortly after Jean died, one of the brothers—Luther—moved in with Laudene. "He just came out of the blue one day and moved in with her," said Martha Holt Nichols, who was Laudene's cousin. "He slept on the sofa. She never knew if Luther was sent as a 'spy' but it was a bad situation."

In Cauthron the Millers "owned hundreds of acres and raised chickens" but the Great Depression took its toll and the family scattered, looking for work. Omer remained in Arkansas but Elmer (known as "E.D.") moved to Erick, Oklahoma, a small town on Route 66 about 150 miles west of Oklahoma City and seven miles east of the Texas state line.[2]

In 1938 E.D. and Omer drove their pickup truck down to Laudene's home in Fort Worth and picked up the three boys. "Elmer was the patriarch of the family," remembered Wendall. "They thought of those boys as 'Millers' and not as 'Holts' so they put us in that pick-up truck and drove us back to Oklahoma. My mother was 23 years old and had been sheltered her whole life and she didn't know anything about the law or that she had a right to keep us. She thought it was just temporary—and she really had no way to support us because the government wouldn't give us any help then. So the Millers took us away: Dwayne, the oldest went to Uncle Emmett in Cauthron, Arkansas, I went to my uncle Omer and Roger went to Uncle Elmer."[3]

According to Martha Holt Nichols, when the Miller brothers came to Fort Worth "it was all sympathy and love. Laudene told them 'You can't split the boys up' and they swore they wouldn't but they got together outside the town and split them up." The Millers "didn't respect women," said Nichols. "They would go into a tirade that women didn't deserve property. Laudene had no say-so when the Millers came and she didn't tell her family, the Holts, because she felt there was nothing they could do."[4]

Omer loaded up everything in a 1935 Ford pulling a two wheel trailer and headed west to California with his family and Roger's brother Wendall, part of the Okie exodus west. In California, Omer found work as a hired hand on farms before he bought a motel in 1948. Roger stayed in Erick with his Uncle Elmer and Aunt Armelia.

Roger Miller's family tree has roots planted in Kentucky, Tennessee, Texas and Arkansas. His paternal grandfather, Elisha "Elijah" Baker Miller was born in Sacramento, Kentucky on March 5, 1850. On March 3, 1892 he married Sarah Cordelia Bales, born March 16, 1873 in Mill Springs, Tennessee. Elisha Miller was a carpenter who built houses and coffins. He and his wife had eight children: Elmer, Margie May, Luther, Rowe, Lou, Emmett, Omer and Jean; all were born in Cauthron, Arkansas, where Elisha and Sarah moved after their marriage. Elisha died on November 25, 1925 and Sarah died on February 13, 1911; both in Cauthron.

Their oldest child, Elmer Dee Miller, was born November 13, 1892. He married Armelia Gray, daughter of David and Armelia Pegg Gray on December 4, 1915. Armelia was born March 29, 1898 in Indian Territory, which later became Oklahoma. Elmer and Armelia had two children; Marion Glenn Miller was born November 14, 1919 and Melva Loree Miller was born November 5, 1922.

Roger's father, Jean, was Elisha and Sarah's youngest child. Jean grew up without his mother, who died when he was a month short of two years old.

Roger's maternal grandfather, Francis Marion Holt, was born February 15, 1879 in Johnson County, Texas; he was the son of William Martin Holt of Tennessee and Florence Pidcock Holt of Texas. He moved to Scott

County, Texas in 1915 before he moved to northwest Arkansas, where he was a farmer. Around 1899 he married Cora Hale, probably from Fannin County, Texas; she was born in August, 1881 in Collin County, Texas. Francis and Cora split and he married Polly Jane Kathryn Martindale on November 10, 1903 in Pecan Gap, Texas; she was born April 2, 1875 in Blanco County, Texas. Francis and Polly had six children; Howard, Martin, Lillie, Johnny, Herbert and Laudene.

Elmer and Armelia Miller have been described as "hard working," "regular common people" and "decent" but "dour." Several of those who knew them compared them to the painting "American Gothic" of a farmer and his wife with a pitchfork. They lived on a farm in the gently rolling hills of west Oklahoma, raising cotton and a small herd of cattle. Like others in western Oklahoma, they struggled to survive the Great Depression and the dust storms in that area.

When Elmer and Armelia took two-year old Roger away from his mother, they did not intend to return him. Laudene and Elmer's sister, Margie went to Erick one weekend to take Roger "but she was told she was not getting the boy back." They disparaged Laudene as "a no good mother and then Laudene started dating and got married again and that was unacceptable. They demonized her."[5]

Laudene married Claude Sims in 1940 and they had two children, Joni (b. 1941) and Bitsy (b. 1947).

Early in 1942, shortly after Pearl Harbor was bombed, six-year-old Roger started school at Hibbard, a one room schoolhouse a few miles from his farm. The original Hibbard School began in 1909; it was a two-room brick building but during the 1920s it was destroyed by a tornado. The school was then re-built as a one-room wooden structure. During World War II Roger walked about a quarter mile, then a bus picked him up and carried him to this school.

In the Fall of 1947, Elmer Miller bought the Holmberg farm from Clarence and Gladys Holmberg for $10,000. Elmer was 56 years old; his son Glenn had married and was running a gas station in Erick while his daughter Melva had moved away. He needed a boy to help him on the farm but 11-year old Roger was not suited to farm life. Roger was in Erick but not of Erick. He lived in a world where people like the Millers respected those who got up early, worked hard all day at manual labor and then went to bed tired at night. That wasn't Roger, a mischievous boy who loved music and dreamed of a life far away from the farm. There was only one tree on that farm and Roger often sat under it, lost in a fantasy world swirling in his head. Elmer Miller didn't have the time or patience for a boy who daydreamed and could not relate to someone who did not accept it as his duty to do backbreaking work from sun-up to sunset as part of a hard scrabble life on a dry Oklahoma farm.

Elmer was tough on the young boy; Roger often got whippings when things didn't go well. Elmer drank, heavy at times, and he let young Roger know that he didn't measure up to what a young man should be. Roger was a dreamer, and that's what a young man should not be. He also loved music and worked for about a year doing odd jobs on various farms to buy an $8 guitar from the Sears and Roebuck catalogue. Roger loved to play that guitar.

Sheb Wooley was a neighbor and remembered that young Roger would be out working in the field "but when something would fly over like a plane, he would watch it as long as he could see it and stand there and daydream. I would yell, 'Roger!' and he would jump and start working again."[6]

Elmer "said Roger would never amount to anything," remembered Pat Henry, a former classmate of Roger's at Erick High. "Elmer said he put Roger out in the cotton patch pulling bolls and the first thing he knew Roger'd be sittin' on his cotton sack with two cotton stalks he'd pulled up, sittin' there beatin' on the ground making music. Elmer used to tell Daddy 'All he wants to do is sit around and plunk that guitar and I made him go to the barn to do it.'"[7]

"Roger just always had music and writing poems and doing this ornery stuff in him and in my opinion Roger would have been better off if he had been placed with younger parents," said Joy Brookshire, a classmate of Roger's at Erick High School. "They'd never seen anything like Roger before and they just didn't know what to do with him. Course I don't know if anybody would have known what to do with Roger. He wasn't happy and that may have been the reason he did those ornery things, because he was an unhappy person."[8]

"Mr. Miller was pretty tough on him," remembered Pat Henry. "He didn't measure up to what they wanted" adding "I remember him as being very poor, not having much of anything." Eldon Hendrix echoed that thought, noting that Elmer Miller "was pretty hard on Roger. That might have been one of the reasons he caused so many problems." Hugh Prather, long-time resident of Erick who drove the school bus that carried Roger to school said, "He was mischief all right ... Roger, he liked to play that fiddle and guitar."[9]

Roger himself told an interviewer, "I just didn't want to milk cows and be in a cotton field all my life. Not that I didn't think there was a future in it—I just didn't want no part of it... I didn't want to work that nine to five and make nothing. I wanted to get out and be world famous."[10]

The Millers "communicated with Laudene," said Wendall. "She wanted to get Roger back but they wouldn't let her have him. She didn't know she had a legal right. She got Dwayne back and raised him but I lived too far away in California. I saw Roger about once a year when we went back to visit. Our Mom would go up to visit Roger because she didn't live too far away but Uncle Elmer never wanted her to come. He was the patriarch of the family and saw his duty as taking in Roger and raising him."

Years later, Laudene Miller reflected that she did not want to give up her children but "it was such a horrible time and I was very young and had never been outside of Arkansas and then I was living in Fort Worth and my husband was dead and this was the Depression and I had no skills. So the brothers came and took my children and never brought them back."[11]

Roger had mixed feelings his entire life about his mother, his uncle and aunt, who he called "Dad" and "Mom" and his life in Erick. He "always missed his mother and always felt abandoned—like he had been left" but he also loved his Mom and Dad. Mom and Dad and Mother; they were each who they were and a part of his life, never to be confused as to who was who and yet conflicted and confused in a young boy's heart and mind. Growing up in Erick, he "always felt like he was displaced and somewhere he shouldn't be."[12]

On May 19, 1949 Roger graduated from the eighth grade at Hibbard and that fall started the ninth grade at Erick High School. Pat Henry remembers that "He really was not a trouble maker but he was just always in trouble. In English class we had an elderly teacher who was crippled and I think Roger instigated putting bobby pins underneath the desks and the kids'd pop 'em and just sit there and look real innocent while this teacher was going crazy."

In September, 1951 when Roger was 15 years old he started his junior year at Erick High School. At the start of the school year each student had to fill out a "Public Information Sheet" and Roger stated that he lived "7 1/2 miles SE of school" and that his home had "no telephone." He listed his father as "E.D. Miller—farmer" and his mother as "Armelia Miller—housewife" but answered "no" when the form asked "Do you live with your parents?"

The form asked "What are your home duties" and Roger answered "milking, feeding all chickens, horses, cows and working in the fields," then answered "no" when asked "Do you earn money?" For "What do you do in your spare time?" Roger answered "Play guitar, violin, harmonica, go swimming and sleep." He stated he was in FFA and wished to learn how to cook and "all about personality manners." Answering the question "What would you like to do when you finish school?" Roger wrote "I would like to have my own band and play over the Radio."[13]

Two days later, on September 6, the students had to write an essay titled "My Life." Roger noted that he was born in Ft. Worth and "I lived there as my father was a baseball player for the Ft. Worth Cats. When I was only 13 months old, my father died of a serious spinal disease. As my mother was unable to care for us, my three brothers and I went to seprate (sic) uncles to live. 1 going to Arkansas, one to California, and one right here in Erick."

Roger wrote that "While I was a freshman, I picked cotton and bought my own guitar. I sat down and learned to play it right away. I now play with a small band sometimes," adding that he had "developed an overwhelming love" for country music "and am going to continue with it after I have finished high school."[14]

In his junior year the English class was assigned to write some poetry. "Roger didn't hand in three lessons in his whole life but on that particular one he did," remembered Pat Henry. "And the teacher just bragged and bragged on him. I think we were supposed to write a poem about each person in the class and his must have really been creative. That was his creative juices just popping out."

Attention Deficit Hyperactivity Disorder (ADHD) hadn't been diagnosed when Roger was growing up but if ever there was a clear case of a child having ADHD it was Roger. The symptoms of ADHD all fit Roger in his childhood. They fit him when he was an adult, too, especially when he was in his 20s and 30s. He was fidgety, energetic and hyperactive, always doing something, mischievous, unable to sit still and incapable of shutting off his mind, which was always playing with words, twisting them around.

Roger Miller may have been a "trouble-maker" and "nuisance" while growing up but deep inside him was a burning ambition. He knew from an early age he wanted to go to Nashville, although he may not have known exactly how he was going to get there. You can't just look at a mischievous teenager and understand Roger Miller because there was a deep seated determination to leave Erick and make his mark on the world. It may not be possible for anyone to truly understand Roger Miller—and Roger probably could never explain himself—but the essence of Roger was a relentless drive to get out of Erick and become known all over the world as a great songwriter.

It may seem that fate had been unkind to young Roger Miller, taking him away from his mother to live on a small farm during the Depression with a couple who valued a life of hard, manual labor. But fate shone a bright light on young Roger because the Wooley family lived about three miles away from the Millers. Sheb Wooley was born April 10, 1921 and sometime around 1936, when he was 15 years old, formed a band, The Plainview Melody Boys, who performed on a weekly radio show in Elk City, about 30 miles east of Erick.

During the late 1930s and early 1940s Sheb worked for the Millers, helping them in their cotton fields, and courted and married their daughter, Melva in 1941. Sheb knew how to play the guitar, was entertaining and funny. He often entertained the Miller family. Roger quickly realized that he wanted to play the guitar and sing country songs like Sheb.

Sheb showed Roger how to play the guitar and also how to leave Erick. The two of them used to sit in an old car on the farm and Sheb would say, "Let's go to Hollywood!" and Roger, sitting beside him, would say, "Yeah—let's go!" and they would pretend to drive to Hollywood. Or Nashville or wherever else their wandering imagination took them.

In 1945, when Roger was nine years old, Sheb left Erick and went to Nashville where he auditioned for a spot on WSM and the Grand Ole

Opry; instead, he was hired by WLAC, where he did two fifteen-minute radio shows, one at 4:45 in the morning and the other at 4:45 in the afternoon. Those shows created a small demand for personal appearances and pictures, which allowed Sheb to earn $30-40 a week. He also made his first recordings for Bullet, a small independent label in Nashville, recording "Oklahoma Honky Tonk Girl."

In 1946 Sheb left Nashville and moved to Fort Worth, where he had a country music radio show, "Sheb Wooley and the Calumet Indians" sponsored by General Foods' Calumet Baking Powder. In Fort Worth, Sheb recorded "Peepin' Through the Keyhole" for the Blue Bonnet label, based in Dallas and this was a regional hit. Hill and Range Publishers signed Sheb to a songwriting contract and negotiated a recording contract for him with MGM Records.

Sheb was on the Fort Worth radio show for three years and Roger listened to it regularly. Sometime during this period Sheb bought a three-quarter sized fiddle for Roger, who quickly learned how to play it.

Musically, Sheb Wooley was pulled in two different directions; on one hand he grew up listening to the Grand Ole Opry and loved the idea of going to Nashville and striking it big. But he tried that in 1945 and early 1946 and it didn't pan out. On the other hand, he also grew up during the heyday of the singing cowboys with Gene Autry, Roy Rogers and Tex Ritter riding across the silver screen and singing country songs. In 1936—the year Roger was born—the Texas Centennial was held in Dallas to celebrate the One Hundredth Anniversary of the Alamo and San Jacinto. During the Centennial, Gene Autry went to Dallas and filmed a movie, *The Big Show*, which featured the Sons of the Pioneers (including a young Roy Rogers) and the Light Crust Doughboys. Sheb wanted to be a singing cowboy too, so in 1950 he headed out to Hollywood.

Unfortunately, Sheb landed in Hollywood as the singing cowboy era was coming to an end. However, he managed to connect with agent Ray Cooper and landed a role in the film *Rocky Mountain* starring Kay Rollins in 1950 and the following year appeared in three films: *Inside the Walls of Folsom Prison*, *Little Big Horn* and *Distant Drums*. His biggest role came in *High Noon* in 1952 when he played the killer Ned Miller, who was gunning for Gary Cooper. For Roger the impossible now seemed quite possible; he knew a movie star, someone who had grown up in Erick, married his cousin who was like a sister and struck it big in Hollywood.

Sheb Wooley was always a hero to Roger and a major influence in his life.

Chapter 2
Erick, Oklahoma

Early in 1952, during Roger's junior year at Erick High, he played fiddle in a band that consisted of Eldon Hendrix on electric guitar, Norris Lucas on steel guitar, Charles Gibson on drums and Pat Sanders, who played acoustic guitar and sang. "Pat Sanders and I graduated in '52," said Eldon Hendrix. "Charles Gibson was a year behind, like Roger. Norris Lucas's dad taught school and was superintendent of schools around Erick but they had been living in Bartlesville, which is where Norris graduated and they moved back to a farm in Erick in May of 1952." That was the Lonesome Valley Boys and "we'd play for whoever would listen," remembered Eldon. "We got to playing music and every school in the country around here wanted us to play at school functions. We even played for the Governor one time when they opened up Route 66 as a four lane that came through here."[1]

"We played real country music," said Eldon. We did 'In the Mood' and a lot of Hank Snow songs like 'I'm Movin' On' and 'Golden Rocket.' Course Hank Williams was hot back then and we played a lot of his stuff, like 'Your Cheatin' Heart' and 'I'm So Lonesome I Could Cry.' Lefty Frizzell and Eddy Arnold songs. 'When My Blue Moon Turns to Gold Again' and instrumentals like 'Steel Guitar Rag' and "Under the Double Eagle.' See, that's the kind of music we grew up with. Pat was the singer and he knew every Hank Snow song there was. Roger didn't sing at that time; he only played the fiddle."

Roger had to borrow Eldon's fiddle to play in that band because his own fiddle—the three-quarter sized one that Sheb had given him—was not loud enough.

Erick was a thriving small town at the time. Route 66, established originally in 1926, had been enlarged to four lanes and ran right through the town; business was good. Everybody in the area came in to town on Saturday afternoons; the men sat on street corners and the women met and shopped. There was a dry goods store on the north side of Route 66 and Eldon Hendrix remembers that "the night watchman would let us hook up and play after they closed. There was Carl's Cafe on the south side, across the street, and at night after nine o'clock he'd let us go in there and play."

It was the Golden Age of radio and Hendrix remembers that "We'd listen to the Opry. That was a big thing in our day when we was growing up. Go somewhere and turn on the radio and sit around it in chairs and look at that radio just like it was a TV. Every Saturday night it was the Opry. We also listened to shows like 'Jack Benny,' 'The Shadow' and 'The Lone Ranger' was a big deal."

Shamrock is about 20 miles west of Erick in the Texas panhandle and "All the kids used to go to Shamrock," remembered Pat Henry. "They had a drive-in over there and a movie theater. They just had more things going on over there than in Erick."[2] Shamrock was also a popular place for Roger's band, The Lonesome Valley Boys to play. They played on a radio station in Shamrock and at a country school in Samnorwood, Texas, about fifteen miles south of Shamrock.

"From May through the Fall of '52 we'd go down there each Friday night," said Eldon. "They'd have different bands—nobody professional, just someone who sang and played. It was all free and that thing would be packed full. No air conditioning. They'd have us start the program and we'd have about 15 minutes per group and then when everybody'd played they'd have us come back and we'd do 15 minutes and close it. We did that all summer."

Most of the time the band traveled in Eldon's 1947 Ford coupe. They would load all their instruments—electric guitar, amplifier, acoustic guitar, steel guitar, fiddle and drums—in the car and head for a gig.

Practices were "usually at Pat Sander's house, sometimes at my house," said Eldon. "I don't ever remember practicing down at Roger's house. Most of the time it was in town." Eldon also remembered that sometimes when the rest of the band members were at school, Roger would be at the Sander's house on the back porch playing the fiddle. "He didn't want to go to school, he wanted to play music," said Eldon, who added, "Roger could play anything. I mean give him 15 minutes, any instrument, and he could play it. One of the sharpest people I ever knew. He was writing songs when he was a sophomore."[3]

There is an undated piece of paper that claims to be Roger's "first song." There is no title, but here are the lyrics:

Sittin' 'neath a golden star
Just a-strummin' my guitar
Thinkin' of you, thinkin' of you
    Thinkin' of you
Got no worries on my mind
Thinkin' of you all the time
Thinkin' of you, Thinkin' of you
    Thinkin' of you
Poor, humble and forgotten
That's the way I feel
Need not be this woe and worry
Guess I've no appeal
Might as well forget the past
Face the future first to last
Quit thinkin' of you
    Thinkin' of you
    Thinkin' of you

In the fall of Roger's junior year he played the lead role of Septimus Green in the school play, "A Little Clodhopper," written by Walter Hare. Pictures in the school yearbook show him as a member of FFA "because that was a big thing with the guys," said Pat Henry. "All the guys were in that club."

Roger ran into trouble in the spring of 1952 during Study Hall. "In the front of the Study Hall was a small library where you check out books," remembered Eldon. "There was a radiator that had openings in it and Roger was sitting in his seat and Miss Garrett, an old maid school teacher, was sitting up by that radiator. He had a fire cracker buried in a shotgun shell and we had all seen that fire cracker. He got up from his seat and come behind this teacher and dropped that fire cracker behind the radiator and went up to the library and got a book and then went back to his seat. Well, that firecracker went off and rattled every window and Miss Garrett didn't say a word. She got up out of her chair, went down that aisle and got Roger by the hair of the head and just pulled him up to the principal's office. Never said a word to him cause she knew who done it." The result was that Mr. Easley, the superintendent, expelled Roger from Erick High School.

Prior to that incident, Roger pulled another prank at Erick High. "In the floor of the Study Hall was a door and down there was like a storage area, a big hole," said Eldon. "One day Roger hid under the floor when school closed and everybody had gone home. Then he took every single chair—they were folding chairs—and put them down under the floor. The next day we went into Study Hall and there wasn't a single chair in that room. They finally found them underneath the floor."

Eldon also remembered that "in that same Study Hall there was big windows—as tall as the ceiling—and they'd be open. I've seen Roger run and jump out of one of those windows and you wouldn't see him back in school for days." Eldon also remembered Roger sitting in Study Hall "and just write song after song after song. He was something else."

In the Fall of 1952, Roger enrolled at Delhi High School for his senior year. During the year he had a part in the school play and Mrs. Bessie Kelly, who taught English at Delhi, gave him encouragement when she told him he was talented and should "do something with it." Roger, yearning for acceptance and encouragement, never forgot those words of encouragement. However, before he graduated Roger was also expelled from Delhi. Stories are vague about the expulsion but apparently it came because things kept missing from the boy's locker room. Finally, the school principal hid to see who was stealing from the other students; Roger was the culprit and that led to the Principal kicking him out of school a few months before graduation.

Roger's former classmates remember him as a "fun loving, funny, easy-go-lucky type of guy who was a goof off and class clown," said Pat Henry. "He was always witty and had a quick come-back. He was a funny character but if we wanted something stirred up, we could depend on Roger to do it. The adults saw him as a goof off and that was a conflict with Elmer."

"Roger had every strike against him," continued Pat. "He wasn't with his parents, he was with people who really didn't want him, they was poor as dirt and he didn't fit because his brain operated different than the rest of us."

"We didn't understand Roger back then," said classmate Joy Brookshire. "Even the kids didn't understand Roger. When we were growing up, sports was the main thing and if you didn't play sports something was wrong with you. And Roger didn't have the least interest in sports. He couldn't have cared less—it just wasn't his thing. The teachers here didn't care much for him either. No one knew what to do with Roger. He just didn't fit. His folks, the Millers, were older and they just didn't understand Roger either."[4]

Eldon remembered that Roger had a passionate love for music but "didn't have a thing in the world to play. He was poor as Job's turkey."

"We was all poor but we didn't know it" is a phrase often heard from people who came through the Great Depression. But Roger was certainly aware that he was poorer than most; Elmer was tight with a dollar and could see no sense in parting with money for Roger to get a musical instrument or some such foolishness. And so Roger was left to find instruments to borrow and play. Most of this time he played a fiddle he borrowed from Eldon Hendrix.

Roger was ambitious to be a musician and grasped any opportunity to play. Bill Mack, a radio disc jockey and aspiring artist and songwriter from Shamrock, played a show in Delhi, Oklahoma and before the show they had a fiddling contest, which Roger won by playing the popular classic "Bile Dat Cabbage Down." After Mack started his show "the first two rows of the audience began shouting 'put ol' Rog on' [so] Mack brought Miller on and he began stomping his right foot and played 'Bile Dat Cabbage Down' fast and loud." Mack then asked Roger to play another song and he reprised "Bile Dat Cabbage Down" because the response was great. Roger played the song a third time and after the show asked Mack if he ever needed a fiddle player. Mack replied he might need a fiddler sometime so Roger gave him a phone number to reach him. Several months later, Mack's regular fiddle player was sick and Mack had a Christmas show scheduled in Childress, Texas so he contacted Roger, who came down to Childress. "We were doing Christmas songs and I asked him, 'Are you sure you know all these songs? My songs?'" said Mack. "He said, 'Yeah, I know them. You just do them and I will do my bit.' And the only thing he played all night was 'Bile Dat Cabbage.'" Bill Mack never hired him as a fiddler again.[5]

Sisters Georgetta and Barbara Crow were two years apart and very close; one night they slipped away from home and went to a bar in Texola on the Texas-Oklahoma line and, according to their younger sister, Phyllis, that's when Barbara probably met Roger Miller. The Crows lived in Shamrock, where The Lonesome Valley Boys often played and, according to Barbara's brother, James, "The Oklahoma boys would come over here and try to steal our girls." That's how James thought they met.[6]

The Crows lived in Magic City, Texas before they moved to Shamrock. George and Pauline Crow had four children, three girls—Georgetta, Barbara and Phyllis—and a boy, James. George Crow worked for a trucking firm which hauled crude oil to a carbon black plant. Carbon black is primarily used in the manufacture of tires to help prolong the life of the tire; it is also used in the production of rubber hoses and belts and in laser printer toner. Working in a carbon black plant is "a dirty, dirty job" remembered James Crow.

Barbara Crow was born August 27, 1938 and attended Shamrock High School. Her brother remembered that she "laughed all the time. She was a happy-go-lucky person who liked pretty clothes and shoes and having a good time."

Roger was "a night owl," remembered James Crow. "He was playing music when he could. There wasn't a lot to do in Shamrock. We'd go to the service station and pitch quarters at a line, then get in a car and ride up and down the streets. That was about it. Roger would bring his guitar over and get with some others in somebody's garage and play." One of the young men Roger played with in Shamrock was Eugene Price, who later played guitar in Merle Haggard's band. The romance between Roger and Barbara blossomed later.[7]

Roger should have graduated in the spring of 1953 but didn't; instead, he managed to obtain some odd jobs in town and continued to play music. The Lonesome Valley Boys began playing bars and dances, which caused Eldon Hendrix to drop out of the group because of his religious faith.

In the summer of 1953 Bob Wills and his family moved back to West Texas from Los Angeles, where he moved in 1943 and spent the war years performing on the West Coast. Wills bought a home in Amarillo and began broadcasting on KGNC on July 16, 1953. Those broadcasts were live and open to the public and Roger Miller attended some of them and hung out with Bob's band members after the shows. Roger loved the hot, jazzy sound of western swing and always loved the songs of Bob Wills.

Roger was liable to run away to wherever Bob Wills was playing. Roger was never shy about introducing himself to musicians, asking to sit in or sing them his songs. He hung out with some of the Texas Playboys and Wills gave him some encouragement with his songwriting, which both thrilled and worried Roger, who wrote a letter to Sheb Wooley in Hollywood asking for advice about protecting his songs. One of his biggest thrills as a young man came when, during a show, Bob Wills pointed his fiddle bow at him, acknowledging his presence. This was what he wanted in life, to have great musicians know that Roger Miller was somebody. Roger was so thrilled and overwhelmed as he stood close to the great Bob Wills that he actually cried.

A third major influence on Roger was Will Rogers, an icon in Oklahoma, who died about four months before Roger was born. The memory of Will Rogers remained strong in Oklahoma during the time Roger grew up and the legendary humorist was regarded as a "hero" to those who remembered him. During Roger's early years, he heard numerous references to Will Rogers; people quoted things Rogers said and talked about him and his wit. Everyone admired and loved Will Rogers and everyone, it seemed, wanted to be like Will Rogers, who was witty, warm, and down to earth with a common touch while he hung out with celebrities and world leaders.

The biggest adventure for Roger Miller in 1953 came when the 17-year old hitch-hiked out west and landed at Grand Canyon Village on the South Rim of the Grand Canyon. At the railroad depot, he asked agent Sam Turner for a job; Turner did not have any to offer but called Jack Verkamp, who ran the Motor Lodge and Jack agreed to hire Roger to work in the store he owned. Jack let Roger stay in a little trailer—roughly eight by twelve—and assigned him the job of pushing a broom to keep the place clean.

Roger brought along his guitar and Jack Verkamp had to stay on him to work; Roger preferred sitting around and playing his guitar. He also had a habit of beating out rhythms with his hands on the glass cases in the store, which nearly drove Verkamp crazy. Roger wasn't adverse to falling asleep during working hours, either; Verkamp once caught him asleep in the basement.

The Verkamps had a family business; Jack and his wife Betty owned the place, and their three children, Susie, Steve and Mike worked there. The store was about 60 feet from the rim of the Grand Canyon in Northern Arizona and was a popular spot for tourists to stop and purchase souvenirs. In the summer of 1953 about 20,000 Boy Scouts descended on the Grand Canyon for a Boy Scout Jamboree. Boys were swarming all over the store and the young ladies were at the counters, trying their best to keep up with the demand for goods. Roger was leaning on the counters, flirting with the girls, when Jack Verkamp told him to leave the girls alone—he needed to be pushing that broom.

Roger loved to flirt and often had a date for the nightly dances at the Bridge Angel Lodge. So it was not surprising that after lunch that day, Jack Vercamp caught Roger chatting with the girls ringing up sales while they tried to keep up with the horde of Boys Scouts who had invaded the store. That was too much for Verkamp, who fired Roger on the spot, ending his employment at the Grand Canyon.[8]

In the Fall of 1953 Bud Keathley became the manager of Roger's band, "Roger Miller and the Western Highlighters." Bud had gotten married on August 22, 1953 and lived in a small house in the 100 block of North Oak, just off Highway 66. That's where the band, comprised of L.A. Norris, Norris Lucas, Chester Cline, Charles Gibson and Roger, practiced. "We made loud music for all the neighbors. I imagine they wanted to run us out of the neighborhood," remembered Bud.[9]

This was the first band where Roger did most of the singing; in the Lonesome Valley Boys it was Pat Sanders who sang and nobody remembers Roger even adding harmony. The Western Highlighters performed some of Roger's original songs. On a sheet of paper dated January 1, 1954, Roger wrote the lyrics to one of his compositions:

Saving All My Kisses
I'm saving all my kisses for
Someone who really cares
I gave away a lot to you
But now no more you'll share
You seem to think it's all in fun
That kisses should be free

But now the price has raised
And I'll start saving constantly
Just like a red of roses
I'm waiting for the rain,
Your little showers,
They didn't help
Your out of luck again
I'm saving all my kisses for
A love that's sweet and true,
I'm saving all my kisses,
And no more shall go to you

Bud and Roger became close and Roger sometimes spent the night at Bud's house. "Roger was ten years ahead of everybody else here in Erick," remembered Bud. "He wasn't one of us; in his mind he was going for bigger things. But he couldn't verbalize it and there was no place in Erick for him to do it." Roger talked "constantly" about going to Nashville and making music a career. "You almost couldn't talk to him about anything except music," said Bud. "That's all he ever wanted to do—play country music."

"He was so talented," continued Bud. "He'd go into Carl's Cafe and get three or four glasses and put so much water in each of them and then get something to tinkle against them and make music. He was so musically orientated. Sometimes we'd go to different people's houses just so he could play." The band played regularly on Friday and Saturday nights, mostly dances although "occasionally something special would come up," said Bud. "We played a lot of Senior Citizens gatherings."

"Roger was a good fiddle player but I never saw an instrument he couldn't play," said Bud. "On 'Bonapart's Retreat' he used to could stand on his head in a corner or up against a wall and hold his fiddle behind his back and play that song and never miss a beat. Roger wrote a song called 'Ya'll Come' and they used to play that at the end of the night; that was the last song they played."

Bud Keathley had negotiated for the band to play at a Dude Ranch in Red River, New Mexico in 1954. "We had made a deal and we were all looking forward to going out there and playing and mingling with the people there because they were going to furnish us with a place to live, our food, room and board and give us $350 a week for eight months. It was just a fantastic deal," said Bud.

In early January Roger got off a Greyhound bus in Erick with a brand new electric Gibson cutaway guitar and a Fender amplifier. Roger had spent that night in a junkyard, sitting in a car, playing that guitar. He was so hungry to play music, to have a nice instrument, that he just stayed in that junk car all night playing.

Roger told Bud Keathley that Glenn, his cousin who had a gas station in Amarillo, had made the down payment for him and he was going to pay the balance in installments. The band, with Roger playing his new guitar, played a date in Cheyenne, Oklahoma at the American Legion Hall on January 11. The following week, a Federal Marshall knocked on Bud's door while Roger was there.

"The Marshall asked if Roger was here and we said 'Yeah,'" remembered Bud. "Roger asked if we'd hide the guitar and amplifier for him but we said 'no.'" It turned out that Roger had broken into a club in Amarillo and stolen the guitar and amp and some stage clothes. The Federal Marshall arrested him and took him back across the state line to Amarillo.

The "Korean Draft" was on and healthy young men were eligible. The judge in Amarillo made an offer to Roger: enlist in the Army and the charges would be dropped. Roger decided to enlist; on March 27, 1954 Roger Miller was inducted into the United States Army.

That ended the band and Bud had to negotiate to get out of the contract with the Red River Dude Ranch. "We couldn't play without our star," said Bud. "He was the band. Red River was kinda complicated to get out of but it was my job as a manager to take care of that. It kinda gave the whole group the blues because everybody thought a lot of Roger."[10]

Chapter 3
Private John Q.

Let's face it: Roger Miller was not cut out to be a soldier.

After basic training he was sent to Fort Lee, Virginia, for Quartermaster Training. (A quartermaster is in charge of supplies for the Army.) After quartermaster school, Roger shipped out to Korea. On the ship crossing the Pacific Ocean, Roger had "the lonesomest feeling that I ever had." He was so far away from everyone he knew and "was so scared because we were on that ship forever and I got so seasick."[1]

In Korea he got a tattoo on the upper part of his arm that said "Korea" because his Army buddies were getting one and told him that he needed to get one too. It was a small tattoo and he hated it his entire life.

The Korean War began on June 25, 1950 but an armistice was signed on July 27, 1953 so by the time Roger arrived the United States Army was an occupying force in South Korea, below the 38th parallel.

Roger's interest in Korea was not in foreign relations or understanding military or political policy; Roger was interested in music. He was assigned to various jobs in the Army—he drove a jeep, worked in an office and was an "infantry man." In the Infantry his primary job was to drive officers around in a jeep. This is what you do with an infantry soldier whose mind can't stay on the task of militarily engaging the enemy. He had played fiddle and guitar back in Oklahoma but noted that in Korea he "met some guys who really knew something about the guitar and they taught me and I learned what I could." He joined a country band in Korea made up of soldiers and saw one of his early dreams come true: he played on the Armed Forces radio station on the base. But that wasn't enough. Roger lobbied the brass to get into Special Services, where he could perform full time.

His wish was granted during his last year in the Army when he was assigned to Special Services at Fort McPherson in Atlanta where he was part of the Circle A Wranglers. This is the same Army unit where Faron Young served while he was in the Army.

On February 17, 1956, just after Roger was transferred from Korea back to the States, he married Barbara Louise Crow in Shamrock, Texas.

Roger was 20 years old and Barbara was 17. Since she was underage, her father and Roger's Dad, Elmer Miller, went with Roger and Barbara to Wellington, Texas, south of Shamrock, for the marriage license with George Crow signing for his daughter. They were married by a Justice of the Peace in Shamrock.

"Barbara was the troublemaker in our family," remembered her sister, Phyllis. "She was always skipping school or doing something. If they got caught, our sister Georgetta would always confess but Barbara would continue to deny. She was very outgoing and fun." Roger was also "fun and outgoing," said Phyllis, who thought they were "a good match." However, "when he came to our house he was always beating on the table, like a drum, which irritated my mother. We lived next door to a Baptist church, which my father helped build, and every time the doors were open we were there. Roger would go in and play the piano, some boogie woogie type stuff and I'd think 'I hope the Lord doesn't strike us.' He was so talented, could play a lot of different instruments. And he would always make weird noises with his mouth. He could imitate a coffee pot percolating."[2]

Phyllis doesn't remember Barbara and Roger writing to each other while Roger was in Korea or even dating much. "It was just 'they're getting married,'" she remembered. And right after they got married, they moved to Atlanta, where Roger was stationed.

Faron Young was an up and coming country star when he received his draft notice in 1952; he had signed with Capitol Records and released his first single, "Tattletale Tears" b/w "Have I Waited Too Long," toured as an opening act for Hank Snow and His Rainbow Ranch Boys and was a member of the Grand Ole Opry. He was inducted into the army on November 16, a little over a month after he recorded "Goin' Steady." That record entered the *Billboard* country chart on January 10 while Faron was in basic training at Fort Jackson in Columbia, South Carolina. "Goin' Steady" was an instant hit; it reached number two on the charts and led the Special Service's division at Fort Jackson to send Faron to New York to appear on "Talent Patrol," a network TV show sponsored by the Army to aid recruiting.

The Army quickly realized that country music could be a good recruiting tool so the Special Services of the Third U.S. Army acquired Faron, replacing pop singer Eddie Fisher, who was mustering out. In June, 1953 Faron was transferred to Fort McPherson, just outside Atlanta, and was cast in a musical variety program, "Showcase." The all-soldier revue, which featured a jazz group, comedian, dancers and circus type acts like fire-eaters and sword swallowers, did up to four shows a day.

The Third Army's emblem was an "A" in a circle so the country band formed at Fort McPherson was known as the Circle A Wranglers. Members of the band wore tan-colored business suits that carried the circle A on their breast pockets.

During his time in the Army, Faron went to Nashville and recorded more songs for Capitol. He had a major fan and ally in Lt. General Alexander Bolling, commanding general of the Third U.S. Army. Bolling believed that morale for Army soldiers was helped by entertainment so the Circle A Wranglers performed on the road for troops and did recruiting shows for the public. At Fort McPherson, the Circle A Wranglers entertained on Saturday nights at the officer's club.[3]

Roger Miller was aware of Faron Young's role as a country singer for the Army's Special Services. "We felt big being in the same group as Faron," he later remembered.[4]

When a country music show came to Atlanta, Roger almost always found a way to attend. At one show held at the old Tower Theater on Peachtree Street he met Bill Anderson, a college student at the University of Georgia who worked as a disk jockey on a radio station in Commerce, near Atlanta. Anderson states that he doesn't actually remember meeting Roger but "it was one of those things where I don't remember ever not knowing him." Anderson states they "probably met at one of the country shows that came to Atlanta, one of the Grand Ole Opry shows or something. They would bring shows to Atlanta every couple of months or so on Sundays. I was working as a disc jockey at a small station close to Atlanta, and Roger and I would meet each other at these shows at the old Tower Theatre in Atlanta. We would hang out backstage and talk about our dreams. We wanted to go to Nashville, we wanted to write songs, and we wanted to perform."

Anderson continued that "Every time a big country show would come to town, we'd be standing off to the side of the stage in the darkened corners and singing each other songs we'd written, dreaming of the day each of us would became a big enough star to step out onto the stage and into the spotlight."[5]

One Sunday afternoon during a touring country show that featured Wanda Jackson, Roger knocked on her dressing room door and wanted to know if he could ask her a few questions, then asked her "all kinds of stupid questions about the music business" before he asked "Would you mind if I borrowed your guitar and sang my friend here a couple of new songs I've written?"

He sang those songs for Anderson, who sang some of his own. "Roger and I made a vow to each other," remembered Anderson. "We promised that we would help each other—whoever got to Nashville first."

Horace J. "Aychie" Burns was a Sergeant at Fort McPherson who served with Roger. Burns was the brother of Jethro Burns of Homer and Jethro, who recorded for RCA. Jethro was the brother-in-law of Chet Atkins; he and Chet had married twin sisters.

Aychie Burns was a talented musician himself. With his brother Kenneth, later known as "Jethro," Henry Haynes, later known as "Homer," and Charlie Hagman they formed "The Stringdusters" and performed on WROL, WNOX in Knoxville and WDOD in Chattanooga. Later, he played with the Colorado Mountain Boys, whose members included Chet Atkins. While Homer and Jethro pursued a career in music, Aychie Burns decided to pursue a career in the Army. He was stationed at Fort McPherson in Atlanta when he met Roger Miller.

Aychie Burns and Chet Atkins formed a tight bond when they were both at WNOX in Knoxville in the late 1940s. It was a difficult time in Chet's life and he was often depressed. Later, Chet remembered "Aychie Burns was my shrink for a long time. Lying on the back seat of his car headed for a personal appearance, I used to pour out my problems to him. He gave me good country philosophy, which is as good as any philosophy if you just take the time to listen." Aychie told Chet that he came across to others "like you're antisocial or something" and encouraged him, when meeting people, "Stand right up there, eye-to-eye with people, and talk to them and let them know you're interested in them."[6]

It was good, sound advice and it turned Chet's life around as he overcame his shyness and insecurities and became more outgoing.

Aychie showed Chet "licks on his bass that I could transfer to the guitar. He was kind to me, and gave me a lot of encouragement." Aytchie also signed a note so Chet could purchase a flattop Gibson for fifty dollars."[7]

Aychie Burns wrote a letter to Chet Atkins on Roger's behalf, telling him about the young singer; this served as an opening for Roger to meet Chet, who was head of RCA Victor's Nashville division and producer of most of the country acts on RCA's roster.

Roger was making $140 a month when he was discharged from the Army in March, 1957. He and Barbara moved to Nashville and rented a room at Mom Upchurch's boarding house at 620 Boscoble Street in East Nashville. Delia "Mom" Upchurch opened her boarding house in 1945 and, in the days before there were plenty of apartments, was known for renting rooms to musicians. In addition to rooms, "Mom's" provided meals.

Roger walked from Mom's to Chet's office, in the Methodist Radio and TV Services Building on McGavock Street and, according to Roger, "I just walked in and said to Chet Atkins, 'I want to audition. I'm a songwriter,' and he said 'Well, where's your guitar?' I said, 'I don't have one' and he said, 'You can use mine.' So there's Chet Atkins and I'm using his guitar and I sang in one key and played in another. It was a disaster." The song he sang was "That's the Way I Feel."[8]

"That's the Way I Feel" has George Jones listed as a co-writer, although that came about because George was the first to record it. The song is an up tempo song with fast paced words about unrequited love; the singer asks the listener if he/she has ever been unwanted and unloved and then says the lady he loves "left me here heart-sick and lonely, that's the way I feel."

Chapter 4
Them Was the Good Old Days

Roger Miller arrived in Nashville at a fortuitous time. On January 1, 1957, the Starday and Mercury record labels merged; the next day the label released its first record, "Don't Stop the Music" by George Jones.

Mercury Records was started in Chicago by Irving Green in 1945. In 1951 they hired D. Kilpatrick, who established the first office in Nashville by a major label. Starday was formed by two Texans; Jack Starnes, the "Star" in "Starday," was a booking agent in Beaumont where he managed Lefty Frizzell. Pappy Daily, the "Day," was a record distributor in Houston. In October, 1953 Don Pierce, formerly with Four Star Records in Los Angeles, joined Starday.

The biggest act on Starday was George Jones, who was produced by Pappy Daily. In 1955 Jones had his first national hit, "Why Baby, Why," which reached number four on the country charts, and in 1956 Jones had four chart records.

During 1956 there was a great deal of turmoil within the country music industry in Nashville. First, Elvis Presley hit big and sold ten million records that year. Elvis had five number one hits on the country chart in *Billboard*: "I Forgot To Remember to Forget," "Heartbreak Hotel," "I Want You, I Need You, I Love You," "Don't Be Cruel" and "Hound Dog." Carl Perkins' "Blue Suede Shoes" and Marty Robbins' "Singing the Blues" were also number one songs on the country chart. These did not sound like country music to those who grew up on fiddles and steel guitars. The previous year Webb Pierce, Carl Smith, Hank Snow, Faron Young, Porter Wagoner, Eddy Arnold and Tennessee Ernie Ford all had number one records; in 1956 none of them did.

The biggest country hit in 1956 was "Crazy Arms" by Ray Price, which remained number one on the country charts for 20 weeks. This country shuffle had a traditional, honky tonk sound, but the second biggest hit, "Heartbreak Hotel," which remained number one for 17 weeks, sounded more like Rhythm and Blues.

There was also a "perfect storm" brewing at radio. Television became popular during the 1950s and the networks shifted their focus from radio to television. Comedy, dramas and musical shows that had been on network radio moved over to television and radio was increasingly concerned about its future. Many openly wondered if there was a future for radio.

The "barn dances," which were live country music shows, usually broadcast on Saturday nights, were phased out as radio discontinued their live shows and switched to records. This meant that from the mid to late 1950s on through much of the 1960s, the only way to have a big hit in country music was for the record to "cross over" to pop/rock radio stations.

In addition to the situation at radio, there was a crisis in the Nashville music community. In August, 1955, Jack DeWitt, president of WSM radio, which broadcast the Grand Ole Opry, issued a memo telling WSM employees that if they had any outside business, they needed to either get rid of that business if they wanted to remain with WSM or else leave WSM and concentrate on their outside business.

Jack Stapp, Program Manager at WSM, started Tree Publishing in 1951 with Lou Cowan, a CBS executive he met while in the army during World War II. In 1953 Stapp hired Buddy Killen to find songs and songwriters for the young company. Killen was a bass player who worked with various acts on the Opry so his work with Tree was part-time. In January, 1956, Elvis recorded "Heartbreak Hotel," which was published by Tree. After DeWitt's memo, Stapp sold his interest in Tree to Lou Cowan, who added a partner, Harry Fleischman, president of Entertainment Productions.

When Jim Denny, who had an outside publishing company but refused to resign, was fired from his job as head of the Opry Artists Bureau in September, 1956, WSM offered D. Kilpatrick the job of booking Opry acts. Kilpatrick accepted, which meant that Mercury needed someone to head their country division in Nashville. In November, 1956, at the annual Disc Jockey Convention in Nashville, Mercury owner Irving Green and Art Talmadge, then vice president, met with Pappy Daily and Don Pierce and offered them a deal whereby Mercury and Starday would merge. Daily was the Mercury distributor in Texas and that would continue; in addition, he booked Grand Ole Opry talent in Texas. Don Pierce took Kilpatrick's place when he moved to Nashville from Los Angeles. By April, 1957, Pierce was in Nashville and Mercury-Starday was releasing product. The company bought a building at 3557 Dickerson Road, about six miles northwest of downtown Nashville.

George Jones stayed at the Clarkston Hotel when he was in Nashville; the coffee shop at the Clarkston was a popular hangout for songwriters and musicians. After he moved to Nashville, Roger Miller landed a job as bellhop at the Andrew Jackson Hotel, about a block away from the Clarkston, and close to the National Life and Accident Insurance Company. The insurance company owned the Grand Ole Opry and WSM Radio, whose studios were located on the top floor of that building. That's where Roger met George Jones and sang him some of his songs. Jones was impressed and told Pappy Daily and Don Pierce about Miller and urged them to audition the young singer.

In a room at the Andrew Jackson Hotel, Daily and Pierce listened as Roger sang his songs. "He reminded me a lot of Hank Locklin," remembered Pierce. "He had a high voice like Locklin. I wasn't blown away, but he was different and likeable."[1]

Pierce was anxious to develop a publishing company; he liked Roger's songs and signed several to his publishing company. The first artist to record a Roger Miller song was George Jones, who recorded four of Miller's songs: "Don't Do This To Me," "Tall, Tall Trees," "Hearts in My Dreams" and "No Use to Cry" at the Bradley Studio on April 23, 1957. A day or two later, Jimmy Dean did two sessions for the Mercury-Starday venture and recorded two of Roger's songs; on the first session he recorded "Happy Child" and on the second he recorded "Nothing Can Stop My Loving You." "Happy Child" became the first song that Roger had released to the public; it was released as a single on May 7 but did not chart, despite promotion from Starday that included several full page ads in the trade press.

Roger Miller wanted to record and Pierce agreed to record him, but it needed to be done in Houston instead of Nashville because in Texas "we could cut for $5 per song per man. In Nashville it was $41.25 per man per three-hour session" because it was a union town.[2]

Roger's first recordings for Starday in Texas were produced by Pappy Daily. On that session he recorded four songs he wrote: "Poor Little John," "My Pillow," "Can't Stop Loving You" and "You're Forgetting Me." His first release was "My Pillow" b/w "Poor Little John"; his second release, in late 1957, was "Can't Stop Loving You" b/w "You're Forgetting Me." None of those songs charted.

Roger worked as a bellhop by day at the Andrew Jackson Hotel and in the evenings he hung out at WSM, about a block away. One evening at the "Friday Night Frolics" he ran into Johnny Johnson, a guitar player on the Opry who was putting a band together for a tour that summer throughout the midwest. They needed a fiddle player and Roger volunteered. According to Roger, that's how he came to back Minnie Pearl on her summer tour of mostly fairs in Illinois and Indiana.

Mel Tillis has a slightly different version of how Roger came to be in Minnie Pearl's band.

According to Tillis, Jim Denny booked Minnie Pearl and arranged for Tillis, who wrote songs for Denny's publishing company, Cedarwood, to join Minnie's band as a rhythm guitar player and singer. Minnie needed a fiddle player and Tillis said he knew one he'd met at the Clarkston Hotel's coffee shop. In their conversations, Roger told Tillis that he played the fiddle.

Tillis told Minnie that he'd go down to the Clarkston "and see if I can't find him." When Tillis arrived, Roger was sitting at a table in his bell hop uniform. Tillis asked Roger if he wanted a job and Roger replied, "Doing what?" "Playing fiddle," said Tillis. "For who?" asked Roger. "Minnie Pearl," said Tillis. "How much does it pay?" asked Roger.

"$18 a show," said Tillis. "If we do one show you get $18. If we do two shows you get $36." "For how long?" asked Roger. "For three months," said Tillis. "All out through the Midwest. Fair dates." "Well, let me run over and give the Andrew Jackson my two-minute notice," said Roger.[3]

Although Roger told Mel Tillis that he played the fiddle, Mel had never actually heard Roger play. "If he said he played the fiddle then I figured he played the fiddle," said Mel. There was no rehearsal; Minnie Pearl assumed he could play the fiddle, too. Their first "rehearsal" came when they set up for their first date in Melvin, Iowa.

The show consisted of Johnny Johnson opening the show, singing a few numbers and then Roger sang "Fraulein," the big hit by Bobby Helm. Tillis had a record out, "Honky Tonk Song" that he sang but, because of his stutter, couldn't talk. Roger would introduce him, saying, "Mel Tillis would like to sing you a song." After Tillis finished, Roger said, "Mel Tillis said 'Thank you.'"

The band also backed Judy Lynn, who won "Miss Idaho" in 1955, which led to her competing in the "Miss America" contest (she was runner-up). In 1956 she signed with ABC-Paramount and was voted "Most Promising Female Vocalist" by *Billboard* in 1957. Judy Lynn dressed in flamboyant western costumes and in 1956 replaced Jean Shepard on the Opry touring show. She served as co-host of the first Grand Ole Opry national telecast in 1957 with Ernest Tubb. "She looked like a star but she couldn't sing worth a damn," remembered Tillis.

In addition to Roger on fiddle and Mel Tillis on guitar, the band was comprised of Howard White on steel guitar and Willie Ackerman on drums. "Howard and Roger were always getting into fights," remembered Tillis.

After Judy Lynn performed, Minnie came on and did skits with the band members—they were the straight men—and then Minnie did her stand-up comedy. Minnie's husband, Henry Cannon, was a pilot and Tillis and Roger sometimes flew with them.

According to Tillis, "That was my first experience with Roger Miller. We traveled with Miss Minnie for three months, and he'd sing them crazy songs. I said, 'You'll never get shit like that cut.' Little did I know!" Tillis and Roger wrote a song together, "That's Why I'm Drinking," but it was never recorded.

"I wouldn't let him drive," said Tillis. "He couldn't keep his mind on what he was doing so I did the driving. We'd pull a trailer and we had a bass fiddle, and its neck went down between us."

Late one night—Thursday, July 24, 1957—Tillis and Roger were driving into Nashville from Kentucky. They were listening to the radio and the disc jockey, Bill Morgan—brother of Opry star George Morgan—played Tillis' record of "Honky Tonk Song" and then announced, "If Mel Tillis is in the area listening, I'd like to tell him that he is the proud father of a baby boy." Tillis pulled off the road and dropped a dime into a pay phone to call collect but when the operator answered "I couldn't say nothing," remembered Tillis, "so the operator hung up." Roger took the phone, put in a dime and called collect to Tillis' father in Florida."

On that call, Tillis learned that he was not the father of a baby boy but the father to a baby girl, which the Tillis's named "Pam."[4]

Roger remembered that Tillis "carried his guitar around in a toe sack, or burlap sack because he couldn't afford a guitar case and he couldn't talk enough to order food. We'd be on tour and all he could order was a grilled cheese sandwich and a Coke. He couldn't even say 'Melvin.'"[5]

The tour with Minnie Pearl ended by October, 1957 and Roger could not find additional work in Nashville. Barbara was pregnant at the time with their first child so they decided to move back to Texas.

Chapter 5
Invitation to the Blues

In the Fall of 1957 Roger and Barbara moved back to Texas and stayed with her parents then, in early December, moved to Amarillo, Texas, where they rented one side of a duplex at 4409 East 18th Street. On December 9, Roger applied for a job as a "Fireman" in Amarillo and indicated that he received "Safety and Fire Prevention Training" while in the Army. A week later, on December 16, he was hired and worked there until February 17, 1958. Roger always said he was "fired" from his job in Amarillo but employment records indicate that he resigned to accept a job in Nashville.

Joy Brookshire, who came from Erick, Oklahoma and knew Roger, lived in Amarillo with her husband from 1957 until 1969.

"When we first went to Amarillo in 1957, Roger was on the fire department there and he was known as the 'Singing Fireman,'" said Brookshire."I worked in the personnel department and one time the old fire chief came into the personnel department and I asked him something about Roger. He didn't get much out of him; he said, 'All he's got on his mind is that music. He sets up there and plunks on that guitar all the time—and that was it. No matter what, he was going to play his music.'"[1]

Roger played in some clubs in Amarillo during the time he was there and James Crow remembered that one night "I got off work early and drove up to hear him in my yellow and white '57 Chevy. He liked to died when he saw me coming because he had a girlfriend with him. Said 'I could just see Barbara and your mother in the back seat' when I drove up."

"Roger treated Barbara good, although he ran around on her," said James. "She probably knew about it. But he never abused her. He was basically a good guy but he didn't let anything stand in his way to success. He knew where the star was and he was going to get there, regardless. He never let anything get in his way."[2]

During the 1950s Ray Price and his Cherokee Cowboys played Texas dance halls, mixing western swing with the honky tonk sound that kept people on the dance floor. Ray Price's recording of "Crazy Arms" was a career-making song for him. The song hit the country chart in *Billboard* on May 26, 1956 and landed in the number one spot on June 23, bumping Elvis out of the top spot. The song stayed number one for 20 consecutive weeks and on the charts for an amazing 45 weeks.

Van Howard sang harmony on Price's "Crazy Arms," which led to him asking Price for credit and royalties on future recordings. This initiated a disagreement between Price and Howard with the result that Howard left the group and Price needed a new singer to sing harmony and open shows for him.

The Cherokee Cowboys were in Amarillo "and somebody said 'there's a guy who plays fiddle and sings at the Fire Department,'" said Price. "So we got hold of Roger and he came out to audition and I liked him right away. But he made a mistake—he wanted to play fiddle right off the bat and when he got through he said 'How'd I sound to you' and I was trying to keep from laughing—he wasn't a great fiddle player—so I said, 'Can you sing and play guitar?'"

Roger made light of the situation—"Well, I messed that up" or something along those lines—and then played the guitar and sang for Price, who hired him.[3]

Ray Price and the Cherokee Cowboys were one of the best, most consistent acts in country music. The musicians were all top notch, the band was tight, and they had a cocky self-confidence knowing they were the best in the business. Their shuffle sound was perfect for the Texas dance halls, and that's where they primarily played. The Cherokee Cowboys attracted some of the best musicians in country music, although simple comradeship and the ability to put up with the crazies of life on the road seemed to be part of their hiring criteria as well.

Roger Miller served as the front man for the Cherokee Cowboys for the rest of 1958 and into 1959.

On the evening of May 6, 1958, Ray Price recorded Roger's song, "Invitation to the Blues" as well as "I've Got To Know," a song that Price is listed as co-writer with Roger. The session started at 10 o'clock that evening and did not finish until one in the morning at the Bradley Studios at 804 16th Avenue South. Produced by Don Law, the session listed four guitar players—Ray Price, Roger, Samuel Pruett and Velma Williams

Smith; Jack Evins was on steel guitar, Joe Zinkan on bass, Tommy Jackson on fiddle, Buddy Harman on drums and Floyd Cramer on piano. Roger sang harmony with Price on "Invitation to the Blues."

Twenty-three days later, on May 29, Price recorded "City Lights," written by Bill Anderson. Roger was listed as a guitar player on this session too, but there was a different line-up of musicians; Ray Edenton played guitar, Jimmy Day played steel, and Bob Moore played bass. Samuel Pruett, Tommy Jackson, Buddy Harman and Floyd Cramer were holdovers from the previous session.

About ten o'clock the following morning Roger called Bill Anderson at the radio station where he worked in Commerce, Georgia and excitedly told him, "Hey, Anderson, guess what. Price cut 'City Lights' last night! It's gonna be his next release. I've got the other side, a new thing I just wrote called 'Invitation to the Blues'! How 'bout them apples?"

This was a huge break for Anderson, who had released the song on a small, independent label. Later that morning, Anderson's publisher in Texas called and then Buddy Killen with Tree called and congratulated him on getting the song recorded. Early that afternoon, Jim Denny called Anderson and said, "If you give me the publishing on your song, I believe I can get Ray Price to cut it."[4]

Roger also sang harmony on Ray Price's hit, "Heartaches By The Number," which was recorded on January 29, 1959 and entered the *Billboard* country chart on May 11 and rose to number two. The song, written by Harlan Howard, remained on the chart for 40 weeks.

In the summer of 1957, Jack Stapp resigned as Program Director from WSM and became general manager of WKDA, a rival station in Nashville. As part of that agreement, Stapp was allowed to own Tree Publishing, which he purchased back from Lou Cowan and Harry Fleischman after Cowan was named president of CBS and had to sell the company. Stapp wanted to keep Buddy Killen as an employee but could not afford to pay him a full-time salary, so he gave him 30 percent of the company. Stapp gave his assistant, Joyce Bush, 20 percent of the company because he needed her help as well.

Buddy Killen often told the story of being in Mom's—later known as Tootsie's—one night when Roger Miller and his wife came in. Miller introduced himself and told Killen that he was a songwriter and needed money because he and Barbara were broke. Barbara would have been nine months pregnant at that meeting. According to Killen, he gave Roger his last five dollars and told him to come to Tree's offices on Monday morning and he would listen to his songs.[5]

Tree's offices were in the Cumberland Lodge Building at 319 7th Avenue, about two blocks from the Ryman Auditorium (and Mom's). Killen related that he was impressed with Miller's songs and gave him a $25 "draw" or weekly advance against royalties. Miller had asked for $50 but settled for $25 while Jack Stapp was upset they had to pay so much for a songwriter.

According to Killen, Miller was an unknown songwriter; however, Miller had been in Nashville and had songs recorded by Jimmy Dean and George Jones as well as several singles released on Starday. A publisher would have known that. Additionally, it probably came up during the conversation between Killen and Miller that Ray Price had just recorded "Invitation to the Blues."

The meeting between Killen and Roger Miller probably occurred on Saturday night, May 10 and came because Roger performed with Ray Price on the Opry that night. Roger and Killen would have met at Tree on Monday, May 12 because in the May 19 issue of *Music Reporter* it was announced "Tree Signs Miller." The article states that Roger's songs have been recorded by Rex Allen, Jimmy Dean, Ray Price and Marvin Rainwater and that Miller had two releases on Mercury-Starday.[6]

Back in Shamrock, Roger and Barbara Miller's first child, Michael Dean, was born May 31, 1958. The child was born with "blue baby syndrome" and never left the hospital; the child died on June 30 and was buried in Shamrock.

"Roger didn't pay the hospital bill or pay for the funeral," said James Crow. "He left a lot of bills unpaid in Shamrock when he left. My parents and I paid them because it was the right thing to do."[7]

Owen Bradley, a big band leader with WSM and his brother, guitarist Harold Bradley, had built two studios; one on Second Avenue, then another in Hillsboro Village before Owen and Paul Cohen purchased an old house at 804 16th Avenue South in December, 1954 to construct a recording studio.[8]

In 1958, Paul Cohen left Decca to begin his own record label and Owen became head of the country division for Decca Records. Owen produced Red Foley, Ernest Tubb and Kitty Wells, some of the biggest acts in country music. Country music was a singles business and the major buyers of country singles were jukeboxes so the key to having a country hit at the end of the 1950s was to get it played on jukeboxes. Bradley was on the look-out to find acts who could cut a hit single and it was beneficial if an artist could write his own songs because that meant a source of material.

In Nashville, Roger often ran around with Ernest Tubb's nephew, Douglas Glenn Tubb and Tubb's son, Justin. Tubb and Ray Price were both booked by Hal Smith and Tubb and Price were often booked on shows together. According to Harold Morrison, a fellow musician and friend of Roger's, Miller wanted to "write something with 'Half a Mind' in it." Nothing came of that writing session but, according to Douglas Glenn Tubb, he and Roger were in Mom's Café one night when Roger said he had an idea for a song and "Let's write it." The idea was "I've got half a mind to leave you, but I've only got half the heart to go."

Roger and Glenn left Mom's and got in Hutch Hutchinson's car, where they sat in the back seat with a guitar and worked on the song while Hutchinson drove. Ernest Tubb recorded "Half a Mind" on June 11, 1958 and Douglas Glenn Tubb was in the studio that evening because Tubb was scheduled to record "Next Time," a song written by Doug. Doug was surprised that his uncle also recorded "Half a Mind" and thanked him for it. Ernest wondered why Doug thanked him and Doug told him he co-wrote "Half a Mind." Ernest replied, "Your name's not on it." Doug replied, "Me and Roger wrote it the other night." Tubb asked what he should do about it—"You want me to throw it out?"—and Doug replied, "No, don't throw it out. It sounds like a hit song to me. If Roger can live with it, I can live without it."[9]

In Ronnie Pugh's biography of Ernest Tubb, Bill Anderson stated that Ernest Tubb wrote the third verse to the song. "Roger for all his talent was somewhat undisciplined, both as a person and as a writer," said Anderson. "Roger would write the 'inspiration' part, but the 'perspiration' part he didn't want to have a whole lot to do with...So he had these great two verses to 'Half a Mind' and Ernest I know wrote the third."[10]

According to Pugh, Roger sang the song to Ernest Tubb over the phone but Buddy Killen claims he took "Half a Mind" to Owen Bradley, who headed A&R for Decca Records and he recorded it on Ernest Tubb. It entered the charts on October 20 and rose to the number eight position; it remained on the charts for eleven weeks. The same week that "Half a Mind" entered the charts, another of Roger's songs, "That's the Way I Feel," recorded by Faron Young also entered the chart and rose to number nine.

In 1959, Buddy Killen brought Roger Miller to Owen Bradley, who signed him to a singles contract to Decca. On June 30 Roger recorded two of his songs for Decca Records at the Bradley Film and Recording Studio. Paul Cohen is listed on the session as producer; the musicians were led by Owen Bradley with Roger, Harold Bradley, Hank "Sugarfoot" Garland and Grady Martin on guitars; Sonny Burnette, steel guitar; Bob Moore, bass; Buddy Harman, drums; and the Anita Kerr Singers on background vocals.

Owen Bradley probably viewed Roger and his song "Jason Fleming" as a way to reach the rock'n'roll world. Roger was young and handsome; "Jason Fleming" is a lively, up tempo song about a good-time fun lovin' woman chasing "swingin' daddy-o" while the flip side, "Sweet Ramona" is a Romeo-Juliet love story.

Roger's record did not excite jukebox operators or hit the country charts, but his songs did well when recorded by other artists. By November, Roger had written a number of chart hits, including "Half a Mind" for Ernest Tubb, "Invitation to the Blues," released by both Ray Price and Rex Allen, "Nothing Can Stop Me" by George Jones and "That's the Way I Feel" for Faron Young. Two more songs by Roger, "Billy Bayou" by Jim Reeves and "Dear Lonesome" by Porter Wagoner were "destined for chart honors," according to a story in a trade magazine.[11]

On July 17, 1959, Roger and Barbara's son, Alan Douglas, was born in Nashville. Things seemed to be going well for the young couple; James Crow and his wife came for several visits "but Roger was gone a lot," he said. "He was on the road." Barbara's sister, Phyllis remembered that after Alan was born, Barbara's parents, uncle and aunt drove to Nashville and stayed a week or so, then her Mom and Phyllis stayed several more weeks, helping Barbara with the baby.

Roger was usually out late at night and liked to sleep during the day, which irked Barbara's Mom because everyone had to be quiet so he could sleep. Besides, the Crows were the kind of people who worked all day and slept at night, so it was upsetting, to say the least, when their son-in-law didn't have that schedule. Still, they got along reasonably well and Phyllis remembered that Roger took her backstage at the Grand Ole Opry where she had stars sign her autograph book.[12]

Roger had written "Billy Bayou" and Chet Atkins produced the recording of that song by Jim Reeves at the new RCA Studio at the corner of 17th Avenue South and Hawkins Street. The building had been built the previous year and the first session there was on November, 7, 1957. Chet's office was in the building, located diagonally across the alley from Cedarwood Publishing and about half a block from Owen Bradley's studio.

When he recorded "Billy Bayou," Reeves changed Roger's line, "The boogie-man will get you" to "a pretty girl will get you." "Billy Bayou" was a big hit for Roger; it entered the charts on November 10 and stayed in the number one position for eight weeks and remained on the charts for almost half a year.

Roger's second Decca session was on December 13; musicians on the session were Hank "Sugarfoot" Garland and Donny Young Lytle (who later changed his name to Johnny Paycheck) on guitars; Jack Evins on steel guitar; Joe Zinkan on bass; Buddy Harman on drums; Tommy Jackson Jr. on fiddle; and Floyd Cramer played piano.

This was a "split session" where Owen Bradley booked two artists into the studio and each recorded two songs. The two songs written by Roger, "A Man Like Me" and "The Wrong Kind of Girl," are both good, solid straight-ahead country songs; the harmony vocals were by Donny Young. (Roger had sung harmony vocal on an earlier Donny Young release on Decca).

Buddy Killen often told the story of Roger—who always needed money—coming to his office and desperately wanting $300. "He was always coming in for money," remembered Killen, "and at one time I think we had advanced him more than we could have sold Tree for, but he still kept coming back. One day he came in and said 'I've got to have

$300.' I thought he really might be in some trouble because he sounded so serious. But I also knew that he hadn't been bringing in any songs, so I told him to get in the other room and write me a hit before I'd see what I could do about it. We had a big argument about it, then finally he just gave me a disgusted look and headed for another office."[13]

Roger went into Jack Stapp's office (Stapp was at his office at the radio station) and came out 20 minutes later with "Home." After he'd written the song—and received his $300 check—Killen asked him why he desperately needed the money. Miller replied that he'd seen a riding lawnmower that he just absolutely had to have.

Bill Anderson had gone by Roger's home, on Dunbarton Drive in Goodlettsville, and was waiting for him when Roger drove down the road in the bright orange riding mower, cut a path to the front door and got off. Barbara was upset; "We can't afford a riding lawnmower," she told him. "It only cost $11," said Roger, then turned to Anderson and said, "Down!"

According to Bill Anderson and others, after Roger got off the lawnmower that day, he never cut grass with it again.[14]

On February 5, 1959, Jim Reeves recorded two Roger Miller songs: "Home" and "If Heartache is the Fashion." At the end of March, "Home" entered the country charts and rose to the number two position where it remained for four weeks.

In 1959 Roger also had hits with "Last Night At a Party" by Faron Young, which entered the charts in January and rose to number 20, and "Big Harlan Taylor" by George Jones, which entered the charts on November 23 and rose to number 19. Roger's song, "Old Man and the River" recorded by Donny Young, also entered the charts briefly that year.

In 1959, Hal Smith and Hayes Jones formed a booking agency. Jimmy Key joined them and was assigned to book Roger Miller, but it was difficult. "We booked him on some package shows," remembered Key, "but we were lucky to get $100 or $150 a night for him. It seemed like everybody liked to be around Roger because he was so funny but a lot of people thought he was a joke."

Key remembered Roger coming into the booking offices in Goodlettsville one day and waving a check that he had received from an insurance company for an accident he was in. "I get more money out of having accidents than I do from you booking me," Roger said. Then, according to Key, Roger left and had another accident a couple of blocks away.[15]

Always looking to acquire a few extra bucks, Roger went to Starday in the latter half of 1959 and recorded some sound-a-likes for producer Tommy Hill. Those were recordings of hit songs by singers who attempted to sound like the original. They were sold at budget prices and the singers were reportedly paid $10 a song. Don Pierce had initiated a series of albums, *Hillbilly Hit Parade*, where singers recorded sound-a-like recordings of hits and packaged these on budget albums. Roger recorded "Country Girl," which had been a hit for Faron Young; "I Ain't Never," a hit for Webb Pierce; "Under Your Spell Again," a hit for Buck Owens; "Jimmie Brown, The Newsboy," a hit for Mac Wiseman; and "Who Shot Sam?" a George Jones hit. Tommy Hill sang harmony vocals with Roger on these songs.

Late in 1959, Roger ran into Faron Young at Tootsie's bar. Roger had a long face and Faron asked him what was going on; Roger replied that he needed a job. Roger had played fiddle on a show with Faron in Indiana but Faron told him he didn't have an opening for a fiddle player but "I need a drummer. Do you play drums?" Miller asked "When do you need a drummer?" and Faron replied "Monday." "By Monday I'll be a drummer," said Roger, according to Diane Diekman in her biography of Faron Young.[16]

Roger asked Faron to buy him a set of drums—which he did at a pawnshop—and then asked for an advance to "buy groceries for his wife and baby, repair his car, and pay his electric bill." Faron paid it all and that week they went on tour.[16]

Sometime late in 1960, Roger went back to the Starday studios and recorded three more sound-a-likes, "Hot Rod Lincoln," a country hit for Charlie Ryan and a pop hit for Johnny Bond; "I Wish I Could Fall in Love Today," a Ray Price hit; and "The Tip of My Fingers," a hit for Bill Anderson. Roger also recorded "Playboy," a song he wrote.

Chapter 6
When Two Worlds Collide

Roger Miller toured with Faron Young, playing drums and singing a song or two before Faron came on, during all of 1960. Also in the band were Donny Young, (Johnny Paycheck), Tom Pritchard on upright bass, Odell Martin on lead guitar and Ben Keith on steel guitar. Dale Porter and Shorty Lavender alternated on fiddle, with Potter performing the bulk of the time.

Each member of the Deputies received $25 a day and had to pay for meals out of that amount. Faron paid for the bands' outfits, which were colorful, sequined suits, and their hotel rooms.

According to Diane Diekman in her biography of Young, "Miller took his turn at the wheel of the limo. But he found a way to shorten his driving stint. He closed his right eye and pretended to fall asleep. While watching the road through his left eye, he'd drop his head and jerk it back up. Faron made him pull over." Faron was quoted as saying, "We went on a five-thousand-mile trip and he drove thirty-seven miles."[1]

Miller wrote songs while on the road and Faron often told the story that Roger wrote "In The Summertime" (You Don't Want My Love)" in the middle of the night and banged on Faron's door to play it for him although Faron, who was inebriated, repeatedly threatened to kick him off the bus. Faron finally woke up and listened to the song but "called it the most horrible song he'd ever heard."

Roger was always full of nervous energy, both natural and enhanced with pills. He was constantly playing his songs for people—artists, friends, neighbors, you name it. Roger was always ready to entertain a crowd, no matter how small, and play the newest song he had written.

Life on the road was fueled by music and pills. The pep pills kept the musicians going; the band usually played a gig, then had to pack up and head to another one, perhaps several hundred miles away. On one trip to El Paso, the band members bought marijuana in Mexico. When Americans crossed the border they had to stop and announce they were Americans before they were waved through.

Faron Young's band members were headed west from El Paso with

Darrell McCall driving and Faron in the front passenger seat. In the middle seat, Roger and steel guitar player Ben Keith pulled a blanket over them and lit a joint. At a construction zone, McCall had to stop the car and, when he did, Young ordered Roger and Keith to "get rid of the weed." Roger stuck his head out of the blanket, saw a man holding a red stop sign, rolled down the window and yelled "American!"

According to McCall, "We'd get to a show date, and Faron would check us in a motel, we'd take our instruments in the room and set there and pick until we had to work the show." The band would play the show, load the car and head out again. "A lot of times we never cracked the covers on the bed," said McCall. "We were crazy on the road."[2]

Although Roger played drums for Faron Young, he also picked up dates with other artists; if an artist had a show scheduled and Roger wasn't booked with Faron, he might go out with them to play. Some artists had bands they toured with regularly but other artists did not keep a regular band; instead, they hired musicians when they needed them. Roger picked up extra money this way.

A number of songwriters—including Willie Nelson—earned money as road musicians while others, like Hank Cochran and Harlan Howard, preferred to stay in town. The advantage of remaining in Nashville was that songwriters were ready to pitch a song whenever there was a recording session. The advantage of road musicians like Roger was that they were with artists on the road for extended periods of time, including times when there was nothing to do but play and sing songs they wrote with the artist listening.

Roger came into Tree's office one day and, responding to Buddy Killen's question of whether he had written any songs, said "I've written this little thing that Skeeter Davis likes." Roger had been playing for Skeeter on the road and sang "In the Summertime" but only had a verse and chorus. Killen informed him he needed another verse so Roger wrote the second verse and they demoed the song. Killen played the demo for Chet Atkins at RCA, who liked the song and asked "Who do you think would be good for it?"

Killen told Chet he thought Roger should do it, although Roger was still on Decca at the time. Killen called Owen Bradley and asked the producer if he would release Roger from his recording contract; Bradley agreed and on August 10, 1960, Roger did his first RCA session.[3] The session was produced by Chet Atkins and split between Roger and another artist. Roger recorded two songs, "You Don't Want My Love" and an old song in the Public Domain that Bill Monroe had recorded in 1945, "Footprints in the Snow." Backing him on the afternoon session were Roy Huskey, Jr. on bass, Floyd Cramer on piano, Buddy Harman on drums, Hank Garland and Ben Schaefele on guitars and the Anita Kerr Singers (Kerr, Dottie Dillard, Gil Wright and Louis Nunley) on background vocals.

"You Don't Want My Love" entered the *Billboard* Country chart on October 31 and rose to number 14, remaining on the chart for 16 weeks. Andy Williams covered the song for the pop market and that version entered the *Billboard* Pop Chart on December 12 and reached number 64. Although the song did not reach the top of the charts, it became popular because Andy Williams regularly sang it on his television show, which was on NBC from September, 1962 until July, 1971.

Songwriter John D. Loudermilk remembers that "Just before they allowed mixed drinks in Nashville, Roger and I used to hang around a bit together. One day he said 'What do you do for entertainment here? There's no bars or anything!' I said, 'Well, I go to Night Court and see what the police bring in.' I told him 'You have to dress up with a suit and carry a clip board so the Judge will think you're a reporter.' So we did that several times. One night we were on the way down to Night Court and a police car came up and said 'I think you ought to follow that car.' They thought we were detectives. I had just gotten a new car so we followed that police car and went to the Capitol Park Inn. We got out and went in and saw the police down at the end of a long hall and they motioned for us to come down so we went there. The police said 'We've got the subject in this room' so Detective Miller and his policeman went around to the outside door and we heard some shooting so my policeman took out his gun and shot the door open. The subject was between the box springs and the mattress and his feet were sticking out and he had on black sox and garters to hold up his sox. Roger and his policeman came in and took the mattress off the guy—and it was the wrong room. Roger looked over at me and moved his head to the side, meaning 'Let's get the hell out of here' so we went back and got in the car and left."[4]

George Hamilton IV had a pop hit in 1956 with "A Rose and a Baby Ruth" on ABC-Paramount. He continued to have records on the pop charts but wanted to be a country singer. His first country chart record was "Before This Day Ends." On the flip side of that record was a song Roger wrote, "Loneliness All Around Me."

"I think he sang it for me," remembered Hamilton, "since that's the way most songwriters pitched songs in those days." That was Hamilton's last record for ABC-Paramount, then he joined RCA where he was produced by Chet Atkins.

"I used to run into Roger at RCA," remembered Hamilton. "Chet always got a kick out of Roger's songs, which were so clever."

"Once my wife, Tink, and I went on a double date with Roger and Barbara to a movie," remembered Hamilton. "They drove over to our house and when we came back Roger said he'd just cut a new session at RCA and asked if we'd like to hear it. We said 'Yes' and Roger got the acetate out of his car and put it on the phonograph in the living room and pantomimed it as it played. He was so funny! He performed for an audience of three like he was on Dick Clark's American Bandstand!"

George Hamilton IV also remembered a tour where Roger, Willie Nelson (who was also on RCA) and he played a package show in Austin, Texas "back when Roger and Willie both had short hair and wore a suit and tie." Also on that show was Bob Wills and His Texas Playboys. Roger came into their dressing room "carrying this really filthy, slimy thing in his hand," said Hamilton, "and we asked 'What is that Roger?' Roger said 'Don't you recognize it? This is Bob Wills' cigar!' Roger had followed Bob Wills around until he dropped his cigar, and Bob Wills chewed a cigar until it was pretty nasty. Roger was carrying it like it was a holy relic. He said he was going to take it home and frame it."

"Roger was a really lovable, likeable guy," said Hamilton. "And he was always so funny!"[5]

Roger's second chart record on RCA was "When Two Worlds Collide," which he wrote with Bill Anderson. The initial idea came from a science fiction movie, *When Worlds Collide*, that Roger loved. Roger wanted that to be the title of the song but Anderson countered with "When

Two Worlds Collide" and as they drove to San Antonio for a series of performances in Texas in Roger's bright green Rambler station wagon, they sat in the back seat and, while Johnny Sea drove, wrote the song.

The song was finished around midnight but they did not have a tape recorder so they stayed up all night, singing the song to each other until they arrived in San Antonio around eight that morning. They checked into their hotel and Roger called Neal Merritt, a disc jockey friend, who brought over a tape recorder so they could record the song.[6]

(NOTE: Neal Merritt later achieved songwriting fame by writing "May the Bird of Paradise Fly Up Your Nose" for Little Jimmy Dickens.)

On February 2, 1961, Roger went into the RCA Studio and recorded two songs: "Every Which-A-Way" and "When Two Worlds Collide." The session was again produced by Chet Atkins, who played guitar, with Bob Moore on bass, Buddy Harman on drums, Floyd Cramer on piano and Hank Garland and Velma Smith on guitars.

Bob Moore remembered that he told Roger that "When Two Worlds Collide" would be a hit—and bet Roger $100 that it would sell 100,000 copies. Roger bet him it wouldn't; Roger lost "but it took a while to collect that bet," said Moore, "because it took a while to sell that many records."[7]

Roger's record entered the *Billboard* country chart on June 5, 1961 and reached number six, remaining on the chart for 18 weeks.

Bobby Bare remembers that "Roger used to make fun of that song. Called it 'Two Worlds Clyde.'"

A little less than two weeks after the recording session—on February 18—Roger and Barbara's daughter, Rhonda was born in Shamrock.

In August, Roger went on a tour of California, booked by Hal Smith with Curtis Artist's Productions. On that tour he played Tinker Air Force Base on August 18, then San Bernardino, Claremont, Ventura, Oxnard, Long Beach, Disneyland, La Puente, Lompoc, Santa Clara, Redding, Lodi, Bakersfield and finished on September 8 and 9 back in San Bernardino. For each of these shows, Roger received $150 and paid 10 percent commission to the booking agency.

Bobby Bare remembers that "Roger was booked at the Red Barrel in Orange County. Willie was out there, too and so was Earl Ball, the piano player. I told Roger 'We'll be out to see you' so I picked up Willie and we drove there. It wasn't a huge crowd but Roger was up there being Roger.

Putting on a show. We sat down and some guy kept coming up to our table and talking and he sat down in Roger's chair. So when Roger came off the stage the guy wouldn't get up and that pissed off Roger so he grabbed the guy by his collar and the seat of his pants and got him going and threw him out the door and the minute that happened, Willie hopped up and ran right behind him to get Roger's back in case anybody else wanted to get in on it. Nothing happened—but I thought 'Those guys mean business.'"

Roger was known to get in fights. "He'd go off sometimes," remembered Bare. "He got in a fight with Sammy Jackson once and Roger wound up with a big black eye."[8]

Chapter 7
When A House Is Not A Home

Roger lived at 4704 Grinstead Place in Nashville. Harlan and Jan Howard had previously lived in this small, two bedroom house in Inglewood. When the Howards moved to a home on Graycroft, "Roger asked if we would leave the deposit so he could move into that house because he didn't have the money for a deposit. That's how Roger and his family moved into that house," remembered Jan Howard.[1]

The house on Grinstead Place was where "I Fall to Pieces" was written and the demo recorded. Hank Cochran came to the house one day and told Jan to "Tell Harlan I got an idea but I can't put it together." Their garage had been turned into an office where Harlan recorded his demos. "I sat on the desk while they sat there and wrote 'I Fall to Pieces,'" said Jan, who recorded the demo and wanted to release it as a single. Harlan promised the song to her, then came home one day and told her that Patsy Cline was going to record it. "That's the day I almost divorced him," remembered Jan. "That happened a lot and eventually we did get a divorce."

After the Howards moved to Graycroft, Roger came over to their house "whenever Barbara kicked him out," said Jan. "He was always calling the house and asking 'Got any peanut butter and jelly? How about some milk?' and I'd say 'Yes.'"

On September 19, 1961, Roger recorded three songs for RCA: "Fair Swiss Maiden," "Sorry, Willie" and "Burma Shave." Guitarists on that session, produced by Chet Atkins, were Atkins, Jerry Kennedy and Velma Smith with Roy Huskey, Jr. on bass, Buddy Harman on drums, Floyd Cramer on piano and the Anita Kerr Singers on background vocals.

Jerry Kennedy grew up in Shreveport and performed regularly on the Louisiana Hayride and traveled with their troupe; he played with Johnny Horton. Kennedy moved to Nashville and soon became a member of the "A" team of studio musicians who played on a number of classic recordings.

Chet Atkins was a hero of Jerry Kennedy's and that RCA session on Roger was the first time Kennedy played on a session for Chet. Kennedy was so nervous that after the session he went outside and threw up. This was also the first time that Kennedy played on a Roger Miller session, but it was not the first time that Kennedy met Roger. That initial meeting occurred outside the Cumberland Lodge Building, where Roger and Joe Tex were trying to put a Tootsie Roll in the tail of one of the stone lions outside that building to make it look like it was taking a crap.[2]

"Sorry, Willie" was about Willie Nelson and his first wife, who were separating at the time. "She was kind of a wild one around Nashville and I just wrote that song," remembered Roger.[3]

"Swiss Maiden" b/w "Burma Shave" was released as a single but did not chart in *Billboard*; however, "Fair Swiss Maiden" reached number 34 on the *Cash Box* charts.

On November 10, Roger moved out of his house with Barbara and their children and moved into an apartment. On November 20, a "Bill for Separate Maintenance" was filed in Davidson County, Tennessee which noted that the couple had two children, Alan, two and a half years old, and Rhonda, nine months and that Barbara was three and a half months pregnant.

The bill stated that Tree Publishing employed Roger and "handles all of his financial affairs." According to Barbara, Roger informed her that "his work comes above everything else and that if it should appear that his home life is interfering with his work that his work comes first whether she liked it or not."

When Roger moved out, he told Barbara that "he was too tied down and that he must be free in order to maintain his position and success in the music business." Barbara stated in the bill that even though Roger generally slept at his apartment, he "returns to their home whenever he needs something done for himself or when he wishes to have intercourse" and that "he sneaks into the house" while she and the children are asleep "which greatly disturbs and upsets" her.

In the bill, Barbara asserts that Roger "has struck her on several occasions," the latest came during "a car ride in August" and that he "possesses a wild and unmanageable temper which goes off when she asks where he is going or why he does not spend some time with his family."

The court document notes that "because of the late hours the defendant is required to keep up in making his personal appearances he began taking some type of drug or medicine which peps him up and keeps him from being sleepy, and that he has begun taking these pills regularly even when he had no need to stay awake and complainant feels that his tantrums might be caused by taking these pills." The bill further states that Roger "possesses little or no sense of value and responsibility in financial affairs and that unless restrained from doing so spends all money available to him without considering the necessities of his family and home." She stated that all of Roger's earning are sent to Tree, which "disburses money to him upon his satisfying them that he needs the money."

Barbara noted that she had to call Tree in order to get money and that the couple owned no property.[4]

Bobby Bare knew Roger in those early days. He lived in California at the time and "When I came to town I'd stay at the Downtowner, which was a motel and you could get crazy there. And we did. Roger and me and Willie and Harlan Howard and a lot of songwriters. I remember sitting around and listening to Tex Ritter talk—we all loved Tex—and he'd talk all night long. It was nuts. It would get really crazy there with women all over the place. In order for me to get any rest so I could record I would go out to Roger's house and sleep. His wife was always pissed off at him because he'd come dragging in and bringing me and he'd been gone for a day or two. That marriage went to hell so he moved in with Bayron Binkley, who had an apartment out on West End. I'd go out there and crash and I remember one time that Roger was getting ready to drive to Albuquerque in his Nash Rambler. He was putting fuzzy stuff on the light switches and he was getting that stuff on just right. Electric fur. Then he was going to rush and pack and drive to Albuquerque."[5]

Bayron Binkley worked as a TV director at WSM; among his jobs was directing Ralph Emery's early morning television show. Binkley first met Roger at the Carousel Club in Printer's Alley. "He played in the Alley quite a bit and sat in with other people on their shows," remembered Binkley. "The big stars hung out at the Carousel and I was there. I had just gone through a divorce and didn't have a place to stay so I was roaming around. When I met him he said 'Where are you staying?' and I told him I didn't have a place to stay so out of the goodness of his heart he said 'You can stay with me.' He lived in a little bitty apartment—just a bedroom, bathroom and sitting room, there wasn't even a kitchen—on West End Avenue behind a funeral home."[6]

Binkley remembered that "One night Roger was doing a one man show at the Carousel and that club had seats right up to the stage. I was sitting on that front row and there was a heckler and Roger asked him to be polite and let him do his show. He did that about three times but the heckler continued so he said 'Bink, you help me' and he got up from the stage, walked over and cold-cocked the guy—knocked him out. Then he jumped off the stage and each one of us grabbed hold of an arm of the guy, who was unconscious, and we dragged him out the front door. It was hard to get him out of the door because his feet were turned out but we finally got him out and then Roger went back in and finished his show."

Roger was still married to Barbara when he and Binkley started running around together. "He got mad at me once because we had an agreement not to interfere with the other's personal life but she called me and I told her that I would try to get Roger to communicate with her and Roger said that broke our agreement. It took a pretty good while to get over that because he didn't want anyone talking to Barbara."

"Roger didn't like to do anything that everybody else liked to do," said Binkley. "Occasionally we went fishing but we didn't know what we were doing. After I got remarried he'd call at like three in the morning and my wife would answer and he'd say 'Nancy, can Bink come out and play?' A lot of times I'd get up and we'd be out all night. A lot of times we would just ride around or go see other people. We'd pop in and a lot of people would tell him to go to bed. He liked to stay up all night, more than I did, but I went with him a lot of times when I'd rather been sleeping."

Roger and Binkley often attended parties in people's homes and "he'd play the guitar and sing—just entertain. He made so many noises with his mouth, like instruments. He'd play the guitar, then do the harmony or string sounds with his mouth. He'd do that in the car when he was writing—he'd put in the turnarounds and fills with noises from his mouth."

"He had a lot of connections with a lot of people and he was quite a ladies' man," said Binkley, who remembered that Roger "liked to write songs riding around in his Cadillac. We'd be out and I'd be driving and all of sudden he'd get an idea for a song so I'd stop the car and he'd get out and open the trunk and get his guitar. Then he'd sit in the back seat and write while I drove."

Roger was in Nashville quite a bit during this period. He didn't have a band but every now and then he'd get booked on a package show "or somebody would just take him because they wanted to have him with them," remembered Binkley. "They just loved to have him around because he was so entertaining and such a good musician. They never knew where he was going to be coming from."

After Roger moved out of his apartment he stayed in motels and Binkley remembered that "he would never wash his underwear. When it came time for fresh underwear he'd buy underwear in those packages of three or four in a pack and then just throw his old ones away. He went through a lot of briefs," said Binkley, who added, "That was a brief moment in the history of Roger Miller."[7]

Nashville musicians were fueled by amphetamines during the late 1950s and on through the 1960s. The "yellow jackets" or "old yellers" were quite popular with session musicians, who often had to play three or four sessions a day, day after day, and the road musicians who had to drive hundreds of miles, play a date, then drive hundreds more miles to the next date.

"There used to be a Foxall Drugstore on Sixteenth Avenue," said Bayron Binkley. "And back then everybody was taking 'old yellers,' which was a diet pill that was a speed pill. Roger didn't particularly care for alcohol but he loved 'old yellers' because he believed they stimulated his creative juices. He'd get diarrhea of the mouth and come up with some of the craziest one-liners from being on those pills. He had a deal with the druggist where he'd go in there behind the counter where all the pills were kept. He knew where they were, what each one was and what it did and he'd place an order. He'd say 'I want some of these and some of those' and point to where each one was. When we walked out of there he'd have a full supply."[8]

Ray Stevens did not take the pep pills but had done three sessions one day and needed to do arrangements for a Brenda Lee session the next day. Another studio musician gave him a "yellow jacket" and "I was up for three days," said Ray.[9] Mother Maybelle Carter needed to drive all night and reportedly took one of Johnny Cash's pills to help her stay awake; she was up for three days.

The pills kept you "up," jumpy and nervous. Ray Stevens remembers running into Roger once when Roger couldn't talk; instead, his teeth chattered and mumbled. During the late 1950s and early 1960s Roger was reportedly taking 70-90 pills a day.

On February 7, 1962 Roger went into the RCA Studio and recorded four songs: "You Can't Do Me This Way (And Get By With It)," "I Catch Myself Crying," "I Get Up Early In The Morning" and "Hitch-Hiker."

The session was produced by Chet Atkins and engineered by Bill Porter; the musicians on the session were Chet on guitar, Joe Zinkan on bass, Hargus "Pig" Robbins on piano, John Greubel on drums, Pete Drake on steel and Jerry Kennedy and Jerry Reed on guitars with backing vocals by Millie Kirkham, Gil Wright, Jr., Louis Nunley and Dottie Dillard.

At the end of April, "Sorry, Willie" b/w "Hitch-Hiker" was released as a single; "Hitch-Hiker" reached number 35 on the *Cash Box* chart but did not chart in *Billboard*.

In March, Jack Parr left as host of "The Tonight Show" and for the next six months, there was a series of guest hosts for that show. Jimmy Dean was a hot artist at that time; his record of "Big Bad John" was number one on the country chart for two weeks and number one on the *Billboard* Hot 100 for five weeks in early 1962. Dean had previously hosted a TV show on CBS and signed with the William Morris Agency, which had strong connections booking TV shows. "Big Bad John" had gotten him booked on "The Tonight Show starring Jack Parr," so Dean was one of those asked to be a "Guest Host" for "The Tonight Show" during the six months they looked for a permanent host.

When Dean came to town for recording sessions he checked into the Anchor Motel on West End Avenue and songwriters came by to pitch their songs. Roger Miller sat with Dean "and sang those funny songs like 'Lou's Got the Flu' and all that stuff and he thought I was the funniest person he'd ever run into," remembered Roger. "He said, 'I'm hosting 'The Tonight Show' in June. Would you come to New York and be on it?'" Roger said he would and that was his first appearance on television, a medium that was made for him.[10]

Roger also appeared on "The Tonight Show" when Groucho Marx hosted and Marx came out and introduced Roger with "Here's a guy they say is wonderful, say he's pretty good but I've never heard of him." When Roger came out he said, "Well, thanks, Groucho. I've never heard of you but I've read your brother, Karl's book." It was a funny line but Grouch deadpanned, "Karl Marx was not one of the Marx Brothers." By that point, "The audience was on my side" said Roger, who became one of the few to win a battle of wits with Groucho Marx.[11]

On August 2, 1962 Roger went into the RCA Studio and recorded two songs, "If You Want Me To" and "Little Star." Produced by Chet Atkins and engineered by Bill Porter, the musicians on the session were Chet on guitar, along with Velma Smith and Jerry Reed, Henry Strzelecki on bass, Jack Greubel on drums, Charlie McCoy on harmonica, and Floyd Cramer on piano.

Six days later, Roger went back in the studio and re-recorded "Hey Little Star" in addition to "I'll Be Somewhere" and "Trouble on the Turnpike." That session was also produced by Atkins and engineered by Porter and featured Atkins, Jerry Reed and Jerry Kennedy on guitars, Henry Strzelecki on bass, Willie Ackerman on drums, Hargus "Pig" Robbins on piano, Bill Pursell on vibes and backing vocals by the Anita Kerr Singers. In addition to the basic rhythm section, a string section was added on "Hey, Little Star" and "I'll Be Somewhere" with arrangements by Anita Kerr.

In between those two sessions, on August 6, Roger was on "The Merv Griffin Show" with Gale Storm, Henny Youngman, Johnny Nash and golfer Sam Snead. Later that month, he was on "The Tonight Show," hosted by Hal March, with guests Abe Burrows, Roberta Peters, Pat Harrington and Joannie Sommers.

"The Tonight Show" settled on Johnny Carson, who had hosted a game show, "Who Do You Trust" with sidekick Ed McMahon. Carson's first night as host of "The Tonight Show" was October 1, 1962; the following night, Roger appeared on the show. Carson was so nervous that "people thought he was waving at 'em," remembered Roger. "I remember saying to him, 'Hey we're gonna be all right.' I wasn't an old pro or anything but I thought he was doing great." Roger was becoming increasingly popular on TV talk shows with his quick wit and funny songs. On November 21, Roger was back on "The Tonight Show" starring Johnny Carson with guests Sam Snead, Patrice Munsel, and Walter Gaudnek. He had met the staff of "The Tonight Show" "and knew everybody so I was like part of the family," said Roger. He also had "great rapport with Johnny," which led to more appearances on that show.

Bayron Binkley remembered that on Roger's first appearance on "The Tonight Show" with Johnny Carson he was late for the rehearsal, so when he got on the air they asked him why he was late. He told them "My roommate has a poodle and he assured me that the poodle didn't get fleas but I found out he was wrong because when I opened my suitcase it was full of fleas. So I had to go out and buy a whole new outfit to wear on the show."[12]

In September, "Trouble on the Turnpike" b/w "Hey Little Star" was released as a single with "Hey Little Star" reaching number 45 on *Cash Box*'s country chart.

Roger Miller had success as a songwriter in the early 1960s but never had a huge, career defining hit. In October, 1960, Roger had "Loneliness All Around Me" on the "B" side of George Hamilton IV's first country record and Ray Sanders' recording of "A World So Full of Love" entered the *Billboard* Country Chart and rose to number 18. Faron Young covered that song and his version entered the chart in January, 1961 and reached number 28; although Roger was the only writer listed on Sanders' record, Faron was listed as co-writer of that song on his record.

On June 26, 1961, Claude Gray's recording of "My Ears Should Burn (When Fools Are Talked About)" entered the *Billboard* chart; it rose to number three and remained in that position for three consecutive weeks, spending 19 weeks total on the charts. Jan Howard recorded "A World I Can't Live In" and Little Jimmy Dickens recorded "A House Is Not a Home."

On December 29, the Grand Ole Opry presented a Carnegie Hall show for the benefit of the Musicians Aid Society. The line-up included Patsy Cline, Jim Reeves, Bill Monroe, Marty Robbins, Grandpa Jones, Minnie Pearl, the Jordanaires and Faron Young. Playing drums for Faron was Roger Miller, in front of a sellout crowd of 2,700 in that august concert hall.

Chapter 8
Smash

In January, 1963, Jimmy Dean spent two weeks hosting "The Tonight Show" while Johnny Carson took a break. He had Roger on the show, singing "In the Summertime" as well as Eddy Arnold, The Jordanaires, Chet Atkins, Anita Bryant and Homer and Jethro as guests. It was a great shot in the arm for Roger and for country music.

On Valentine's Day, Roger went into the RCA Studio and recorded three songs: "Lock, Stock and Teardrops," "But I Love You More" and "I Know Who It Is (And I'm Gonna Tell On Him)." Chet Atkins produced the session with engineer Bill Porter; the line-up was familiar; on bass was Henry Strzelecki, Floyd Cramer played piano, on drums was Willie Ackerman, playing guitars were Ray Edenton and Wayne Moss with Pete Drake playing "talking steel."

Roger was friends with Patsy Cline and her husband, Charlie Dick "and used to come around to the house a lot," remembered Dick. "He'd come over to the house to jam because everything shut down at midnight so you'd have to either go to an after hours club or somebody's house. Roger was dating Anita Carter and brought her around a couple of times. He was a good friend."

Charlie Dick remembered that "Roger had just bought a new 1962 car and a little while after that I bought a brand new 1963 car at the end of 1962. One afternoon I was in Tootsie's and Roger came running in the door and said, 'Come out here—I want you to see this' so we went outside and he showed me my car and said 'I've got to have one.' He'd just gotten a new car but he went out and bought one like I had. Buddy Killen was always flipped because Roger was always wanting to buy something."[1]

According to Roger, Patsy Cline wanted to record "Lock, Stock and Teardrops" but on March 5, less than three weeks after his session, the plane carrying Patsy, Hawkshaw Hawkins, Cowboy Copas and Randy Hughes went down in Camden, Tennessee and all four were killed.

"Roger, Billy Graves and Hubert Long came over to the house when they heard the plane was missing," remembered Charlie Dick. Roger,

Graves and Long went down to Camden and joined in the search during the period when no one was sure of what happened or where the plane was.

"I looked for that wreck all night. It was raining hard, and I just had this picture in my mind that they were hurt and laying out there in the rain," remembered Roger. "I never had any experiences with accidents or stuff like that. So we went through the woods yelling their names all night. It was daybreak next morning before I could climb a fire tower. I saw some tore up trees. We ran over there, and there it was."[2]

"Roger was a good guy but wild," said Charlie Dick. "He wasn't the world's greatest singer or greatest musician but he was funny and people liked having him around. Everybody liked Roger."[3]

In April, RCA released "Lock, Stock and Teardrops" b/w "I Know Who It Is (and I'm Gonna Tell on Him)" and it entered the *Billboard* country chart on June 1 and hit number 26 for one week; however, it stayed on *Cash Box*'s chart for 15 weeks and reached number 11.

In 1960 George and Pauline Crow moved to Duncan, Oklahoma. "It was easier to live in Duncan because of the drive he had to make hauling crude oil to the carbon black plant," remembered James Crow. Roger and Barbara's marriage was off-and-on; they would split and she would go back to her parents in Duncan, then they'd get back together in Nashville. On May 13, 1963 their third child, Shari, was born in Duncan.

"Roger never liked Barbara pregnant, so every time she had a baby she went back to Duncan," said Phyllis. After Shari's birth, the couple reconciled and Barbara came back to Nashville. Barbara knew that Roger had girlfriends and it upset her; "it really hurt her self-esteem," said Phyllis. "But she really loved him."[4]

In 1963 Felton Jarvis moved into an office at 1007 17th Avenue South on Music Row. Jarvis had been hired by ABC/Paramount Records as a staff producer and had just moved to Nashville. One evening, around 7 or 8 o'clock, Roger stopped by Felton's office and inadvertently parked in a way that blocked a neighbor's driveway. That man became angry at Roger and pulled a knife on him—moving towards Roger with the knife while Roger walked backwards up the street. Doug Gilmore, who owned the building where Felton rented an office, saw what was happening and came out of his office and broke up the altercation.

Roger then went up to see Felton and when he came back down, stuck his head in Gilmore's office and offered to buy him a beer. Gilmore agreed and they headed to a downtown bar where a number of men in the real estate business gathered. Gilmore had graduated from Vanderbilt in 1958—he was quarterback on the Vanderbilt team that went to the Gator Bowl in 1955—and was in the construction business. There was a hat on a table and Gilmore picked it up and—attempting to be funny—put it on Roger's chair as he sat down. Roger crushed the hat when he sat on it, then took it out and began trying to get it back in shape when the guy who owned the hat took offense at Roger and "next thing I know they were in a fist fight rolling around on the floor," remembered Gilmore.

The bouncer came over, grabbed Roger and pinned his arms back "which gave the other guy a free shot at Roger," said Gilmore, "but I happened to catch him just before he got to Roger and popped him." Gilmore then looked at Roger "who was in hysterics, laughing, and said 'You've saved my life twice in one day.'" That was the beginning of the friendship between Roger Miller and Doug Gilmore.[5]

Both Roger and Gilmore were going through divorces so Gilmore arranged for Roger to stay in an apartment he owned in East Nashville.

The Urban Folk revival was going strong, especially with college students. In July, 1963, the folk movement reached its apex at The Newport Folk Festival when Pete Seeger hosted an event that featured Bob Dylan and Joan Baez, the reigning king and queen of folk music.

Folk music was so popular that in April, 1963, the ABC network telecast "Hootenanny," a Saturday night show hosted by Jack Linkletter. Folklorists connected country music to the folk movement, which brought attention to country music from academics and college students, and Johnny Cash headlined a show at the Hollywood Bowl billed as "The First Giant Folk, Western, Bluegrass Spectacular." In the line-up of artists were Cash, the Carter Family, Johnny Western, Merle Travis, Patsy Cline, Flatt and Scruggs, Gene Autry—and Roger Miller.[6]

On September 10, there was a hootenanny held in Centennial Park in Nashville, headlined by "The Clown Prince of Country Music" Roger Miller. The event was sponsored by the morning newspaper, the Tennessean and featured, in addition to Miller, Fred Carter, Walter Forbes, Alan Reynolds, The Boys From Shiloh, The Cape Gay Trio and 13-year old Bobby Watral.

The Tuesday night event was a free "back to school" concert and, according to the newspaper article, received "wild cheers." The show ran for almost two hours before Roger Miller took the stage and sang "Lock Stock and Teardrops," "You Don't Want My Love" and "I Know Who It Is" in addition to country standards like "Ya'll Come."

Folkies liked acoustic instruments and most folk artists performed with a minimum of accompaniment, but Miller was backed by a band that included Billy Rainsford on electric piano, Jack Eubanks on electric guitar, X. Lincoln on bass and Larry Graham on drums.[7]

On September 27, Barbara Miller filed a "Bill for Separate Maintenance" against Roger. The couple had three minor children: Alan was four, Rhonda was two and a half and Shari was 16 months old. The bill stated the couple had lived in Nashville for six years and that Roger's estimated income was over $50,000 a year, although Barbara really did not know how much money he made.

The bill stated "That despite the fact sums of money earned by the defendant and coming into his hands, he, perhaps because of his artistic nature, has little comprehension of the needs of his wife and children and has so neglected their needs that they are deprived of the basic necessities of life, including food at times." At the time of the filing, Barbara did not know where Roger was.

The court awarded Barbara $650 a month, to be paid on the fifteenth of each month in addition to providing transportation and paying her lawyer $100.

By this time, Barbara lived at 4605 Log Cabin Road in Nashville.[8]

Sometime in September or early October, Roger made an appointment with Jerry Kennedy at the Mercury offices across the street from the Quonset Hut studio. In 1962 Columbia Records purchased the Bradley Recording Studio, generally known as "The Quonset Hut," and house in front of it and established their Nashville headquarters there. Mercury continued to record in the Quonset Hut studio because it remained open for outside bookings.

Roger told Jerry that he was dissatisfied with RCA and would like to record for Mercury. Jerry agreed—he knew Roger was a huge talent and had played on several of his sessions for RCA.

Jerry Kennedy learned a valuable lesson from Owen Bradley about how business was conducted in Nashville soon after he arrived. Mercury signed Roy Drusky, who had been on the Decca label, without informing Bradley of their intentions. Bradley called Kennedy's office and demanded that Jerry see him as soon as possible. Jerry went to Owen's office and Bradley gave him a dressing down, telling him that was "not the way we do business in Nashville," recalled Kennedy. "I didn't have anything to do with that signing—Shelby Singleton did that. But Owen let me know that everybody worked together in Nashville and kept each other informed about what they were doing."[9]

That led Jerry Kennedy to call Chet Atkins and ask if Roger could be released from his contract from RCA. Chet agreed, saying "New York doesn't believe in him. It will probably be a good move for Roger."

The failure to get hits on Roger Miller was a major regret in Chet Atkin's career and life, according to Ralph Emery. "Chet knew Roger had talent and believed in him, thought he could be a star, but it never worked out. He recorded a live album on him to capture his wit but it never came out."

According to Emery, Chet decided to do live albums—back to back— on Porter Wagoner and Roger Miller. Porter insisted that no food or drink be served before his album was recorded because that created too many distractions. So Porter recorded his album, then the food and drink came out and Roger recorded his album, but it had to be shelved because of the distractions.[10]

"Chet knew that Roger was talented but he was like Willie—they didn't know what to do with them," said Bobby Bare. "I'm surprised because Roger's record 'In the Summertime' should have been a big neon light flashing. I'm amazed that Chet didn't see that and run hard with it. I don't know why he didn't key in on that kind of stuff with Roger. Roger was loaded with wit."[11]

Mercury had A&R meetings in Chicago where they discussed potential artists to sign to the label. Jerry Kennedy told Charlie Fach, head of Smash Records, that he wanted to sign Roger Miller and Fach replied, "Is that the crazy guy I see on Carson?" Kennedy replied that he was, indeed, the same person who appeared on "The Tonight Show." Fach agreed to sign him "but didn't do anything for three or four weeks," remembered Fach.[12]

In October, it was reported that Roger had signed a personal management contract with the Joe Wright Talent Agency, which also handled Leroy Van Dyke. The announcement stated that "Negotiations are underway for Miller to do a string of network teevee appearances, including one possible acting assignment."[13]

Mercury had a problem with radio programmers: They did not want to program too many records from a single label because it looked like they were favoring one company over another. The "payola scandal" of the late 1950s had extended into the 1960s and disc jockeys were alert to any problems that attracted the attention of Congress or the FCC. This problem led Mercury to create a new imprint, "Smash." That way, a radio station could play more records from a record company like Mercury if those records were issued under different labels. Mercury was no longer an independent American label; in 1961, owner Irving Green sold Mercury to Philips, the electronics giant headquartered in The Netherlands.

Shelby Singleton was involved in the launch of Smash in the Spring of 1961. Singleton was one of the iconic "record men" of the independent label era. A "record man" was someone who was saturated with the record business, immersed in it to the point that they could produce a session, get a record pressed, call on radio stations, jukebox operators and retailers to get the record played and stocked and then count the money when it came in. These were men who were not musical aesthetes—many could not even play an instrument or hum a tune—but they had "ears" and knew a hit when they heard it. They defined a great record in terms of sales; the more it sold, the better it was.

Shelby Singleton was born in Texas and moved to Shreveport when he was 15; he married in 1948 when he was 17 and his bride, Margie, was 13. Back in Shreveport after the war, Shelby bought his wife a guitar and she learned to play and write songs. The "Louisiana Hayride" was in Shreveport and Shelby managed to secure a spot on that radio show for Margie. Backstage at the Hayride he met Pappy Dailey, owner of Starday

Records and manager of George Jones, and arranged for Margie to record for Starday in Houston. Her third single reached the national charts.

Shelby promoted his wife's records and secured bookings for her. This impressed Pappy Dailey, who called one day and told him that Mercury was looking for a promotion man. When Mercury and Starday merged, Shelby Singleton joined as a promotion man, whose job was to get records played on the radio. At first Shelby worked the state of Louisiana, then branched out to cover the entire southeast, later adding Texas, Oklahoma and the Ohio markets.

After a year or so, Mercury promoted Shelby to regional manager in charge of sales and promotion. Along the way, he fell into A&R and producing when David Carroll, who was supposed to produce a session on Rusty Draper, was grounded by a snowstorm in Chicago and couldn't make it to the session. Someone from Mercury called Shelby and told him he'd have to produce the session. Shelby countered that he wasn't sure if he could do that, which was countered with "If you know how to get the record on the radio and jukeboxes and then get people to buy it, then you ought to know how to make the record."

On that session Rusty Draper covered a Hank Locklin hit, "Please Help Me, I'm Falling" and "Mule Skinner Blues" by the Fendermen. Shelby took an acetate from the session, got on the telephone and on a plane and worked that record hard; it reportedly sold over 150,000 units.[14]

Because Shelby was so energetic and successful, the Mercury headquarters in Chicago gave him free rein to sign who he wanted and do whatever it took to make a record a hit. As long as he made them money—and he did that consistently—Shelby Singleton could do as he pleased.

In November, 1962, Shelby was named a Vice President at Mercury. With the promotion to Vice President, Shelby had offices in New York and Nashville and commuted regularly. He brought Jerry Kennedy, a guitar player on the Louisiana Hayride, up from Shreveport to help in the Nashville office and run it while he was not in Nashville.

In addition to Jerry Kennedy, Singleton hired Ray Stevens to work in A&R; he also played piano on studio sessions. When Stevens left, Shelby replaced him with Jerry Reed, who also became a noted studio musician and artist.

When Smash was created, Charlie Fach was named to head the label.

In November, 1963, the annual Country Music Disc Jockey Convention was held in Nashville and Fach was there along with Irving Green, head of Mercury in Chicago, and Shelby Singleton. Fach, Singleton, and Green walked into the Brass Rail in Printer's Alley for dinner; also having dinner there were Buddy Killen and Roger Miller.

Shelby, Fach and Green noticed Roger and Killen and Shelby said to his dinner partners, "You know, we probably ought to sign him. I think he's going to be a star." Green and Fach said, "Well, go see if you can sign him" so Shelby went over to Roger and Killen's table, spoke with them for a few minutes, then returned to his table and told Fach and Green, "We've got a deal."[15]

The decision was made to record an album on Roger Miller, even though country music was a singles business during the 1950s and 1960s. In fact, it was not until 1964 that *Billboard*, the trade magazine for the music industry, instituted a country album chart. Prior to that time, only a relative handful of country acts had recorded an album that reached the pop chart; Chet Atkins had charted eight albums on RCA, but he was an instrumentalist whose appeal went beyond the country audience. Eddy Arnold had released four chart albums, but, again, his appeal extended beyond the traditional country audience.

What Singleton, Fach and Green envisioned when they signed Roger Miller to a recording contract was a comedy album. There had been a number of successful comedy albums during the previous several years. *The Button Down Mind* and *The Button Down Mind Strikes Back* by Bob Newhart were both number one albums (the first was number one for 14 consecutive weeks in 1960-61 and remained on the charts for 108 weeks). Newhart's next two albums, *Behind the Button-Down Mind of Bob Newhart* and *The Button-Down Mind on TV* also did well on the charts.

Allan Sherman had a string of number one albums—*My Son, the Folk Singer, My Son, The Celebrity* and *My Son, The Nut* during the 1962-1964 period and his single, "Hello Muddah, Hello Faddah," reached number two on the *Billboard* Hot 100 chart in the summer and fall of 1963. Vaughn Meader's album *The First Family*, a spoof on the Kennedy family when John Kennedy was President, was the number one album on the LP charts for 12 consecutive weeks in 1962 and stayed on the chart for 49 weeks; it won the Grammy for "Album of the Year" in 1962. *The First Family,*

Volume Two, was on the pop chart the evening the Mercury executives walked into the Nashville restaurant; it reached the number four position before the assassination of President Kennedy on November 22 ended Meader's career of releasing Kennedy spoofs.

This DJ Convention, known officially as the Grand Ole Opry's 38th Birthday Celebration, began on October 31 and finished on November 2. Headquarters for the convention was the Andrew Jackson Hotel, located a block from the WSM Studios, and events were held in several other downtown hotels, including the Hermitage Hotel as well as the new 10,000 seat Municipal Auditorium a couple of blocks away.

BMI hosted an awards dinner with awards for songs based on radio airplay and Bill Anderson and Harlan Howard each took home four. An advertisement in *Billboard* from Tree noted that several Roger Miller songs were being released, including "When a House is Not a Home" by Jean Shephard and "That's Why I Love You Like I Do" by Rusty Draper. Tree had moved to a building at 905 16th Avenue South, just a block from the offices of Columbia, Mercury and Capitol Records, the Quonset Hut Studio, RCA's studio and Cedarwood Publishing. All congregated into the area that was becoming known as "Music Row."

Roger had grown frustrated with his musical career; he seemed to be stuck. He'd had some hits and was getting booked, but there wasn't a big "breakthrough" record that launched him as a country music star. He appeared regularly on top rated television shows like "The Tonight Show," but he was still a struggling country singer.

"People would always tell me what a character I was," said Roger. "And I thought maybe I could go out to Hollywood and capitalize off that and learn how to work it."[16]

There was nothing to hold him to Nashville; things weren't going well on the home front and his wife had left and moved back to Oklahoma. He could still pick up some bookings and he'd receive his song royalties no matter where he lived, so he decided to move to Los Angeles and study acting.

The desire to move to L.A. meant that Roger needed money so he asked Jerry Kennedy for an "advance" of $1,600. Kennedy relayed the request to Charlie Fach who responded, a few days later, with an agreement that he would give Roger an advance of $100 for each song he recorded so if he recorded 16 songs, he would receive $1,600. Roger agreed.

On November 6, Roger Miller recorded his last session for RCA. The line-up was a bit different; Bob Ferguson was the producer and Ron Steele engineered with Jack Clement as session leader on guitar. Others on the session were Bob Johnston, Ray Edenton, Norman Blake and Wayne Moss on guitars, Roy Huskey, Jr. on bass, Kenny Buttrey on drums, Hargus "Pig" Robbins on piano and two members of the Jordanaires—Gordon Stoker and Ray Walker—along with Jerry Crutchfield and Anita Carter provided background vocals. Roger recorded two songs: "Part of Me" was written by Ray Pressley and Speedy Price while "It Happened Just That Way" was penned by Roger.

On December 10, Barbara Miller took her children and moved in with her parents in Duncan, Oklahoma. She drove to Duncan in Roger's 1963 Cadillac that Tree had given him and he couldn't get the car back. "I remember they were hiding the car," said Phyllis. Apparently, Roger sent someone to retrieve the car but Roger did not go to Duncan himself.[17]

There was another problem brewing for Roger. He had been having an affair with Anita Carter of the Carter Family, who were traveling with the Johnny Cash Show. Anita and Roger were passionate about each other; sometime in November, around the time she sang on Roger's last RCA session, Anita became pregnant with Roger's child.

Shelby Singleton and Jerry Kennedy wrapped up Roger Miller's recording contract by Christmas, then left for Shreveport for the holidays. Right after their Christmas break, they went to Chicago for meetings with the top brass at Mercury to discuss the sales and marketing for their acts during the coming year.

Chapter 9
Dang Me

Shelby Singleton was determined to obtain publicity for Roger so he arranged for an interview with Charlie Lamb, editor of the trade magazine, *Music Reporter*. The article noted that Shelby "predicts big things for the likeable artist-writer." Discussing his songwriting, Roger stated, "I just sit around and think oblong thoughts. The Lord put a little thing up in my head. I can look at something as it is or I can go around to the other side and look at it that way."

"I had a bad personality when I was a kid," added Roger. "I never had much to say and when I did it was wrong. I always wanted attention... Always was reaching and grabbing for attention. I guess everybody is a ham—but you don't have to be a hog about it."

An unidentified "sidekick" said of Roger that "He's very funny on the outside and this is the impression you get when you meet him. But he's been knocked around a lot in life and on the inside he's full of a lot a hurt. Sometimes this comes out in his songs."[1]

On Thursday, January 9, 1964, Roger and Jerry Kennedy met in Jerry's office and went over the songs that Roger wanted to record. Roger sang the songs and Jerry listened; when he heard "Less and Less" he heard a straight-ahead country song whose tag line "more and more I think about you less and less" sounded commercial. He knew he would concentrate on this song as a potential single for country jukeboxes and radio.

Kennedy received a copy of "Ain't That Fine" from publisher Al Gallico and thought it could be a hit. The song was written by Dorsey Burnette, who began his career in Memphis with the Burnette Trio, consisting of brother Johnny and Doc McQueen. Jerry thought that "Less and Less" and "Ain't That Fine" would be a great, two-sided record.

"I totally missed 'Dang Me,'" remembered Jerry. It was easy to miss; there were 16 songs to be recorded over the next two days.[2]

The next day Roger went into the Columbia Recording Studio and recorded three songs: "Ain't That Fine," "Why" and "Less and Less."

On Saturday, Roger had two back-to-back sessions and recorded twelve songs. Here is where the real Roger Miller emerged; all of those songs he wrote that weren't considered "complete" or "commercial" by the pro's on Music Row were part of who he was. Out of this session, Roger became a superstar country and pop act, but that could not be predicted going into the session.

"We worked our butts off that day," remembered bassist Bob Moore.[3] None of the musicians had heard any of the songs before they gathered in the studio. The Nashville studio musicians listened to each song in the studio—Roger sang his songs live—and then started "running it down" or practicing it. They did not write anything down; instead, they kept it all in their head. (The Nashville number system was not in practice for musicians at this point.) At the end of two run-throughs, the musicians were usually ready to record a master on tape. Usually, there were three or four songs on a session so there was a little time to relax between songs, but cutting 12 songs in one day meant that it was a constant grind on the musicians to listen, learn and record each song, then get on to the next one.

The first song recorded on Saturday was "Chug-a-Lug," which was based on real experiences in Roger's past. Bud Keathley, the manager of Roger's old band in Erick, could drink a beer in three seconds or less; he called it "chug-a-lugging." Roger remembered "the Gibson twins, who with a friend of their's named Charlie Rawlson, made some wine and brought it to school in a Mason jar" as well as "a little bar joint on the state line of Oklahoma and Texas on Highway 66 where an uncle of mine sneaked me in. I was about 14 or something like that."[4] That was probably the same bar where Roger and Barbara Crow first met. Roger was in the FFA during his high school years and they took field trips, which is alluded to in the second verse.

The second song on the session was "I Ain't Coming Home Tonight," followed by "Lou's Got the Flu," "The Moon Is High (and So Am I)," "Got 2 Again," and "Feel of Me." Next came "That's Why I Love You," "Squares Make The World Go Round" and then came "Dang Me," the ninth song that day and the twelfth song during those two days of sessions.

Roger wrote "Dang Me" while sitting in a booth in a bar in Phoenix, Arizona but, in his mind, he was sitting in a booth at Tootsie's. The song describes a wayward husband and father who wasn't taking care of his wife and family back home—which was a pretty accurate self-appraisal of his life at the time.

In late summer, 1963, Bobby Bare filmed a Warner Brothers western, *A Distant Trumpet* with Troy Donahue and Suzanne Pleschette. The filming was done in the Painted Desert and Bare remembers that "Roger was always real curious about movies. I think he wanted to get in movies. He flew in to Flagstaff and spent about three days with me there. When you sent your shirts to the laundry they'd come back with a piece of white paper stuck to the back and Roger had a piece of that paper with lyrics written all over it. He said it was 'Dang Me.' He said he and Dorsey Burnette had been working on it. He was there for two or three days and then I came in one day from filming and he was gone."[5]

This may have been the period when Roger wrote "Dang Me" because he was in Phoenix during that time in addition to being in Flagstaff.

Harold Bradley, who played guitar on the session and sat next to Roger during the recording, remembers Roger running "Dang Me" down and playing that string bending riff off the E chord that opens the song. Roger "had an Epiphone gut string that kind of looks like Willie Nelson's guitar," remembered Harold. "I was playing a real nice, Nylon string guitar and Roger said, 'Harold I want you to play this' and he played this 'bap-ba-ba-ba-da-da-da-da" and I'm looking at him and I know there's no way I can play it like he's playing it because he's hitting it and the strings are going down and 'bappin' off the fret and I'm sideways, I'm a polite picker. I asked Roger if he could play it again and he did and I'm sitting there puzzled so I call Jerry Kennedy over and said, 'Jerry, Roger wants me to play this—what do you think?' Roger played that intro again as Jerry listened and immediately told Roger, 'You've got to play that' because it was funky sounding. So I said, 'Okay!' and thank God he played it because I could never have played it like he did."[6]

Roger played that distinctive opening as well as the scat singing end on the guitar of that recording and, in the lyrics, rhymed "purple" with "maple syruple."

After "Dang Me" came "Private John Q," which harkened back to Roger's days in the Army, and then "If You Want Me To" and "It Takes All Kinds (To Make a World)," which ended the session. He had recorded 15, not 16 songs, but that $1,500 would get Roger to Los Angeles.

After the sessions, Jerry Kennedy added strings to "Less and Less" to get it ready for a single release.

The first time Kennedy listened to the session, he had the songs on a seven inch tape reel but only had a five inch take up reel, so he could not listen to the entire session. Later, Kennedy took the tape of those sessions to his home at 209 Green Acres Court in Goodlettsville, just outside Nashville, and listened on a reel-to-reel tape recorder that had a take up reel for a seven inch tape.

Since "Dang Me" was the ninth song on the Saturday session, and twelfth song they recorded over that two day period, Kennedy did not hear it when he first played the tape with the smaller take up reel. However, when he played it on his home tape recorder, his three young sons immediately "went wild" with excitement when "Dang Me" came on. Seeing their reaction, Jerry knew he had something special. He also knew he had to stop the release of the scheduled single.

Jerry called Charlie Fach and told him he wanted to cancel the release of "Less and Less" and replace it with "Dang Me." "I had copies of the record with 'Less and Less' and 'Ain't That Fine' pressed for the disc jockeys and ready to send out when Jerry Kennedy called and said his kids were going crazy when he played 'Dang Me' and thought that should be the first single," said Fach. "I told Jerry, 'Mr. Green will kill me if I pull that record now' so Jerry said he'd call him and, when he did, Mr. Green agreed to put out 'Dang Me.'"[7]

Meanwhile, Roger had left for Los Angeles in a 1954 two-toned green Ford; his wife had his Cadillac and he couldn't get it back. Somewhere along the line, Roger had met Lee Hazelwood, who invited him to Los Angeles and offered him a place to stay in his guest house while Roger took acting lessons. Doug Gilmore remembers that he lent Roger $1,500 to move to L.A. and, just after he'd handed over the money, ran into Merle Kilgore who asked, "How's your new best friend?"

"Well, he's moving to L.A.," replied Gilmore.

"Well, I hope you didn't loan him any money," said Kilgore. "The sonovbitch won't pay you back." (Roger did pay him back.)

When Roger arrived in Los Angeles, he enrolled in acting class and studied camera technique with James Best, later known as Sheriff Roscoe on "The Dukes of Hazzard" but, at that time, a struggling actor.[8]

Barbara and Roger had their final reconciliation in California; Barbara moved out there with him but it was soon apparent the marriage was over. "Roger was messing with another woman—Barbara saw a picture of them—and she called Dad," remembered her sister Phyllis. "Dad sent them money and they flew home. Barbara was very down, she was struggling. When she left, she had everything moved out of their place except a blanket and a pillow. She could be ornery like that."[9]

Chuck Blore was a legend in pop radio. In the book, *The Hits Just Keep On Coming: The History of Top 40 Radio*, author Ben Fong-Torres states that the term "genius has been applied to Blore so often that he could be mistaken for Ray Charles."[10]

Blore was one of the top programmers of Top 40 radio in the United States; his influence was felt—and his station copied—by radio stations all across the country. He left radio because, according to Blore, he thought the advertisements on radio were "crap" so he formed an advertising agency to produce radio ads.

Early in 1964, Blore hired Glen Campbell to play guitar on a radio ad for Hoffman's Candy Bars. Campbell brought along Roger, who had been staying at his house. "I used Glen as my lead guitarist on almost everything I did," said Blore. "This was when Glen was a studio session player, before he became Glen Campbell the big star. In those days, to save money, we doubled everything. So Glen says, 'Roger plays pretty good guitar' and I said, 'Well, I can't pay you much' and Roger said, 'That's O.K. I just want to learn.'"

"Well, we did the basic tracks and then there was a chorus, 'Hoffman Candy Bars are good to your tummy, they're chocolate and yummy' or whatever it was. Roger and one girl sang it and we doubled it so it sounded like a huge choir. I'd written the copy which went over the musical bed and, after we finished the music, Glen and Roger decided to hang around and see how the whole thing turned out. So I'm reading this copy that says 'I was sittin' and lickin' my last piece of a gold candy bar' when the talk-back opened up and I said 'WHAT?!' I was in the middle of a take. And Roger said, 'How'd you like to have that done authentic?' I said, 'You think you can do this better than me?' and he says, 'Oh, hell yes.' So he came into the studio, looked at the copy and did it and sure as hell it was a lot better so we said 'That's great.' We had him do three spots that day and just before he left he said, 'Hey, Chuck, how much money do you think I made today?' Back in those days we paid 50 bucks a spot. So I told him he'd made $150. He said, 'Do you think I could get it quick?' and I said, 'You can get it right now' and we wrote him a check right there. We gave him the check and he said, 'Call me whenever you want and I'll come running.'" [11]

The day that "Dang Me" was released, Roger, scrambling for money, played a club in San Francisco for $75; there were four people in the audience and the check bounced. The first time he heard the song on the radio came while he was driving on the 405 Freeway in Los Angeles.

In the May 16 issue of *Billboard*, "Dang Me" was featured in a country singles review. The review states, "Very clever song taken from Roger's newest LP. In the light-vein it revolves around a really bad guy; 'Daddy was a pistol, and I'm a son-of-a-gun.'" On the "B" side was "Got 2 Again." Both songs were short; Dang me was 1:47 and "Got 2 Again" was 2:17. [12]

"About ten days after the record was released I got a phone call from Ken Dow, a program director in Dallas," said Charlie Fach. "I thought, 'This is strange' because usually we were always calling them trying to get a record played and here was this guy calling us. The one stop, which distributed records to jukeboxes, had put 'Dang Me' on some jukeboxes and the records were flying out of the one-stop. This alerted radio that this was a hit and Dow wanted to make sure there were plenty of records in stock before he put it on the air because if he played it and people couldn't buy it, that put him in an awkward position—people got mad at the radio station!" [13]

Howard Bednoe was a promotion man for Smash and he got the record on WLS, the 50,000 watt station in Chicago, then Fach flew to Little Rock where he convinced KAAY, another 50,000 watt station, to program the record. Buddy King in Little Rock called a friend of his in Oklahoma who put it on that 50,000 watt station "so within three or four weeks we had 'Dang Me' on a number of 50,000 watt stations in the Midwest," said Fach. From that point, the record took off.

On the West Coast, Lou Dennis was the promotion man for Smash. A former DJ, he started with Smash in October, 1963 as the West Coast Regional representative. Their distribution company in San Francisco was owned by Al Bramey and Tony Valerio; the promotion man for the distributorship was Pete Marino, "The best promo man on the coast—plugged into everybody," according to Dennis. Charlie Fach told Dennis to take Roger up to San Francisco for an appearance on a local television show, hosted by Dick Stewart on KPIX and visit some radio stations. Dick Stewart wasn't on TV that day; instead, Don Sherwood, the morning DJ on KSFO, the top rock station in San Francisco was there and he interviewed Roger, who performed "Dang Me."

Sherwood loved Roger and "Dang Me" and invited him back the next day. He also played the fire out of "Dang Me" on KSFO. Ironically, the nationally televised "Tennessee Ernie Ford Show" was taped at the same studio as the local TV show. Billy Strange was in charge of the music on the Ford Show and he and Roger knew each other so Strange arranged for Roger to appear on the Ford Show—which gave him and "Dang Me" national exposure.[14]

"It was one of those lucky breaks," said Lou Dennis. "That local show in San Francisco was the same show that gave Rich Little his first shot."[15]

On June 6, "Dang Me" debuted at number 41 on the Country Singles Chart in *Billboard*; number one that week was "My Heart Skips a Beat" and number two was "Together Again," both by Buck Owens. In that same issue, "Dang Me" was listed as a "Breakout Single" for pop releases with Seattle and Houston noted for their activity.[16]

Jan Howard was signed to Capitol Records and recorded at the Capitol Studio in Hollywood. For her sessions in L.A., she rented an apartment for two weeks. One day, while she was talking with her husband, Harlan, on the phone, Jan heard a knock on the door, opened it and there was Roger. "I'm working out here," Roger told her. "Come go with me tonight and then we'll go to Las Vegas." Jan agreed and they went to the club where Roger was playing, which was located about 60 miles north of Los Angeles.

"The club was run by Willie Nelson and Tommy Alsup and Bob Wills was supposed to be the main act that night," remembered Jan. "Bob Wills was drunk and I'm not sure if he ever showed up but Roger did his little bit and it really was a little bit. He had 'Dang Me' out. After he finished playing he came off stage and said 'Wait while I get paid and then we'll take off for Vegas.' He went upstairs to get paid and when he came back down he looked down so I asked, 'Did you get paid?' and he said 'Nope.' Then he went over to where the stage and outdoor lights were plugged in and there were a lot of wires. He switched all of those wires around and then we left."

"Johnny Cash was working in Vegas and it was one of those times when he couldn't sing so he wanted Roger to fill in for him," continued Jan. "We drove to Victorville, at the edge of the desert and both of us were tired so we stopped at a truck stop and got some coffee and Roger said 'I don't think we can make it to Vegas tonight.' I said 'I don't think so either but we can't check into a motel because that would get back to Nashville before we turned the light out.' He said, 'Yes, I know that's true' and then he said 'There's a flight leaving out of L.A. at seven o'clock for Vegas' so we turned around and drove back to the airport in Los Angeles and took the seven a.m. flight to Vegas. As we were taking off, Roger leaned back, closed his eyes and I said 'Are you O.K?' He said, 'Yeah. The first seven minutes and the last seven minutes are the most dangerous so I'm praying.'"

In Las Vegas they "teamed up with Luther Perkins and his wife, Margie, and played black jacks," said Howard. "I took a nap later but he never went to bed. Roger filled in for Cash that night and then flew to Tucson because he had to work a date there. Then he came back to Vegas and we drove back to L.A. I don't know what kept him going. That was just one experience with Roger."

"Everybody loved Roger, everybody did," said Jan. "He was funny but he had a serious side. I recorded a song of his in one of my albums, 'A World I Can't Live In.' It took him two years to write that three verse song; it was a very simple song but he put a lot of thought into his ballads. He could write those 'Dang Me' songs in two or three minutes."[17]

In June, Roger did a ten day promotional tour of the mid-west, starting in Denver and stopping at radio and TV stations to plug his song. On June 18 he appeared on "The Mike Douglas Show," which provided national exposure for "Dang Me."

On June 13, "Dang Me" debuted at number 94 on the *Billboard* Hot 100 chart; the following week, it jumped from number 40 to 27 on the country singles chart. Several years earlier in Nashville, Roger sang the line "I'm a walkin' talkin' cryin' barely beatin' broken heart" to Justin Tubb, son of Ernest and an artist in his own right as they were riding around in a car. Justin wanted to co-write the song with Roger but Roger begged off so Justin wrote the verses and he and Roger are listed as co-writers of that song. On the *Billboard* country singles chart of June 20 was "Walkin' Talkin' Cryin' Barely Beatin' Broken Heart" by Johnny Wright and the Tennessee Mountain Boys at number 22.

On July 4, "Dang Me" was number six on the *Billboard* country chart behind "My Heart Skips a Beat" and "Together Again" by Buck Owens, "Burning Memories" by Ray Price, "Memory #1" by Webb Pierce and "Wine, Woman and Song" by Loretta Lynn. On July 7, Roger sang "Dang Me" on "The Andy Williams Show"; on July 18, "Dang Me" sat at number one on the country singles chart in *Billboard* but his album, *Roger and Out*, was not on the album chart. On July 30, Roger was on "The Tonight Show" starring Johnny Carson.

In the August 1 issue of *Billboard*, "Dang Me" peaked at number seven in the Hot 100 chart, behind "A Hard Day's Night" by the Beatles, "Rag Doll" by the Four Seasons, "Little Old Lady From Pasadena" by Jan and Dean, "Everybody Loves Somebody" by Dean Martin, "Where Did Our Love Go" by the Supremes" and "Wishin' and Hopin'" by Dusty Springfield. Following "Dang Me" on the pop chart were "I Get Around" by the Beach Boys, "Memphis" by Johnny Rivers and "Girl From Ipanema" by Stan Getz and Astrud Gilberto.

On August 8, the *Roger and Out* album entered the *Billboard* country chart at number 15; Buck Owens, Johnny Cash and Jim Reeves each had two albums on that chart. "Dang Me" was still number one on the Country Singles chart; it would remain in that position for six consecutive weeks and 25 weeks total.

In addition to Lou Dennis on the West Coast, Alan Mink in Cleveland and Doug Moody in New York were the radio promotion men for Smash who worked hard to get radio airplay for "Dang Me" and broke Roger Miller as a major star in 1964.

With "Dang Me" hitting, Roger needed a band and "hired his band off Ralph Emery's show," according to Bobby Bare. "He had Thumbs

Carlille and Bobby Dyson and a drummer," said Bare. "We were doing a show with Buck Owens in Madison, Wisconsin. Buck was on and I was standing on the side of the stage watching Buck with Roger and I asked Roger 'How do you like your band?" Roger said, 'That Thumbs is great and Dyson is good but that drummer cannot keep a beat. I'm going to have to fire his ass and get me a good drummer.' He didn't know that the drummer was standing right behind us on the other side of the curtain and he heard what Roger said and it broke his heart. I told Roger, 'I think he heard you' cause the drummer walked off. Roger said, 'Me and my big mouth.'" It was over for the drummer; he went out and got drunk. That's what led Roger to hire Jerry Allison, formerly with Buddy Holly's Crickets, to play drums.[18]

On August 10, 1964, a boy was born to Anita Carter. Johnny Cash had confronted Roger about Anita's pregnancy and Roger replied, "I'm going to have to put that on the back burner for now." The child was born autistic and Roger never acknowledged that he was the father. The day after the child's birth Roger went into the Quonset Hut studio and recorded three songs: "Do Wacka Do," "Hard Headed Me," and "Reincarnation."

As "Dang Me" was hitting, the label knew that Roger needed management so Charlie Fach and some others approached Frank Freed with Triangle Management in Chicago, who handled the Chad Mitchell Trio, but he wasn't interested. Irving Green contacted Joe Glaser, who had managed Billie Holiday and was managing Louis Armstrong but Glaser wasn't interested either.

Don Williams, brother of Andy Williams, received a call from the head of Screen Gem Music because "I had done him a big favor to help his son," said Don, "so he called and said "I'm going to do you a big favor. There's a guy named Roger Miller who's playing at the Troubadour. You need to check him out because I believe he's going to be big." This was probably in July as "Dang Me" was hitting.

Don, along with Alan Bernard and Jerry Perenchio, went to the Troubadour to see Roger "who just killed me," remembered Don. "He had about a ten minute act—mostly songs that were half-written and I said 'I've got to sign him!'" Bernard and Perenchio asked "Why?" and

Don replied, "Because he is such a talent." Charlie Fach remembered that during the show at the Troubadour Roger "was hilarious" and spent most of the show "talking to his guitar."

Williams arranged for Roger to come to their offices for a meeting and they signed him. Bernard and Williams was comprised of Alan Bernard, who handled Mary Tyler Moore—then playing "Laura Petri" on "The Dick Van Dyke Show"—and Andy Williams, Don's brother. Williams was one of the hottest acts in the entertainment industry at that time with a top rated television show on NBC and a string of hit records that included "Days of Wine and Roses" and "Moon River." In 1960, Andy Williams had a significant hit with Roger Miller's "In The Summertime," also known as "You Don't Want My Love." Although Bernard and Williams did not book Andy Williams, they were friendly and often helped each other and traded favors.

After Don Williams signed Roger to a management contract he went with Roger to Nashville for the recording session with Jerry Kennedy that produced "Do Wacka Do."

"That was an interesting trip," said Don, "because in those days you had to have your visa stamped to get into Nashville. I went into the recording studio and Jerry Kennedy was the only guy who would talk to me, even though I was his manager. There were some real interesting people on that record date."[19]

A question perplexed Jerry Kennedy and Smash executives: How can you best capture Roger Miller? It was like trying to capture lightning in a bottle. He was funny, entertaining and off the cuff so the decision was made to record a live album. On August 22, sound equipment was set up at the Carousel Club in Printer's Alley in Nashville. Kennedy and Shelby Singleton were there for the recording but, listening to the playback, they decided the album could not be released; the tinkling of glasses and other noises from the bar proved to be too distracting. That recording was put on the shelf.

On August 29, "Dang Me" dropped out of the number one slot on the country singles chart and was replaced by "I Guess I'm Crazy" by Jim Reeves. *The Roger and Out* album was at number six; Johnny Cash's album, *I Walk the Line* held the number one slot.

In late August Roger went to New York and taped appearances on

"The Steve Allen Show," which was broadcast on September 2, and "The Jimmy Dean Show," which was broadcast on September 19.

"The Jimmy Dean Show" was the most important and influential country music show on television. Hosted by Dean, whose easy going style made him an ideal host, the show featured a who's who in country music. Regulars on the show included singer Molly Bee and Rowlf, the Jim Henson Muppet. The show that aired on September 19 featured Roger, who described his playing as "depressive jazz." Roger's quick wit and relaxed manner went over well for TV audiences.[20]

Also in September, an answer song to "Dang Me" was released. "Dern Ya" by Ruby Wright, daughter of Johnny Wright and Kitty Wells, told the "Dang Me" story from a woman's point of view.

"Chug-A-Lug" was released on September 19. The song caused some consternation in the Nashville offices of Roger's record label because the country audience is a rather conservative audience. The idea that "wine" in a song might be offensive caused Jerry Kennedy to go into the studio and edit that lyric out of the song; however, Charlie Fach was convinced it would be a hit with college students. He was right; "Chug-a-Lug" became an anthem for college students and country fans enjoyed it too.

Chapter 10
King of the Road

Through the years there have been a number of stories of how "King of the Road" was written—and a number of people who claim to have been in the room when Roger wrote it—but Roger told Otto Kittsinger that he had played a date in Davenport, Iowa and was driving to Chicago to catch a plane when he saw a sign, a few miles west of Chicago, that said "Trailers for sale or rent." Roger said that he "just thought it would sound good in a song and two or three weeks later I was in Boise and it all came together."

Actually, Roger wrote the first verse in the Boise Hotel—Room 622—and then was stuck. It was unusual for Roger to stay with a song for a long period of time but he "knew it was good" and kept working on the song for three weeks. He went to a store and bought a hobo—that statue is still around—"and stared at it until the rest of the tune came to me." He finished the song in Kitchener, Ontario.[1]

The song breaks the traditional rules of writing a country song where there's a verse, then a chorus, maybe a bridge, but usually another verse and chorus. "King of the Road" really doesn't have a chorus, just a phrase at the end of each verse, "I'm a man of means by no means, King of the Road."

On election day 1964—Tuesday, November 3, when President Lyndon Johnson defeated Republican nominee Barry Goldwater—Roger Miller was in the Quonset Hut studio for a recording session. As they ran down "King of the Road," looking for an intro, Bob Moore played a jazz run on his upright bass. "That's it," said Jerry Kennedy and Roger. They were working up the song in the key of B flat, with a full step modulation to C after the second verse but decided to start the song in the key of B and modulate a half step for the third verse. They needed to do that because there was no chorus with a distinctive change of melody in the song. The opening in B created a bit of a problem for bassist Bob Moore who said, "The fingering for that run is different in B than B flat."[2]

Roger often introduced the song as being in his favorite key, "B natural."

The session began with "As Long As There's a Shadow" before they did "King of the Road," then "That's the Way It's Always Been" and "You Can't Roller Skate in a Buffalo Herd." The day before, Roger recorded "Atta Boy Girl."

The Grand Ole Opry Birthday Celebration—the thirty-ninth—occurred November 5-7 and a number of State Governors—including Governor Frank Clement in Tennessee— declared November "Country Music Month."

The *Billboard* Country Music Awards—a forerunner to the Country Music Association Awards—were voted on by the subscribers to *Billboard*. The number one country singles artist was Buck Owens, followed by Ray Price, Jim Reeves, Johnny Cash and Loretta Lynn; Roger Miller finished at number 36 in that poll. The top country album for the year was *Ring of Fire* by Johnny Cash and the top album artist was Buck Owens, followed by Johnny Cash, Hank Snow, Loretta Lynn and Chet Atkins; Roger finished at number 24 in that survey.

The *Billboard* Disc Jockey Poll had Roger Miller at number one for "Most Promising Male Artist" and number three in the "Favorite Country Songwriter" category, behind Bill Anderson and Harlan Howard.

About 3,500 attended the DJ Convention, the informal name of the gathering, where *Your Cheatin' Heart*, the movie about the life of Hank Williams starring George Hamilton premiered. It was announced that a building housing Country Music Association's museum, Hall of Fame and offices would be constructed the next year.

The November 7 pop charts in *Billboard* did not contain any single by the Beatles—the first time that had occurred since January 18. However, Roger Miller continued his presence on the *Billboard* Hot 100 with "Chug-A-Lug" at number nine, right behind Dean Martin's "The Door is Still Open to My Heart" at number eight and just ahead of "We'll Sing in the Sunshine" at number ten by Gale Garnett while "Baby Love," by the Supremes sat in the number one position.

The November 21 issue of *Billboard* featured a pop single review of "Do-Wacka-Do," calling it "a clever, wacky novelty!" The "B" side was "Love Is Not for Me."[3]

In early December, Kentucky Governor Ned Breathitt bestowed the honor of "Kentucky Colonel" on Roger and on Sunday, December 6, fans in Hammond, Indiana saw Roger on a Christmas Special concert hosted by Uncle Len Ellis of WWCA. Also on the show were Skeeter Davis, Charlie Louvin, Kitty Wells, Bill Phillips, Tompall and the Glaser Brothers and Johnny Wright and the Tennessee Mountain Boys.

On December 12, "Chug-A-Lug" was at number 22 while "Do-Wacka-Do" made its debut at number 43 on the country singles chart. Charlie Louvin's recording of Roger's song "Less and Less" was at number 41 on the chart.

At the end of 1964, "Do-Wacka-Do" was at number 43 on the *Billboard* Hot 100 chart. The number one song was "I Feel Fine" by The Beatles, followed by "Come See About Me" by The Supremes, "Mr. Lonely" by Bobby Vinton, "She's a Woman" by The Beatles, "She's Not There" by The Zombies, "Goin' Out of My Head" by Little Anthony & the Imperials, "Ringo" by Lorne Greene, "Dance, Dance, Dance" by The Beach Boys, "The Jerk" by The Larks, and "Time Is On My Side" by The Rolling Stones.

On *Billboard*'s country chart, "Chug-A-Lug" was at number 23 and "Do Wacka Do" was at number 39. The number one country song was "Once a Day" by Connie Smith and the number one album was by Buck Owens, who also had albums in the number four and seven positions; albums by Jim Reeves and Johnny Cash were in the number two and three positions, respectively. Roger's *Dang Me/Chug-A-Lug* album—the title had been changed from *Roger and Out* to capitalize on his hit singles— was at number twelve.

The top two singles of 1964, based on *Billboard* chart activity from radio airplay, were "I Want To Hold Your Hand" and "She Loves You," both by the Beatles. These were followed by "Hello Dolly" by Louis Armstrong, "Oh, Pretty Woman" by Roy Orbison, "I Get Around" by The Beach Boys, "Everybody Loves Somebody" by Dean Martin, "My Guy" by Mary Wells, "We'll Sing in the Sunshine" by Gale Garnett, "Last Kiss" by J. Frank Wilson and "Where Did Our Love Go" by the Supremes.

The top albums of 1964 were *A Hard Day's Night*, *Meet the Beatles* and *The Beatles Second Album* by The Beatles; two releases of *Hello Dolly* (original cast version and Louis Armstrong's); *People* by Barbra Streisand, *The Singing Nun* and *The Beach Boys In Concert*.

Roger Miller held his own in this company; "Chug-A-Lug" and "Dang Me" were both among the top 100 records of 1964 and they received BMI Citations for the amount of radio airplay they received.

During the first week in January, 1965, Roger Miller debuted "King of the Road" on "The Jimmy Dean Show."

On January 23 *Billboard* reviewed "King of the Road" as a pop single, stating it was "a change of pace from past hits." On the "B" side was "Atta Boy Girl." Charlie Fach had saved the record release number "1965" for "King of the Road" so the single was released on "Smash 1965."[4] On January 30, it debuted on *Billboard's* Hot 100 Chart at number 63 and was listed as a "Breakout Single," indicating wide acceptance at radio.

Roger's career success helped his producer's career; it was announced in January that Jerry Kennedy had been promoted to "A&R head" at Mercury from "A&R assistant."

The year 1965 began with "I Feel Fine," a Beatles single at number one on the Hot 100 and six Beatles albums on *Billboard's* LP chart. On February 6, "King of the Road" jumped from number 65 to 39 on the singles chart and his second Smash album, *The Return of Roger Miller,* debuted on the LP chart at number 135; Roger's previous album, *Dang Me/ Chug-A-Lug* was at number 140. The following week *Billboard* reviewed his new album, stating, "All the personality, wit, charm, vocal and writing talents of this well-rounded music man are captured here."[5]

On February 11, Roger went into the Quonset Hut studio in Nashville and recorded the Elvis hit "Heartbreak Hotel," "Engine Engine No. 9," "The Good Old Days," "Water Dog," "Big Harlan Taylor" and "One Dyin' and a-Buryin'." Recordings of three of the songs—"This Town," "Engine Engine No. 9" and "The Good Old Days" were not released because of Roger's intake of pills; he just wasn't in top form that day for recording.

Roger Miller was the hottest country act in America, although he was considered "pop" as well, which led the *Saturday Evening Post* to put him on the cover for a story about Nashville and country music in their February 12 issue. The article, by Charles Portis, was titled "That New Sound from Nashville."

The article stated that country music was hot and that country artists were raking in millions of dollars; like a number of other articles from New York and Los Angeles writers, this writer had "discovered" country music and found it didn't quite fit the stereotype of poor, backwoods, barefoot, moonshine swilling rednecks but instead had some pretty sophisticated members in its community. The reason those stereotypes had fallen—at least according to this article—was because of Roger Miller, who had just completed a television special for NBC and there was talk that he would star in a regular weekly series.[6]

The money in country music wasn't in the same league as the money in pop and rock music. Country artists made their money on the road but, except for Roger Miller, Eddy Arnold, Johnny Cash and Buck Owens, most artists saw little if any money from record royalties. Jukeboxes were the major buyers of country music, which was a singles business.

In the February 13 issue of *Billboard*, "King of the Road" jumped to number 22 and debuted on the country singles chart at number 31 (out of 50). During this period, the country chart for singles and albums lagged behind the pop charts with Roger's records. The next week, "King of the Road" moved up to number 17 while *The Return of Roger Miller* jumped from number 104 to 70. On the country singles chart, "King of the Road" was at number 20 but the album had not yet charted. A week later, "King of the Road" was number ten on the *Billboard* Hot 100 and his album was at 61; the record entered the country singles chart at number nine and the album chart at number 20.

On March 1, television viewers watched Roger on "The Andy Williams Show." In *Billboard's* March 27 issue, "King of the Road" was number one on the country chart and number five on the Hot 100; on the country album chart, *The Return of Roger Miller* was at number six on a chart where Buck Owens had four albums, Jim Reeves had three and Johnny Cash and Ray Price each had two.

In the March 30 edition of *Billboard*, "King of the Road" peaked at number four, behind "Eight Days a Week" by the Beatles at number one, "Stop! In the Name of Love" by the Supremes and "The Birds and The Bees" by Jewel Akin. Below "King of the Road," in descending order, were "Can't You Hear My Heartbeat" by Herman's Hermits, "Ferry Cross the Mersey" by Gerry and the Pacemakers, "My Girl" by The Temptations,

"This Diamond Ring" by Gary Lewis and the Playboys, "Goldfinger" by Shirley Bassey and "Shotgun" by Jr. Walker and the All Stars.

The Return of Roger Miller album was at number 33 on the pop album charts. On the country chart, "King of the Road" was at number two, behind "I've Got a Tiger By The Tail" by Buck Owens with the album at number seven.

Roger had a strong, well-connected manager—Don Williams—but he did not have a long time relationship with him so he called Doug Gilmore, invited him to dinner and asked, "What would it take to get you to move to Los Angeles with me? I've got Don Williams and the management company who tell me stuff and I believe it but I'd like for you to be me in dealing with Don and the management company."

"I thought that would go over like a fart in a diver's helment," said Gilmore, "but Don and I hit it off."

One of the first things Williams did was arrange for Roger to play Las Vegas, Tahoe and Reno—the supper club circuit. "That management company had a lot of leverage because they had Andy Williams and Andy was big money," said Gilmore. "Andy was playing Vegas and they went to those guys and said, 'If you want Andy, you have to take Roger' and they did. So Roger went from $150 a night to $25,000 a week. He worked 18 weeks a year—three weeks in the Spring for Vegas then three weeks in the fall. The same with Tahoe and Reno. So that's 18 weeks for about $450,000 and then there was the royalties."

"I used to go by Roger's house almost every day," remembered Gilmore. "And one day I got the mail out of his mailbox and there was about $250,000 in royalty checks in his mailbox. Soon after that he was on the 'Tonight Show' and Johnny Carson asked him 'When did you really realize that you'd made it' and Roger said 'The day I got $250,000 worth of checks in my mailbox.' Then he said, 'I can have drawers full of sox!'"[7]

In April, Tree Publishing announced that Roger Miller, Justin Tubb and Joe Tex had signed long term writer deals.[9] In March, Jody Miller—no relation to Roger—released "Queen of the House," an answer song to "King of the Road." This song was also a hit, reaching number five on the country chart and number 12 on the *Billboard* Hot 100 chart.

The other labels that Roger had recorded for lost no time capitalizing on his success. RCA released two albums and Starday released singles of the songs Roger covered; in August, they released "Country Girl" b/w "Jimmie Brown the Newsboy" and soon after that released "The Tip of My Fingers" b/w "I Wish I Could Fall in Love Today."

On April 2, 1965, Roger Miller married 23-year old Leah Kendrick in Las Vegas. Leah was born on December 10, 1941. Her father, Ranzel Murrah Kendrick, was a major investor in the American arm of Fina Gas and she had been raised in "society." Roger met her after one of his shows and they carried on a heavy romance. Roger was running wild and things were happening fast in his career. It was no time to try and settle down, but he loved Leah and she was three months pregnant. It was not the most opportune time for a wedding; Roger had to leave the day after their vows for England.

The Hoffman Candy Bars commercial was only supposed to run for three months on Los Angeles radio stations but the ads were so popular, due to Roger's ear-catching delivery, that the ads were introduced by announcers saying "Now here's Roger Miller for Hoffman Candy Bars."

"They were getting all that for nothing," said Chuck Blore. "So the Hoffman Candy people called the ad agency and said 'We'd like to get Roger to do another ad for us.' I had told the agency about Roger and so they called me and said 'We want Roger to come back and do this.' I hadn't seen or talked to Roger since that day in the studio and I'm thinking 'We can't get Roger to do this. He's had all those monster hits. You're crazy!' but the agency said, 'Well, you told us that he said if you wanted him to do it again he'd coming a-runnin.' Remember that?'"

"I didn't have a number on Roger," said Blore, "so I called Glen Campbell and he gave me a number and I called it but no Roger, this was his agent. So I told him about wanting Roger to do another ad and he said, 'Sure, we'll do it again. How much are you going to pay?' and I said, 'Well, the first time he did it was for $50 apiece but that was before he hit big.' And the agent said, 'Well, it's got to be a minimum of $15,000.' So I called Glen back and said 'You gave me the number for Roger's agent' and Glen said, 'That's the only number I have' and then he says, 'Wait—

hang on a minute and then he found another number. I called and it was Roger and I told him the whole story and he said 'I remember all that' and then he said 'How much did you pay me that day?' and I said '50 bucks apiece, $150.' He said, 'O.K. That's all I'm going to take, and I'll come runnin'. I said 'Roger, we can't do that' and he said, 'The hell we can't' and he came in and did another ad for Hoffman's Candy Bars for $150."

At the end of that year, "That little spot that Roger did won every major advertising award there was," remembered Blore.[8]

Don Williams developed plans for Roger to go to England for promotion when "King of the Road" came on the British charts. RCA lost no time in taking advantage of Roger's success and packaged his recordings from that label on an album for their budget label, Camden.

Roger was reluctant to go to England, remembered Williams. First, he had just married Leah the day before the tour of England. "Get married and then go on a bridal trip solo," remarked Roger. Instead, he went to England with Don Williams and Thumbs Carlille.

"Nashville people don't like to be away and he didn't like to be away without Leah," remembered Williams. "I told him, 'I'm going to get a limousine and take you and show you London' and he said 'I don't want to see it.' I said 'Well, you're going to see it.'" Williams took Roger and Thumbs Carlille on a tour of London but Roger had his hands over his eyes.

"Roger was sitting in the front seat with the driver and Thumbs and I were in the back," said Williams. "Roger said 'I'm not going to look' and I said, 'O.K.' So he's sitting there and we go along and I'd say, 'Thumbs, look over there—that's Scotland Yard and if you look straight ahead that's Big Ben and right next to Big Ben is Westminster Cathedral and you could see Roger peeking through his fingers while Thumbs is sitting up going 'Oh, my God.'"[9]

Roger did a number of television shows in London and one in Manchester. He did "Pop Inn," "Parade of the Pops," "Scene at 6:30" and on April 9 he appeared on "Top of the Pops" with the Rolling Stones. "I almost hit Mick Jaggar," remembered Williams. "He was such an asshole, taking up all of our time and everything."

The "Top of the Pops" appearance resulted in two more appearances before the British television audience when it aired two more times that month.

In Manchester, Roger "saw two bobbies on bicycles going over this little bridge—it was a very short bridge—and he thought that was fantastic, bobbies on bicycles two by two," said Williams. "In London I took him down to Covent Garden at three in the morning and we saw a little baby in a carriage. It was pretty chilly, we had jackets on, but this baby was lying there with just a little flimsy garment and had big rosy red cheeks. Roger loved that—here we were shivering and there was this baby not feeling a thing, just as happy as can be. As we were walking he said, 'I'm writing this song about England' and he sang some of it to me. He asked, 'What do you think of this line?' and he sang 'the amplified pickers with the amplified hair'—he was thinking of the Beatles. That line never got in the song but he was writing that song in his mind as we were walking along."[10]

The next day, Saturday, April 10, Roger, Thumbs and Don Williams flew back to the States. Three days later Roger was in Nashville for the Grammy Awards.

Chapter 11
The Grammys

The first Grammy Awards, held May 4, 1959 in the Grand Ballroom of the Beverly Hilton Hotel in Los Angles, had 28 categories. There were no awards for rock'n'roll and just one for "Country and Western." Frank Sinatra received 12 nominations but won only one award (for album cover art) while Elvis, who accounted for over half of RCA's sales, received no nominations. "Best Country & Western Performance" was awarded to "Tom Dooley" by the Kingston Trio.

The second Grammy Awards were held a little over six months later in two locations. There was a gathering at the Beverly Hilton Hotel in Los Angeles and at the Waldorf-Astoria in New York in November. There were some adjustments made for the second awards show. First, NARAS created an award for rock—sort of—called "Best Performance by a Top 40 Artist." The winner that year was Nat King Cole. The urban folk movement was going strong so NARAS created a "Best Performance, Folk" award; they also created a "Best New Artist" award. The creation of the "folk" category allowed the crossover hit, "Battle of New Orleans" by Johnny Horton to win the second Grammy for "Best Country & Western Performance."

The music business establishments in Los Angeles and New York dominated the early Grammys but leaders felt they needed to include Nashville so there were some overtures made and in 1960 a "hillbilly music" chapter was established; however, the Nashville chapter was not allowed any representation or vote on the Academy board. The Nashville music community knew the L.A. and New York music industries looked down their noses at "the hillbillies" and so the "hillbilly chapter" folded after six months.

By 1964 Nashville had established itself as a music industry power to be reckoned with and the major labels either had offices there or were looking for a place and person to establish a presence. Country music was doing quite well; "The Jimmy Dean Show" was on ABC pulling in good ratings, "The Ballad of Jed Clampett" by Lester Flatt and Earl Scruggs was heard each week on "The Beverly Hillbillies" TV show and Bakersfield,

California based Buck Owens was outselling most pop artists on Capitol. The 1963 Grammy for "Best Country & Western Record" had gone to Bobby Bare for "Detroit City."

It was glaringly obvious that it was time for NARAS to have a presence in Nashville and for Nashville to have a more prominent role in NARAS and the Grammy Awards. Wesley Rose, head of Acuff-Rose, the music publishing company that published "Tennessee Waltz," the songs of Hank Williams, Roy Orbison's songs ("Oh, Pretty Woman," "Only the Lonely," "Running Scared" and others) and songs like "Bye Bye Love," "Wake Up Little Susie" and other Everly Brothers hits was the person the NARAS executives had to deal with in establishing a Nashville chapter. A delegation of three emissaries from Los Angeles came to Nashville and met with Rose.

Rose was a powerful and shrewd negotiator who bargained from a position of strength. At the end of their discussions, NARAS agreed to add six awards for country music: album, single, song, new artist and male and female vocalists. This gave country music more Grammy Awards than rock'n'roll, R&B and jazz combined.

In March, 1964, when the NARAS emissaries arrived, there were less than fifty members of NARAS from the Nashville community; by May, because of intense recruiting, there were a hundred.

The 1964 Grammy Awards, which rewarded recordings released between December 1, 1963 to November 30, 1964, was held on April 13, 1965 in four different locations. The Los Angeles ceremonies were held at the Beverly Hilton Hotel, the New York awards were presented at the Astor Hotel, there was a dinner at the Millionaires Club in Chicago and in Nashville the awards were held at the Carousel Club in Printers Alley in front of about 300 people.

Roger Miller and "Dang Me" won five Grammys that evening: for country song, single, album, male vocal and new artist, sweeping all of the country awards except the one he was ineligible for: Female Vocalist (Dottie West won that). Roger insisted that his producer, Jerry Kennedy, also come to the podium and receive credit for the wins. The crowd in Nashville cheered every time Roger's name was called and at the end of the evening, emcee Ralph Emery quipped "Thank you, folks, for coming to the Roger Miller awards dinner."

An article the next day in the *Nashville Banner* noted that eight years ago Miller was a bellhop at the Andrew Jackson Hotel and now he was staying at that same hotel—but in their most expensive suite, which rented for $30 a night. His new bride, Leah, was with him. In an interview, Roger stated "I'm really shook. I'm thrilled shook. It's been a long, hard and hungry journey. Back there in the late '50s and early '60s after I had come to Nashville there were days when I didn't know where my next meal was coming from and nights when I didn't know where I would sleep. A lot of folks still around here will attest to my poverty during that period."

Commenting on whether his lyrics were autobiographical, Roger noted that "The songs are messages. They relate stories about what could happen, and what did happen to a lot of us."[1]

Roger also pointed out to a journalist that his "songs, although delivered with a whimsical humor, have a serious message, often of waste and tragedy."[2]

The fact that Roger Miller won five Grammys raised some hackles because many in the NARAS community thought the Board had given up too much and made too many concessions to get Nashville into the fold.

On Thursday, April 15, two days after his Grammy haul, Roger recorded "Engine, Engine Number 9." He had seen that title in the December 5, 1964 issue of *Saturday Evening Post* for a short story that Roger never read; he was just inspired to write the song. That was the first song on the session, held at the Quonset Hut in Nashville, which included four other songs, "The Last Word in Lonesome Is Me," "Guess I'll Pick Up My Heart (And Go Home)," "Swing Low, Swingin' Chariot" and "It Happened Just That Way." "Engine, Engine Number 9" was also the last song recorded on that session. Producer Jerry Kennedy was not satisfied with the first take so he asked Roger to record it again; he did and the second version was the one released as a single.

That same week, "King of the Road" jumped from number 26 to 14 on the British chart while "Ticket To Ride" by the Beatles debuted at number one. On the May 13 British charts, "King of the Road" was number one, followed by "Ticket to Ride." "King of the Road" was also the most played song on BBC radio and number one in sheet music sales in England.

In the *Billboard* issue the week before the Grammys, "King of the

Road" was number six on the Hot 100 and *The Return of Roger Miller* was number nine on the pop LPs chart. The week following the Grammys "King of the Road" dropped to number 11 but the album rose to the number four slot. On the country singles chart "King of the Road" was still number one.

"King of the Road" dropped off the Hot 100 chart on May 1 and fell to number three on the country chart. In that issue of *Billboard* was a pop review of Roger's next single, "Engine Engine Number 9," which noted it was "another original, offbeat piece of material with a top performance." The "B" side was "The Last Word in Lonesome Is Me."

"The Last Word in Lonesome is Me" is a songwriter's song. Songwriters, whose stock in trade is to be clever and zero in on what others overlook, kicked themselves when they saw that song title. How could they not notice that the last word in lonesome is me? There was a depth to that line that went beyond mere cleverness and Roger Miller is the one who brought it to everyone's attention. "Dang Me" and "Chug-a-Lug" made Roger Miller a hit songwriter; "King of the Road" and "The Last Word in Lonesome is Me" made him a great songwriter.

In May, Roger was back on "The Andy Williams Show" along with guests Tony Bennett, the Count Basie Orchestra and the Osmond Brothers. His single, "King of the Road" was certified "Gold," signifying sales of over a million copies. On the last day of the month Roger recorded "Kansas City Star" and "The Good Old Days" in Nashville.

Television was reluctant to broadcast music awards shows live so the broadcast of the Grammy Awards occurred on Tuesday, May 18 on NBC. The agreement to broadcast the show after the awards was an attempt by NARAS to elevate the Grammys to the level of the Oscars, Emmys and Tonys.

Roger Miller sang "Dang Me" and "King of the Road," Petula Clark sang "Downtown," Henry Mancini played "The Pink Panther Theme," Gale Garnett sang "We'll Sing in the Sunshine," Bill Cosby did a bit from his *I Was Born a Baby,* album, Stan Getz and Astrud Gilberto did "The Girl From Ipanema" and Jimmy Durante, subbing for Louis Armstrong, sang "Hello Dolly." There were tapes of performances by The Beatles and the Swingle Singers from England.

The hour long show, called "The Best on Record," was sponsored by Timex. The problem was that the audience already knew the winners by the time the show aired and the songs performed were a year old. The other problem was that the "performances" generally consisted of the performers lip-synching their Grammy hit, which was not a format for exciting TV viewing. Still, it gave Roger Miller more exposure to a national television audience.

The Country Music Association promoted country music by making presentations to advertising agencies and advertisers. The purpose was to encourage advertisers to buy ad time on radio stations that played country music. Many ad agencies and advertisers held the view that the country audience was not the audience they wanted to appeal to. The stereotypical image that country music was sung to poor, illiterate rural farmers sitting in a shack by a radio was widely accepted as fact by the "cultured" and "sophisticated" urban dwellers, so country music was dismissed. The CMA wanted to demonstrate that money spending consumers could be reached through country music on the radio. To that end, the CMA staged shows in New York and Detroit. In June, 1965, they went to Chicago.

The show in Chicago on June 17 was emceed by Andy Griffith and featured performances by Roger Miller, Roy Clark, Dottie West, Tex Ritter, Johnny Bond, the Anita Kerr Singers and an orchestra of Nashville musicians headed by Bill Walker. Called "The Sound of Country," the show was well received by the audience of 750 sales and marketing executives. Tex Ritter announced to the crowd that "Country music has come of age. No longer is the country entertainer a barefoot rube with hayseed in his hair."[3]

During the show, Mercury presented Roger a "Gold Record" for sales of a million copies of "King of the Road." There were a number of "door prizes" given out; the top prize was a Tennessee Walking horse, given at the end of the presentation with the stipulation "you had to be present to win" so people would stay.[4]

The story of Roger moving to Los Angeles and then having huge pop success is the classic story of the boy from the country learning city ways. Roger had grown up in the country and he knew country ways; in Nashville, he was part of the country music community. That community was centered in a small geographic area in terms of business—Music Row and the Grand Ole Opry—and performers played in clubs, at fairs and on package shows where the audiences were generally blue collar, salt of the earth, working class Americans. Country artists and country fans were proud of the fact that they were simple, down home, nothing fancy average folks but they had dignity and wanted respect.

In Los Angeles and Las Vegas, Roger became part of a different world, a high-powered world with a veneer of culture and sophistication, where people were hip and worldly. It was a world filled with Big Stars and Big Money. Most of the inhabitants of this world tended to look down their noses at country music and country people. Country artists felt this scorn for years; in that world, it was almost embarrassing to be a country artist. The pop world made you feel that country music was an inferior music, that country performers were not quite as good and certainly not as "hip" as pop performers and the country audience was a bunch of unsophisticated yokels.

Roger loved playing in Las Vegas because there was action 24 hours a day, seven days a week and he stayed awake—through his use of amphetamines—to be part of that action. When he played Vegas, "There wasn't any set schedule," remembered Doug Gilmore. "He'd do two shows and after the second show his dressing room in the Sahara would fill up with women and well-wishers and hanger's on and he'd hang around for a few minutes and then say 'I'm going to the room so get rid of 'em and come on up. If there's a couple of girls you want to bring, then bring 'em.' So we did that, night after night. Usually we'd meet up in somebody's room and pick and sing or we'd take our rolling revue to other shows. We watched Duke Ellington and Don Rickles and whoever was playing. We had a limo driver who took us everywhere we wanted to go and Roger and all of us would go in a club and watch. All the clubs wanted Roger to be seen in their club."

There were some interesting events along the way. "One night, we went to Caesar's Palace," said Gilmore, "and Joe Louis was the greeter there and he said something to Roger like 'I listen to you on the radio' and Roger said to him, 'I used to listen to you on the radio.'"

Roger loved to watch Don Rickles "but Rickles never picked on Roger or any of his guys like he picked on others," said Gilmore. "For some reason, Roger was off base and I think one of the reasons is that Rickles was a little Jewish guy and he was afraid that us rednecks would kick his ass if he messed with us. But he was always nice to us."

Roger was often gone from his hotel room for days at a time—even when Leah was with him. On one date in Las Vegas, Roger and drummer Jerry Allison were out "roaring" for several days before Roger returned to his hotel room. He did not have a key so he banged on the hotel room door until Leah opened it. When she opened the door, Roger looked straight at her and yelled "Where the hell have you been?" Leah slammed the door in his face.[5]

With the pop success of his singles and albums, Roger thought of himself less as a country artist and more as a pop act. He was traveling in new circles and his clothes reflected that. He wore alpaca sweaters and, increasingly, aligned himself with Hollywood more than he did Nashville. Roger had physically left Nashville early in 1964 when he moved to Los Angeles; by late 1965 he had left it mentally. He still recorded in Nashville at the Quonset Hut, but his home was now in fast-paced Los Angeles.

Chapter 12
England Swings

On June 12, "Engine, Engine Number 9" was at number seven on the *Billboard* Hot 100 and the album, *The Return of Roger Miller* was at number 12 on the LP chart. The following week, "Engine, Engine Number 9" dropped a notch to eight on the Hot 100 but held at number five on the country singles chart; the *Return* album remained at number 12 on the Pop LP charts and number four on the country albums chart.

In the July 7 issue of *Billboard*, "Engine, Engine Number 9" was number 38 and falling on the Hot 100 but at number three on the country singles chart. Roger's next single, "One Dyin' And a Buryin'" b/w "It Happened Just That Way" was reviewed in *Billboard*. The review called it a "deep meaning ballad lyric of lost love and its tragic results." The flip side was "another clever piece of rhythm novelty material."

"One Dyin' And a Buryin'" entered the *Billboard* Hot 100 on July 10; during the period of July 13-24, Roger played the rodeo in San Jose, California. Roger's third album for Smash, *The Third Time Around* was reviewed in *Billboard* and cited "Engine, Engine #9," "This Town," and "Water Dog" as evidence of Roger's "brilliance."

In July, the radio station, WCMS brought a lawsuit against Roger in United District Court, charging him $1 million for not showing up for a performance in Norfolk, Virginia on Sunday, June 20. According to the suit, Roger's luggage showed up at the airport but the airline was requested to send it on to Washington. The promoters were unable to get hold of Roger and had to refund tickets to the crowd of 3,000 that showed up. There was a report that Roger had been in a Washington nightclub partying at the time he was supposed to be on stage in Norfolk.[1]

Charlie Dick remembered that "We were in Washington and Roger wanted to hire me as his road manager, but it didn't happen. He was getting hot and we were in a club and he said he wished he didn't have to leave but he had to play in Norfolk. Somebody said he should call the guy and get out of the deal so, finally, Roger called him and said he was cancelling the date. The promoter said, 'Oh, sweet! You can't!' and then Roger hung up. We had a big party."[2]

This was unusual for Roger who, although he was known to take copious quantities of pills, always showed up for a performance and did the show—no matter what his condition. Doug Gilmore remembers a concert at the Circle Star Theater in San Mateo, California soon after he joined Roger as tour manager. They had been there six days "and Roger hadn't even been to his room," said Gilmore. He found Jerry Allison who told him, "Don't worry about Roger. He'll show up for the gig and he'll be on time. He might be stoned out of his mind but he'll do the show so don't worry about that." Gilmore then asked Allison, "Well, how long can he stay up?" Allison replied, "I don't know. I've only been with him a year and a half; I don't know how long he was up before then."[3]

During the summer of 1965 Roger played the Carter Baron Amphitheater in Washington D.C. June 21-27; he performed in Camdenton, Missouri July 6-10; the Safari Room in Los Angeles July 26-August 1; then did fair dates during August and September; in October he played the prison rodeo in Huntsville, Texas. He was so busy he had to turn down a request from Bob Hope to accompany him on his annual Christmas tour overseas to military bases. Roger was disappointed; he remembered when he served in Korea and the lack of American entertainers who performed for the troops. Debbie Reynolds was the only American performer who appeared during the time when Roger was in Korea.

In August, Roger and Leah bought the house formerly owned by Clint Walker, who starred in the TV series "Cheyenne." It was on Penrose Avenue in the Woodland Hills area of Los Angeles.

In September, Roger went to the Music Operators of America Convention in Chicago where the nation's jukebox operators gathered. At their awards banquet on the thirteenth, Roger Miller was named the most popular artist based on jukebox play and "King of the Road" was the most played song on American jukeboxes.[4]

That same month, Roger Miller was scheduled to perform for two days at the New Mexico State Fair for $7,400. There were advanced sellouts of 11,800 each day—but Miller cancelled because he was "ill with a strep throat." A press release stated that Roger's physician "would not let him sing or talk for at least a week" and that the singer was confined to his bed. The matter was taken to the state's attorney general for investigation; meanwhile Ken Curtis and Milburn Stone, the "Festus" and "Doc" of "Gunsmoke" agreed to extend their performances two additional days to fulfill the commitment.[5]

Before the Country Music Association established their awards show, the top honors in that field were the *Billboard* Awards, presented each year in October during "Country Music Month" when the Grand Ole Opry Birthday Celebration, better known as the DJ Convention, was held. The 1965 Awards show was taped as part of "The Jimmy Dean Show" to be shown later. That year the event ran October 17-24; convention headquarters was the Andrew Jackson Hotel, with events also held at the National Life and Accident Building at Seventh and Union, the Hermitage Hotel and the Municipal Auditorium.

On October 15, 1965 Roger Miller stepped to the podium three times at the Grand Old Opry House, now known as the Ryman, to collect trophies for "Most Promising Male Artist" and "Favorite Country Songwriter." "King of the Road" was declared the "Favorite Single Record of the Year." It wasn't the only honor he received that day; out in Los Angeles his son, Roger Dean Miller, Jr. was born.

Jim Reeves, who died in an airplane crash a little over a year earlier, won three plaques at the *Billboard* Country Music Awards, which were accepted by his widow, Mary Reeves. In addition to Miller and Reeves, other award winners were Kitty Wells, Connie Smith, Jim Ed and the Browns, Buck Owens and the Buckaroos, Chet Atkins, and the duo George Jones and Gene Pitney. Edwin Craig, honorary chairman of the National Life and Accident Insurance Company, which owned WSM and the Grand Ole Opry, was named "Special Country Music Man of the Year."[6]

Presenters that evening included Frances Preston, Minnie Pearl, Tex Ritter, Buck Owens, Roy Acuff, Ott Devine, Jimmy Dean and Governor Frank Clement. The show was broadcast a week later, on October 22. Ernest Tubb became the fifth member of the Country Music Hall of Fame, joining Hank Williams, Fred Rose, Roy Acuff and Tex Ritter.

During the DJ festivities in Nashville, Roger was interviewed by Paul Ackerman with *Billboard* about his songwriting. Miller told the reporter that "I had the songwriting bug at the age of five...and my mind became a net which would catch phrases to be used in the songwriter's art."

Miller stated that Will Rogers made him realize the value of humor in songwriting because "Humor is the shock absorber."

"Creative writing, to me," said Roger, "is a matter of allowing your imagination free rein. One absorbs impulses and impressions, and the mind fastens upon phrases...and we create situations, much as a fiction writer does. If you have the song idea clearly in your mind, the actual writing can be done rapidly. Sometimes I carry an idea around in my mind for some time. Sometimes a single phrase is the catalyst and the words flow and I began to wonder how a cheap hotel room might be."

Miller said that Hank Williams was a major influence on him and during the interview he picked up his guitar and sang several of Hank's songs: "Window Shopping," "I'm Sorry For You, My Friend" "I'm So Lonesome I Could Cry," "Hey, Good Lookin'" and "Honky Tonk Blues," the last two in a jazzy presentation, saying "See, songs become new all over again with a fresh presentation or interpretation. I'm a jazz buff; I like the attitude of the jazz field; it's a free mind."

"The seed—the desire to be a writer—is something innate," observed Roger. "You are born with it; you have it or you do not." He continued that "I'll never be satisfied with my work. That's death! Songwriting is a continuous challenge...there's always another hill to climb."[7]

At the BMI Awards Dinner, held at the Belle Meade Country Club and hosted by Board Chairman Sydney Kaye with vice-president of the Nashville office Frances Williams Preston, Roger Miller received three citations for radio and television airplay—for "Chug-A-Lug," "Engine, Engine Number 9" and "King of the Road."

The Nashville chapter of NARAS had initiated a drive to enroll over 500 members, which allowed them to have six trustees on the NARAS Board (instead of their current two) and more impact on Grammy Award voting. Chapter President Eddy Arnold solicited potential members to join the chapter's current 160 members and pay $15 in dues.[8]

On November 6, "England Swings" made its debut on *Billboard's* Hot 100 chart at number 81; "Kansas City Star" was at number nine and Roger's album, *The Third Time Around* was at number seven on the Pop LPs chart. The Mercury executives had decided to release several greatest hits packages as "Golden Hits" and the following week Roger's newest album, T*he Golden Hits of Roger Miller* was reviewed in *Billboard*; the review called it a "blockbuster package of the magical Miller hits" which was "aimed right at the top of the charts."

At the end of 1965, "England Swings" was at number eight, it's peak position on *Billboard's* Hot 100 chart. Number one was "Over and Over" by the Dave Clark Five, followed by "Turn! Turn! Turn!" by the Byrds, "I Got You (I Feel Good)" by James Brown, "Let's Hang On" by the Four Seasons, "Sounds of Silence" by Simon and Garfunkle, "Make the World Go Away" by Eddy Arnold, and "Fever" by The McCoys. After "England Swings," "Ebb Tide" by the Righteous Brothers and "I Can Never Go Home Any More" by the Shangra La's rounded out the top ten.

On the pop LPs chart, *Roger Miller's Golden Hits* was at number 18. The number one album was *Whipped Cream and Other Delights* by Herb Alpert and the Tijuana Brass.

The top country singles of 1965, based on *Billboard* chart activity, were "What's He Doing in My World" by Eddy Arnold, "I've Got a Tiger By the Tail" by Buck Owens, "Yes, Mr. Peters" by Roy Drusky and Priscilla Mitchell, "Bridge Washed Out" by Warner Mack, "The Other Woman" by Ray Price, "Then and Only Then" by Connie Smith, "Before You Go" by Buck Owens, "King of the Road" by Roger Miller, "You're the Only World I Know" and "I'll Keep Holding On" by Sonny James. "Engine, Engine Number 9" was ranked at number 25.

On the list of top country albums for 1965, *The Return of Roger Miller* ranked number four and *The Third Time Around* was ranked number twelve. Of the fifty albums listed, Buck Owens had five, Jim Reeves and George Jones had four, while Eddy Arnold, Sonny James, Johnny Cash and Ray Price each had two on that list.

Much has been written about the British Invasion of America during the 1960s—especially the period after 1964 when the Beatles hit American shores—but little has been noted about the Nashville invasion of Britain during that same time.

In the Spring of 1965, 30 out of 100 records on the American pop chart were by British acts. In England, RCA Camden released albums by Don Gibson and Perry Como and London Records released a series of albums titled *Country Music Who's Who* comprised of recordings leased from Starday. On the London compilation album was Jimmy Dean singing "Happy Child," a song written by Roger. There were albums from Porter Wagoner and Ernest Tubb and RCA released their Roger Miller album, *Songs I Have Written.*

On the British Pop Singles chart, Jim Reeves had two songs, "Not Until the Next Time" and "It Hurts So Much," Roy Orbison had "Goodnight," and Roger had "King of the Road." Roger Miller, Jim Reeves, Johnny Cash, Roy Orbison, the Everly Brothers, Elvis Presley and Brenda Lee—all Nashville-connected acts—were doing well on the British charts in the Spring of 1965.

In May, there was another *Country Music Who's Who* compilation album released on the London label and Roger's "Poor Little John" was on it. Philips, which owned the Mercury and Smash labels, released Roger's first album, *Roger and Out*, which did not have "King of the Road."

The review of *Roger and Out* by the British magazine *New Music Express* stated, "Roger Miller is highly talented in his particular sphere, which lies somewhere between country and western and comedian singers. His lyrics are often hilariously funny and this is an album that will stand the time-test as a sort of updated Stan Freeberg. Particularly on 'Private John Q' and 'Lou's Got the Flu,' Miller links vocal gymnastics excellently with some funny verses. Don't miss this one if you go for light country tinged music coupled with some pretty far-out storylines."[9]

In May, RCA released "You Don't Want My Love" by Roger and it was added on Radio Luxembourg, which also played "King of the Road" and the answer song, "Queen of the House" by Jody Miller.

Back in the States, Roger was on "The Andy Williams Show," with Tony Bennett, the Count Basie Orchestra and the Osmond Brothers.

In England, *Record Retailer* reviewed "Engine, Engine No. 9" and stated, "As with his last number one the number is slightly out of the ordinary without being uncommercial." The flip side, "The Last Word in Lonesome is Me" was described as "a C&W ballad to Hawaiian guitar accompaniment."[10]

In May, Radio Luxembourg was playing "Can't Stop Loving You," a song Roger recorded in Houston in 1957. The British magazine *Melody Maker* had a weekly feature called "Blind Date" where a popular artist reviewed records released that week. In the "Blind Date" section Dave

Clark, leader of the Dave Clark Five, reviewed "Can't Stop Loving You" and asked, "American, isn't it?" before commenting, "Not my sort of music. Is this the chap that did 'King of the Road'? I like Roger Miller but this isn't commercial and it has a very thin sound, not a studio sound. It could have been recorded in somebody's bedroom." Actually, it almost was recorded in a bedroom; those earliest recordings of Roger's were made in primitive conditions.[11]

In England, Roger's second Smash album, *The Return of Roger Miller* was reviewed in *Record Retailer*, with the reviewer observing "It is a welcome album from the country star with the weird titles. Here, along side 'King of the Road' he features such bizarre sounding numbers as 'Do-Wacka-Do,' 'Reincarnation,' 'You Can't Roller Skate in a Buffalo Herd' and 'Atta Boy Girl'—plus eight more orthadox tracks."[12]

"Kansas City Star" entered *Billboard's* American and British charts in September. In England, *Record Retailer* labeled it a "Hit!' and wrote about the song, backed with "One Dyin' and a-Buryin,'" "Roger in his cowboy voice drawling on a-hurryin' through another useful, though deliberately dragging song" then added that "One Dyin' and a-Buryin" was "A talkie cowboy piece."[13]

In the "Blind Date" in *Melody Maker*, Beatles manager Brian Epstein reviewed "Kansas City Star" and said "Oh no! It's not even interesting enough to talk about. It could be a fluke hit but it's not one I would choose." (He loved "Do You Believe in Magic" by the Lovin' Spoonful.)[14]

"England Swings" entered the American charts in November and a British review noted that "Our Mr. Miller paints a rather rosy picture of England, which he reckons swings like a pendulum" where "even the whistling passages come up as a duet!" adding that the flip side, "The Good Old Days," "is nostalgic."[15]

Beatle George Harrison was the guest reviewer for "Blind Date" in December and said of "England Swings," "Oh, it's that Roger Miller bloke. Take it off, it's crap! I don't like it at all. It is Roger Miller, isn't it? I didn't like the first hit he had 'King of the Road,' but at least I could see why it was a hit, but this...nothing. Might be good for the country and western fans, but it's no good for the mass public. Sounds like Roy Rogers at the beginning—or Trigger!"[16]

It was "swinging London" during the 1960s, young people who were hip and cool while Roger's "England Swings" was a nostalgic look at "Olde England." The young people didn't particularly care for the images of "bobbies on bicycle two by two" defining what was the coolest place on planet.

At the end of 1965, "We Can Work It Out" b/w "Day Tripper was the number one song in England; "Make the World Go Away" by Eddy Arnold was number six and "England Swings" was number 23 on the British charts. Americans loved the quaint images in "England Swings"; it rose to number two on the country charts and number seven on the pop charts in the United States.

It had been a whirlwind year for Roger Miller. Three labels were releasing records; RCA and Starday were mining their vaults; Starday released some of the sound-a-likes that Roger recorded, "Country Girl," "Jimmie Brown the Newsboy," "The Tip of My Fingers" and "I Wish I Could Fall in Love Today." Roger was angry with this but Don Pierce said the anger subsided "when we paid him."[17]

Money was coming in by the buckets full; he made several hundred thousand dollars in songwriting royalties, he appeared on a number of television shows and was a top concert draw. His band was small; he had Thumbs Carlille on guitar, Bobby Dyson on bass and Jerry Allison on drums.

Chapter 13
Husbands and Wives

On January 2, 1966, Roger Miller turned 30 years old. He quipped about his stardom that "I may have to petition to be a state," "I need to get an unlisted driveway" and, later, "I used to be Elvis."

One week later he recorded "I've Been a Long Time Leavin'" and "Husbands and Wives" and the next day he recorded "Train of Life." According to Roger, he wrote "Husbands and Wives" while driving on the freeway in Los Angeles with his wife.[1]

When Roger played "Husbands and Wives" for Jerry Kennedy the day before the session, the producer told him the song wasn't finished—it needed a bridge—and he should write something that night. Roger's nightime activities eliminated songwriting that evening so, the next day in the Quonset Hut studio Kennedy told Roger again the song wasn't finished. Roger went out of the studio, down the steps to the area where there were ping pong tables and came up about an hour and a half later with the bridge: "a woman and a man, a man and a woman some can and some can't and some can." Then it was time to record the song.[2]

Roger told Harold Bradley "I want a Dave Brubeck intro on this one," remembered Bradley. "I was pretty astonished to hear that because Brubeck was such a great jazz piano player. So I asked the famous question that session musicians ask all the time: 'How about playing it for me?' So Roger picked up the guitar and played the worst assortment of disconnected notes I'd ever heard in my life. It was so disjointed that there was no way to even remember what it was. So I'm sitting there thinking to myself, 'I'm dead again!' So I called Jerry Kennedy over and said, 'Jerry, Roger wants a Dave Brubeck intro on this' and Jerry said, 'How does it go?' and Roger played it for Jerry and there was stunned silence. Even Jerry was stumped. Then I said the other magic words: 'How does the song go?' and Roger started singing 'Husbands and Wives.'" Roger had written the song in 5/4 time. Harold countered with "'How about this' and I did a jazz waltz—played 'ba-dum-ba-dum, ba-dum-ba-dum' and Roger said, 'Oh great' and that was it. I played the gut string on that song."[3] The song was now in 6/8 time but Jerry Kennedy still felt it wasn't complete.

The mandolin-like instrumental break was played by Ray Edenton on a steel string guitar with a high G string—where the normal G string is replaced with a string that's the same gauge as the high E string and is tuned an octave higher. That's how Edenton got that mandolin-like sound for the break.

On January 19, Roger Miller's TV "Special" was broadcast on NBC. Miller's label, Smash bought a full page advertisement in *TV Guide* to promote the 30 minute special and full color point of purchase material—posters and album flats—were sent to record stores. There were ads in trade magazines and a press kit containing a bio, photos and a copy of *The Golden Hits of Roger Miller* were sent to 450 TV editors at newspapers.[4] The show received great ratings.

Prior to his TV Special, Roger appeared in a "Country Music Spectacular" at the Houston Astrodome where 30,389 fans saw him with Minnie Pearl, Webb Pierce, Faron Young, Red Sovine, Jimmy Dickens, Kitty Wells, Johnny Wright, Bill Phillips, Ruby Wright and Justin Wilson perform. The three-hour event was the kick-off to the seven day Houston Boat and Sports Show.[5]

The day after his TV Special aired, Roger opened a two week stand at Harrah's Club in Reno, Nevada. On February 3, Roger was on Dean Martin's television show then, on February 7, Roger began a ten day stand at the Latin Casino in Merchantsville, New Jersey before he began a 23 day college tour, sponsored by the Ford Motor Company.

In January, "England Swings" moved from 31 to 13 over four weeks on the British charts; in the United States the year began with "England Swings" at number nine on the *Billboard* Hot 100 chart. Number one was "Sounds of Silence" by Simon and Garfunkle and number two was "We Can Work It Out" by the Beatles. There were several other songs from Nashville in the Hot 100; Eddy Arnold's "Make the World Go Away" was at number ten and "Flowers on the Wall" by the Statler Brothers was at number twelve.

On the pop album chart, *Roger Miller's Golden Hits* was at number 14; at the top of the chart was *Whipped Cream and Other Delights* by Herb Alpert and the Tijuana Brass, followed by the soundtrack to *The Sound of Music*.

In the first week of February, "England Swings" peaked at number 17 on the British charts, then began to fall; in the United States and England, "Husbands and Wives," b/w "I've Been a Long Time Leaving (But I'll Be a Long Time Gone")" was released. The British publication *New Music Express* said of "Husbands and Wives," "Dreamy, drawly sort of Miller on this one…A saga of marital 'bliss' taken at slow tempo….Very charming and with poignant lyrics."[6]

Roger was the subject of Hedda Hopper's syndicated gossip column in January and Hopper noted the singer had sold eight million records "without letting his hair grow down to his shoulders and using a lot of gimmicks of today's popular singers."

At the time of the interview, Roger was "wearing an orange sweater with gray slacks and noted 'I always used to dress in black and gray.'" Hopper asked "What are you aiming for?" and Roger replied, "I'd like to be like Will Rogers, who was a country boy but could reach everybody because he was honest. If you have something to say, if you can polish yourself to where you can communicate with everybody, it's a great feeling. But if you try things that aren't true, or honest, you don't get away with it."

The column noted that Roger could not read music, dropped out of school after the eighth grade and "it took me seven years to become an overnight success in the music business. During that time I performed in every kind of dive, bar joint and dance hall in America. I wouldn't want to go through it again but the background of experience it gave me is invaluable."

The article states that he was set to do a western, *Eli Koch* starring Jim Coburn (the title was changed to *Waterhole #3*) and "had been offered the role of a singing troubadour in the sequel to *Cat Ballou* but hadn't made up his mind about that." Roger said about his songs and performances "I create my own music and ad-lib as I go along, sort of. It's prepared ad-lib; the music comes out that way" and admitted "I always wanted to be an entertainer and song writer, since I was knee high."

"I'm sort of a Jekyll and Hammersmith; my music is depressive jazz," said Roger. "I said that one night on stage and it sounded funny—I just couldn't think of the word progressive. It caught on, so I leave it at that.

It's a form of jazz and to me jazz is a kind of self-expression. I came to Hollywood to study acting; when I was working in Tennessee for several years I was basically a writer. Now I have trouble with writers in Hollywood: they want to write lines for me to say and it's very difficult. When you go on somebody's show they tell you 'You say this' but usually I can't say it that way because it's not me. Sometimes I compromise and say it their way until it's time to tape—then I do it my way."

Hopper described Roger as "tall and lean with blue eyes and light brown hair" with "a basic wisdom about him and an uncompromising honesty. Not a voluble man, he sometimes restates things which he feels may be slightly exaggerated or not meticulously correct. He says he isn't shy or afraid of people, but finds that sometimes he doesn't have much he really wants to say."

Hopper noted that Roger was slow to trust people because "I've been taken by everyone there is to be taken by. I don't consider myself a good businessman but am satisfied that I have good people working for me and leave details to them."

The columnist informed her readers that Roger had been married for about a year, had a son, Dean, who "looks like me except that I'm a little taller." She stated that Roger met his wife in San Antonio and asked Roger if she was "an heiress and her father owns oil wells?" Roger replied, "I don't really know. I'm afraid to ask. She's somewhat of an heiress, I guess, but I told her I wasn't interested in her money because I wanted to make my own."[7]

Roger's publishing company, Tree, was the hottest music publisher in Nashville, thanks largely to Roger. Among the non-Roger hits from Tree were "Green Green Grass of Home," and an R&B song, "Hold On to What You've Got" by Joe Tex on Tree-owned Dial Records.

Curley Putnam, who wrote "Green, Green Grass of Home" was a shoe salesman in Huntsville, Alabama, when he met Roger in 1958. Roger came through town playing with Ray Price and, after the show, the two struck up a conversation. "He was real easy to talk to," remembered Curly, "and we just struck up a friendship and went back to the hotel where they were staying—Ed Hamilton was with us—and tried to write a song. We had some ideas, but nothing came of it."[8]

Roger told Curly to look him up if and when he got to Nashville

and Curly, anxious to break into the music business as a songwriter—
"wherever there was music, that's where you'd find me"—did. Roger
introduced Curly to Buddy Killen, which led to Curly landing a job at Tree
Publishing. In early 1966 Putman was named "Professional Manager" of
the publishing company.

In February, "Husbands and Wives" debuted on the *Billboard* Hot 100
chart and was number fifteen on the "Easy Listening" chart. *Roger Miller's
Golden Hits*, was number seven on the Pop LP chart; the following week
it moved up a notch to number six. "Husbands and Wives" debuted on
Billboard's country singles chart on February 26. On February 28, Roger
hosted the popular television show "Hullabaloo."

"The Ralph Emery Show" was a popular early morning show on
Nashville television. The hour long show ran from six to seven and on
Tuesday morning, March 8 at six o'clock, Roger was on the show with
Ralph and Charlie Louvin. Also with Roger were band members Thumbs
Carlille—wearing a Batman shirt—bassist Bobby Dyson and drummer
Jerry Allison.

Roger looked down and mumbled a lot on the show when Emery
announced that the Grammys were a week from that day and that Roger
had been nominated in nine categories. Ralph asked him how he felt and
Roger replied, mumbling, "It's quite an honor so I don't know how to
feel. So I just feel happy."

Emery hosted a popular all night radio show on WSM that ran from 10
p.m. until 4 a.m. and Roger had stopped by the show to chat, then stayed
up for the TV show. Off the air, Roger told Emery about his television
show, which was scheduled to premier in the Fall. Roger admitted that
he "cried" when he received the news via a phone call from an NBC vice
president. Ralph asked, "Were you sitting on pins and needles" and Roger
replied, "No, I was sitting on the side of the bed."[9]

After he heard the news, Roger called to his wife, Leah, "Come here"
but she replied, "I'm changing the baby." Roger then said, "Well, bring
the baby" and told her that NBC had committed to him doing a show and
that "it would be on at 8:30."

Emery continued to praise Roger while Miller said, "Ralph, you're
embarrassing me." Emery invited him to sit down, saying "Take this stool"

and Roger said "Do you, Roger, take this stool" as he sat down. When Ralph asked him how he was handling the success that came his way, adding that "It must be difficult to take it all in stride," Roger demurred, then answered, "Marry a nagging wife and let her take your mind off it."

There were problems in the marriage. There were two sides to Roger; his background was country but he wanted to be part of the social elite. When he married Leah, he married who he yearned to be but couldn't. Roger was a down-home people person and could never be a social snob; that was an awakening that occurred after he married Leah.

Roger said that he was putting together a book of philosophical musings that he wanted to call "Viewpoints from the King of the Road." Among his musings were "To be high strung is the hunter's gun to he who seeks to create," "From the seeds of disillusion grow the weeds of discontent" and "Every day is Saturday to a dog," and that he "wants to be an actor." As he lit a cigarette, Emery asked about his acting career and Roger replied "We've had offers but I let my managers take care of that."

Ralph then asked him about meeting with Otto Preminger, one of the top directors in Hollywood. Preminger had been directing movies since the 1930s and by the time he met Roger had directed films such as *The Man With the Golden Arm, Porgy and Bess, Anatomy of a Murder, Exodus* and *Advise and Consent*. Roger admitted that it was true, he met with Preminger and when Preminger had to take a phone call, Roger fell asleep. Preminger then told him, "Why don't you go home and get some sleep." Roger then added, "The bigger they are the less I care."

Although he had problems with his voice—he said he'd had laryngitis the previous week and that Emery was "taxing the golden voice of the '60s"—Roger sang four songs on the show, "Husbands and Wives," "Do Wacka Do," "King of the Road" and "Engine Engine Number 9." Additionally, Charlie Louvin sang an abbreviated "Less and Less," written by Roger that was a hit for Louvin. Thumbs Carlille did an instrumental, "Candy Girl," from his new album, *Roger Miller Presents Thumbs Carlille.*

Later that day, despite having voice problems, Roger recorded a song he co-wrote with Curly Putman, "Dad Blame Anything A Man Can't Quit," re-recorded "Less and Less" and recorded "You're My Kingdom."

The following day Roger was at the Fontainebleau Hotel in Miami for the NARM Convention. NARM, the acronym stands for National Association of Record Merchandisers, is the trade association for retailers and distributors who sell recordings. Roger performed before that audience of industry heavyweights, along with Herb Alpert and the Tijuana Brass and Nancy Wilson. Roger was given two awards, one for being the most played artist on jukeboxes and the other for "King of the Road," which was the most played song on jukeboxes.

The big topic at the NARM convention was tape cartridges and their future in terms of sales. There were two models—the 4-track, which was developed first, and the 8-track tape, which was introduced to the market the previous September and was forecast to develop into a top-of-the-line product. Ford had agreed to install 8 track tape players in their top of the line models and other car companies were falling in line to install tape machines in their top line of models. Mercury Records announced that it was releasing some select albums on 8 track tape, including Roger's *Dang Me/Chug-a-Lug* album on March 25. It would retail for $6.95.[10]

In a survey of college campuses in 1966, "Favorite Male Vocalist" was Andy Williams; Roger Miller came in at number 21.

There was a huge audience of young people on college campuses so it made sense for Roger to do a college tour. The tour was sponsored by Ford, who used "King of the Road" in their advertising and the car company, according to Doug Gilmore, paid Roger $10,000 a day for the series of concerts. The tour began on March 10 with a two night stand at Drake University and ended on April 3 at Penn State. In between Roger played Butler, Notre Dame, Old Dominion, the University of South Carolina, Florida State, Columbia, University of Maryland and the Naval Academy in Annapolis, Maryland in a series of one nighters. Four days after he finished his college tour, he opened a ten day stand at the Fairmont Hotel in San Francisco.

Roger was booked by General Artists Corporation out of Beverly Hills at this time.

During the Spring of 1966, songs related to the Vietnam War on the country charts included "Ballad of Green Berets" by Barry Sadler, "Dear Uncle Sam" by Loretta Lynn, "The One on the Right Is On the Left" by

Johnny Cash, "Private Wilson White" by Marty Robbins, and "Viet Nam Blues" by Dave Dudley. Johnny Wright's album *Hello Vietnam*, named after his hit single the previous year, and Dave Dudley's *There's a Star Spangled Banner Waving Somewhere,* named after the popular World War II hit that Dudley recorded, were on the country album charts.

Roger Miller was apolitical; he was more interested in having fun and being an entertainer. Although his early song, "Private John Q" on his *Dang Me/Chug-A-Lug* album was a humorous look at the lowly soldier, it was never released as a single. In the Spring of 1966, Roger's hit was "Husbands and Wives" b/w "I've Been a Long Time Leaving (But I'll Be a Long Time Gone)" and there were no political songs on his albums and no political comments during interviews about the Viet Nam conflict.

In March, The Southern California Country & Western Music Academy, later known as the Academy of Country Music, held an awards dinner to celebrate their first anniversary as a trade organization. Held at the Palladium in Los Angeles, the organization honored Roger as "Man of the Year" as well as top songwriter. Buck Owens won two awards, for "Male Vocalist" and "Best Band" while Bonnie Owens, ex-wife of Buck and current wife of Merle Haggard at the time, received honors for "Best Female" and "Best Vocal Group" with Merle.

Host for the evening was Lorne Greene, star of the hit TV series "Bonanza." A 27 piece orchestra led by Bill Liebert entertained the 1,200 guests. Performers included Roger, Glen Campbell, Tex Williams, Buck Owens, the Dillards, Rex Allen, Freddie Hart, Tennessee Ernie Ford and Lorne Greene.

Presenters that evening included Jerry Dunphy of KNXT, Jimmy Bowen, Donna Douglas, Chill Wills, Buddy Ebsen, Nelson Riddle, Dick Clark, Jim Nabors, Irene Ryan and Anita Kerr.[11]

Chapter 14
It Happened Just That Way

The Grammy Awards for 1965, held on March 15, 1966 at four different locations—the Beverly Hilton in Los Angeles, the Hotel Astor in New York, McCormack Place in Chicago and the Hillwood Country Club in Nashville—was "one of the most controversial—and, some critics say, embarrassing—years in Grammy history."[1] The problem, according to Grammy critics, was Roger Miller.

Of the 47 Grammy categories, Roger was nominated in ten of them, including four nominations in the rock'n'roll categories—which weren't supposed to go to a "country" artist. Roger's "King of the Road" triumphed over "Yesterday" by Paul McCartney for "Best Rock'n'Roll Single" and "Best Male Vocalist in Rock'n'Roll." Roger won in the "Best Country & Western" categories for Album, Single, Song, and Male Vocalist—giving him six Grammys that year and a total of eleven for two years. Roger was so dominant that year that "Queen of the House" by Jody Miller (no relation), the answer song to "King of the Road," won the "Female Vocalist" honors in the country category.

(Roger lost "Pop Record of the Year" to Herb Alpert and the Tijuana Brass, "Pop Song of the Year" to "The Shadow of Your Smile," and "Best Vocal Performance, Male" to Frank Sinatra.)

To add insult to injury to the rock crowd at the Grammy Awards, the Nashville based Anita Kerr Quartet beat the Beatles for "Best Performance by a Vocal Group" and the Statler Brothers beat the Beatles, Herman's Hermits and The Supremes for "Best Rock'n'Roll Performance by a Group." Additionally, there were a number of Nashville acts, like Eddy Arnold and the Statler Brothers, nominated in the "pop" and "rock" categories.

There were a lot of complaints from the Los Angeles and New York contingents—as well as music critics—about the 1965 Grammys. First, it was labeled "a Confederate forage into pop territory."[2] Ignored that evening were Bob Dylan, the Beach Boys and the Rolling Stones.

The Nashville ceremony at the Hillwood Country Club began without Roger, who did not arrive until after eleven that evening. He had done a concert in Charleston, Illinois, then chartered a private jet to bring him to Nashville, where he had a police motorcycle escort from the airport to the ceremony. His wife, Leah, accepted his first Grammy that evening but Roger picked up his second Grammy at 11:20 p.m.

An article in the *Tennessean* noted that Roger "literally ran out of ways to say 'thanks'" and that "he apparently got a little tired of walking up to the stage and walking off…between his fifth and sixth awards, Miller perched beside the stage to wait."[3]

The Tuesday night event was held before "a tuxedo and mink-clad crowd" of over 400 and presided over by Eddy Arnold, president of the Nashville chapter of NARAS. The Nashville event presented sealed envelopes in all 47 categories as the winners were announced after a 20-member big band, under the direction of Owen Bradley, played an overture.

At the end of the evening, Roger took the stage and, calling up some of the studio musicians who played on his records, did an impromptu performance of "King of the Road."

Among the presenters that evening were Minnie Pearl, David Cobb, Tupper Saussy, Bill Porter, Ray Walker and Gordon Stoker of the Jordanaires, Mary Reeves, Ray Stevens, Don Light, Mary Lynch, Archie Campbell and Carl Smith with Goldie Hill. Entertainers that evening—who played between presentations—included Chet Atkins, Boots Randolph, Don Bowman, Don Gibson and the Statler Brothers.[4]

During the BMI Awards ceremony in New York to award citations based on radio and television airplay for pop songs, Roger Miller received three. Top songwriters for 1965 were the Motown team of Lamont Dozier, Brian Holland and Eddie Holland with eight citations; John Lennon and Paul McCartney received five and joining Roger with three awards were Sonny Bono, Smokey Robinson and the Rolling Stones songwriting team of Mick Jagger and Keith Richards.

Roger was booked for a ten day engagement at the Fairmont Hotel in San Francisco April 7-17. On April 16, "Husbands and Wives" was number four on the "Easy Listening" chart in *Billboard*; number one was "I Want To Go With You" by Eddy Arnold.

A brief article in May noted that during the Illinois Fair in Peoria, where Roger was scheduled to give nine performances, a heavy downpour hit the outdoor crowd of 7,000 just as Roger started his show. While his band members ducked for cover, Roger stood in the rain and sang for more than the 20 minutes he was scheduled to perform while the crowd cheered him on.[5]

Once again the telecast of the Grammy Awards came after the actual event. On May 16, a one hour special on NBC featured performances by Roger, Herb Alpert and the Tijuana Brass, Duke Ellington, Anita Kerr and Jody Miller. The telecast was a huge success; it was one of the top rated shows of the season. Among the highlights were Tony Bennett singing "The Shadow of Your Smile," Herb Alpert and the Tijuana Brass doing "A Taste of Honey" and Bill Cosby's comedic monologue.

Bob Hope opened and closed the show. However, once again the show came under fire because the performers lip-synced their performances, which lost the impact of a live performance.[6]

When "Dang Me" came out, Captain Kris Kristofferson was an Army Ranger, flying helicopters in Germany. Kristofferson immediately related to the song; he, too, had been "sittin' around drinking with the rest of the guys" instead of taking care of his family at home. He connected with Roger Miller immediately and began making plans to come to Nashville.

Kristofferson moved to Nashville in September, 1965. About six months after arriving, around the first of February, 1966, Kris landed a job at Columbia Studios as "Set Up Man" which he generally referred to as "janitor." Actually, it was a bit more than being a janitor; the set-up man was responsible for getting the mics and music stands ready for a session, for running errands for engineers and producers (everything from food to demo tapes to getting equipment). The pay was $85 a week and the job opened up because Billy Swan, who had the job, quit.

Roger Miller came in on a Saturday to record and Kristofferson volunteered to work that day so he could meet him. Someone introduced them—"This is Kris Kristofferson"—and Roger replied, "What's he pissed off about?" Kristofferson remembers that "I was the only guy there that realized he was referring to what my name sounded like." Roger was in no shape to record—or remember—so he cut no songs that day and did not remember meeting Kristofferson.

After the Grammy event at the Hillwood Country Club, publisher Marijohn Wilkin, Roger Schutt—a local radio disc jockey known as "Captain Midnight"—and Kristofferson walked into Linebaugh's, a popular hangout for country stars, located on lower Broadway, down a block and on the opposite side of the street from Tootsie's. They saw Roger Miller sitting at a table by himself reading a newspaper.

Marijohn, Roger and Kris sat down. Captain Midnight said "Roger Miller!" and Roger looked up, then came over and sat down with them. Midnight introduced Kris who, prompted by Captain Midnight, said ""Glad to meet you, Roger. When are you going to pay Captain Midnight that twenty-five dollars you owe him?" Without missing a beat, Roger looked at Kristofferson and said, "Captain Midnight can take that twenty-five dollars and shove it up his ass!" Fortunately, things got better after that.

The root of that story went back to when Midnight was working for *Music Reporter*, a trade magazine, and publisher Charlie Lamb assigned him to write a bio of Roger Miller. It was arranged that Schutt would be paid $25 for the bio.

The next morning at nine Roger picked up Midnight in his Cadillac convertible and they spent two days together—popping pills to stay awake. Finally, Roger asked the Captain, "Do you want me to drop you off at Charlie's or do you want me to take you home?"

Midnight wrote the bio but never got paid. According to Midnight, Roger told him "My manager will pay you" while the manager said, "Roger will pay you." Midnight never got paid and it became a long running jibe; whenever Midnight saw Roger, he asked about that $25. And Midnight always told everyone who was going to see Roger to ask him about the $25.[7]

"You Can't Roller Skate in a Buffalo Herd" was a song that Roger recorded back in 1964 on the same session that he recorded "King of the Road" and was included on his second album. A story has long circulated that, because Roger did not like to co-write with other songwriters, he often suggested the title "You Can't Roller Skate in a Buffalo Herd" when a songwriter approached him about writing together. Roger eventually wrote the song, which was popular on his shows and demonstrated Roger's humor, wit and off-beat way of looking at life.

The song was so popular with radio programmers and fans that Mercury decided to release it as a single in June, 1966. The other side of the record was a serious song with depth, "Train of Life." On July 9, "You Can't Roller Skate in a Buffalo Herd" entered the *Billboard* country chart and reached number 35, only staying on that chart for five weeks. On the pop side, it reached number 40.

A singer must be very careful of what he or she records because, if the song is a hit, they will have to sing it for the rest of their life. Roger grew to hate singing "You Can't Roller Skate in a Buffalo Herd" night after night after night. Later in life, Roger Miller commented that if he had known that song was going to be a hit, "I would never have recorded the sonovabitch!"

In late August, Roger received a Gold Album for sales of half a million units for his *Dang Me/Chug-A-Lug* album; this was his third Gold Album award, *The Return of Roger Miller* and *The Golden Hits of Roger Miller* had already been awarded gold status.

"My Uncle Used to Love Me But She Died" was released and *Variety* reviewed the single, stating it was "a way-out country song, sort of a backwoods stream-of-consciousness with sound that could hit big." The flip side was "You're My Kingdom."[8]

In Nashville, a membership drive for NARAS resulted in 200 new members. In Los Angeles, the NARAS organization had altered some of their rules in response to Roger's eleven Grammy wins during the past two years.

First, NARAS reduced the number of Grammys from 47 to 42 and eliminated two country Grammys to give that field four while adding three more for Rhythm and Blues and Rock/Pop. The "Best New Artist" awards were transferred from the membership to special trustee selections because the 1965 Grammys overlooked Bob Dylan, one of the most influential artists in pop music during the year. Finally, they established a rule that an artist could only be nominated in one genre; thus, Roger Miller—or anyone else—could not be nominated in both the country and pop categories.[9]

During an interview a reporter asked Roger how long he thought his success would last and Roger answered, "Until the public gets tired of peanut butter, they don't want mayonnaise." The reporter noted that Roger "made close to a half million dollars in the past year" but Roger countered that he "doesn't like to think past one hundred dollars."[10]

Chapter 15
"The Roger Miller Show"

Roger's variety television series, "The Roger Miller Show," began taping in August and the first one did not go well; it took about 13 hours in the studio to finish the show because of problems with the set, with the lighting and with sound. It was a harbinger of things to come.

The show had Gary Smith as director and Dwight Hemion as producer—two of the best in the business—and the writers included Mason Williams, Bernie Kukoff and Jeff Harris.

"The Roger Miller Show" debuted on NBC on Mondays from 8:30 to 9 p.m., Eastern time. The studio bio released to the media noted that, for the interview Roger was dressed in a "soft blue cardigan sweater over a white button-down shirt and he looks like the clean-cut All-American nice guy." The bio stated that Roger "admits he used to write songs out of desperation, and that he still writes best when he's depressed." The show's opening showed Roger, wearing a tuxedo, running through a train yard as the orchestra played "King of the Road" before he stopped on top of a box car on the set. Roger then sang "This Town." On the show Roger introduced the "Doodle Town Pipers," about 20 or so clean cut young men and women in matching outfits.

Bill Cosby was Roger's guest on that first show and Bill sang some nonsense lyrics before he and Roger sang "If My Friends Could See Me Now." This was followed by a string of "I was so poor" jokes. Roger acted tired and bored during this segment.

Roger then did "Dang Me" with Thumbs Carlille, Don Bagley (who replaced Bobby Dyson on bass) and Jerry Allison. This was followed by "My Uncle Used To Love Me (But She Died)" which Roger introduced by looking into the TV camera and saying it was NOT about his Dad. Roger then introduced Wes Harrison, who made "sounds" (like train whistles). Roger sang "Yesterday" with young people gathered in a circle around him. At the end of the show, Roger was back on top of the box car saying "good night."

The theme song for "The Roger Miller Show" was "King of the Road" and The Eddie Karam Orchestra and The Doodletown Pipers were the regulars.

The ratings for the first night of the Fall season showed that NBC did not have a single show win during its time slot. In the 8:30 time slot, "The Lucy Show" on CBS received a 21.4 rating and 37 share; that was followed by "Rat Patrol" and then "The Roger Miller Show," which received a 13.7 rating and 24 share from Nielson. Another rating service, Trendex, showed Roger's show received a 12.2 rating and 22.3 share.[1]

(NOTE: Rating is based on total population while share is based on those watching television, so when "The Roger Miller Show" received a 13.7 rating, it meant that of all the people in the country, 13.7 percent watched that show. The 22.3 share meant that of all the people in the country watching television, 22.3 percent watched "The Roger Miller Show.")

After the next week, it was obvious "The Roger Miller Show" was in trouble with its ratings and share. *Variety* reported that shows who failed to have less than a 25 share of the audience were considered "early season losers" and listed Roger Miller's show in that group, along with "The Monkees," "I've Got a Secret" and "Please Don't Eat the Daisies."[2] However, *Billboard* ran an article praising the first show, stating that Roger's "relaxed style is perfectly suited for TV screens and the railroad yard background was a swinging setting for the fast-paced show," concluding that "The only negative comment is that Miller mumbles on occasion. If he could only prevent that, he'd have it made."[3]

In October, 1966, the top shows based on Nielson ratings were named and Roger's show wasn't among those listed.[4]

October in Nashville meant the Disc Jockey Convention and country music awards. The Country Music Association (CMA) Awards would not begin until the next year so the 1966 awards came from *Billboard*. Most of the events in 1966 were held at the Municipal Auditorium rather than in hotels. Roger was not nominated for top male, single or album and was not present for the awards; however, he won "Favorite Country Songwriter."

Minnie Pearl was voted "Country Man of the Year" at *Billboard's* nineteenth annual Country Music Awards, held at the War Memorial Auditorium on Wednesday, October 19, which preceeded the convention October 20-22. The awards were broadcast on Dick Clark's "Swingin' Country Show" on NBC on November 8. Over 4,500 attended the Nashville convention, including a number from the pop music world who came to see if they could capture some of the Nashville magic.[5]

There were four new members voted into the Country Music Hall of Fame: Jim Denny, Judge George D. Hay, Uncle Dave Macon and Eddy Arnold.[6]

Roger attended the BMI Awards banquet where he was honored with five awards for "England Swings," "Husbands and Wives," "I've Been a Long Time Leaving," "Kansas City Star" and "The Last Word in Lonesome Is Me."[7]

That event was held at the Belle Meade Country Club and before the ceremony Roger made the rounds at the tables, shaking hands and greeting old friends. Someone asked him, "What about your TV show? We've heard it's in trouble." Roger replied, "It's shaky. There is talk that it will be moved to another night." Roger then smiled before saying, "If it is bad—just suppose if it had been an hour show. It would have been twice as bad."

During the evening Roger stated that "a song is a lot like a handshake. You have to stick it out and see if anybody grabs it." In answer to how he writes songs, he said, "How I write a song is between me and God and He doesn't talk much about it." He noted that he'd recently entertained President Johnson and his family at the White House. "After I was through, the President never said a word. He just stood there and picked me up by the ears," an allusion to criticism that President Johnson faced when cameras caught him picking up his beagle dogs by their ears.

Someone overhearing those remarks said, "If they'd let him talk like that on TV his show would be one of the highest rated!"[8]

In November, Roger's recording of Elvis's former hit, "Heartbreak Hotel" entered the country chart but only stayed for three weeks, rising to number 55; it reached number 84 on the pop chart. His album *Words and Music* entered the country chart on November 26 and reached number 32.

Jan Howard remembered an incident with Roger around this time, when Roger had started flying to dates in Lear Jets.

"I was on the road and called home," she said. "I had three sons and a housekeeper, Solona. I called home every night if I possibly could and spoke with the boys or the housekeeper. One night Solona answered the phone and I asked if everything was O.K. and she said it was and then I said, 'Let me speak to Jimmy,' who was my oldest son. 'Well, he's not here, Mrs. Howard,' so I said 'Then let me speak to Corky,' my middle son. 'He's not here, Mrs. Howard.' So I said, 'Let me speak to David,' who was the youngest. I knew he'd be there. There was a pause and she said 'No, he's not here either' so I asked 'Where is he?' and she said 'He went to Washington D.C. with Mr. Miller.' I said 'He did WHAT?'"

"Roger had come by and picked up David and took him to Washington on his Lear Jet. David took lots of pictures on that trip. When they got to Washington—Roger was working up there—Roger turned the limo over to David and told the driver to take David to all the monuments and everything. So that's what David did for three hours while Roger did his show. When David got back I asked him 'What was your biggest thrill?' He said 'Pulling up to the drug store in a limousine and going in there and buying film.'"[9]

During the time his show was running on NBC, Roger continued to perform in Las Vegas in a tuxedo with band members Thumbs Carlille and Jerry Allison.

In an article in *TV Guide*, Roger was quoted as saying he "gets so tense I can hear my blood rushing around. Sounds like it's going through dry leaves" and that "I was like a suede football. They didn't know what to do with me on the Opry. I wasn't country, and I wasn't western. Hell, I still don't know what or who I am." The writer noted that "Roger is easy to talk to but hard to keep on the subject, any subject."

Discussing his success, Roger stated, "When the money started rolling in, I'd rush around to the stores and go crazy. I'd say gimme some of those and those and some of that there. And four or five of them. (he laughs) You got any in green? How 'bout some blue ones?"

The writer noted that "Ambition drove Roger for years. He could be coasting now, but he isn't. When the show ends he goes to the clubs. Not to drink but to listen and to play. He'll play and sing all night, sleep in his suit for two hours, change shirts, drink a Coke and start all over again."

Success had its drawbacks; salesmen chased Roger, offering deals and opportunities for a ranch, cattle, insurance, a Mercedes, a Rolls-Royce, a Lear jet. "Everybody's my closest friend," Roger told the reporter. "Man, I ain't got time to breathe."

Commenting on his show at the Sahara, the reporter noted that Roger "forgets lines, songs, jokes, where he is. He clutches and begins talking into his armpit. Depression rides him like a monkey. His throat closes up and he drinks water and makes a bubbling noise in the mike. He goes into his imitations: an electric bear at the Greyhound Bus Station shooting gallery, a kid revving up a Harley-Davidson, a bullet ricocheting off a rock. A 'pucker string' runs through many of his songs, revealing much about him."

It was painfully obvious that the television show wasn't going well. The article stated, "A lot of people figure the weekly television show submerges him. That chorus line and 20 singers, balloons rising and streamers falling and choreography cluttering up an acre of stage with 400 gimmicks, time steps and vaudeville hokum, make his show look just like any show, and it's common knowledge that his TV effort isn't long for this world. Others hope that as long as he has a guitar and a mike he will remain Roger Miller and that's all they want."

The article concluded that Roger is "all alone out there on his own cold tar-mixed road, double-clutching and highballing, and no one can touch him...Like Picasso and Satchel Paige, there's no one like him. All you can do is point and say there it goes. And later, when the lyrics and rhythms have settled down in you and you realize he not only sings these songs like nobody on this here earth but that the son of a gun wrote them from the bottom up, you shake your head and wonder why the whole country doesn't quit whatever it's doing and sit back and listen."[10]

On Roger's second TV show were the Geezinslaw Brothers and Jack Jones; Vince Edwards and the Jim Kweskin Jug Band were on the third show; Peter, Paul & Mary and New York Yankee manager Casey Stengel were on the fourth show, followed by Jack Burns, Arthur Godfrey and Avery Schreiber on the fifth show. The sixth show had Liberace and Wes Harrison as guests, the seventh show featured Soupy Sales, the eighth show had Brasil '66 and Arthur Godfrey, the ninth show had Richard Pryor and Petula Clark while Bobby Darin was the guest on the tenth show on November 14.

The November 21 show had George Carlin and The Kingston Trio as guests, while Nancy Ames was the guest during the twelfth week. Charles

Aznavour was on the first show in December, Frank Gorshin was the guest on Roger's December 12 show and on Roger's fifteenth show were Joanie Sommers and Gaylord & Holiday.

The end of the year was the end of "The Roger Miller Show" on NBC. The last show was broadcast the day after Christmas in its usual slot on Monday night at 8:30 Eastern time. On that show was just Roger and his band—Thumbs Carlille on guitar, bassist Don Bagley and drummer Jerry Allison. Roger sang a batch of his songs on the final show: "King of the Road," "Atta Boy, Girl," "Chug-A-Lug," "In the Summertime," "Do Wacka Do," "Husbands and Wives," "England Swings," and "My Uncle Used to Love Me."

The show was a struggle for Roger; he was simply out of his element. The writers were writing humorous things for him to say, but Roger wasn't the type of person whose humor relied on saying somebody else's words. Roger had a quick, spontaneous wit but television is geared for scripts. Plus, the Hollywood crowd never quite understood what appealed to a country music audience; further, they really didn't want to. This was, after all, L.A.

NBC saw the show as an opportunity to promote other shows on their network so they regularly scheduled an actor or actress to appear on Roger's show to boost their other shows. Most of them did not fit with Roger and Roger didn't fit with them.

Another problem with the show was that Roger continued to perform during the time he was taping the show, so there was no time to really sink himself into the television show and give some input into what worked. Roger was probably intimidated by the television writers, directors and producers—this wasn't his world—and then he came to a taping where he had to drop into a world that was foreign to him and he was uncomfortable.

Roger's genius was never captured on "The Roger Miller Show." Instead, it became a prime example of how not to present Roger Miller. He was a man who did not work well within a structure and the TV show was highly structured. When you made Roger conform to a structured situation, you lost the magic and genius of Roger Miller.

On the personal side, Roger was taking too many pills to function effectively during his television tapings. Back home, he had an unhappy home life; he and Leah would often blow up at each other, Leah would move back to San Antonio, then they'd make up and she would return to Los Angeles. It kept Roger in an emotional turmoil. It made it difficult for him to write songs—his bread and butter—and caused him to leave behind who he was and try to become what the TV world wanted him to be. It was a recipe for disaster and Roger soon grew tired, then frustrated and then angry.

His frustration led him to disappear one day—he was found in Las Vegas—and had to pay $40,000 in production costs incurred from his flight. For his last show, he and Roy Clark sat in a dressing room until Roger said, "Well, let's get this thing over with."[11]

The set for "The Roger Miller Show" had a train that he stood on and sang. After he knew his show had been cancelled, Roger blew up the train set. It was his way of venting his frustration with the whole ordeal and a final farewell to "The Roger Miller Show." Roger commented later about his TV show that "My face was on everyone's lips."[12]

The most successful TV show featuring country music was "The Jimmy Dean Show" on ABC, which had a major impact on country music because Dean was an affable host who booked country artists, interacted with them but generally let them shine. It is difficult to stress how important that television show was to Nashville and country music during the mid-1960s. Country music was really coming into its own; there were more radio stations programming country, the Country Music Association was actively working with advertising agencies to buy more time on radio, the CMA established their awards in 1967 and built the Country Music Hall of Fame in Nashville, the Nashville Sound emerged, which down-played the whiney twangy country sound in favor of a smooth, pop oriented sound with strings that made it more palpable to the American middle class, and artists like Roger Miller and Eddy Arnold crossed over into the pop world with hits on pop radio and appearances on the top TV shows of the day.

Jimmy Dean brought country music into America's living rooms on a weekly basis and showed Americans that country music had top flight entertainers and great songs. Dean worked with his executive producers, Bob Banner and Julio DeBenedetto and producer Tom Egan to book talent and, although they booked some talent outside of country music, Dean made sure that country music remained at the core of his show. Roger Miller was so appreciative of Dean that he gave him a "Golden Door Knob" award "for opening so many doors" for him; it was an actual door knob mounted on a wood plaque that hung on Dean's wall.[13]

"The Roger Miller Show" did not book country talent on its show; Roger had no say-so in who was booked. Roger had always been someone who reacted to his surroundings and the situations he found himself in; his humor and wit was based on that. He did not want to carry too much responsibility with his TV show because that got in the way of having fun, and because he was simply too busy being an entertainer. As a result, he was in over his head; he was just not ready to host a weekly television show but then, bang, there it was and he had to carry it off.

Country music performers began wearing tuxedos during the 1960s. Eddy Arnold performed in concert in a tuxedo, the BMI Awards during DJ week in Nashville was a formal affair, and Roger Miller wore a tux on his show. There's nothing wrong with dressing up now and then and it was especially important during the 1960s when country music struggled to shed its hicks and hayseeds image. But it's one thing to wear a tuxedo and another to let the tuxedo wear and define you; a country singer could wear a tux if he remained "country" but he lost the country audience if he allowed the tux to move him away from his roots.

Roger Miller was living in the fast world of Hollywood and Las Vegas at the end of 1966 and, although his music was played on country radio, and although his roots were deep in country music, Roger himself preferred the fast lane to a winding cow path. He wanted to leave the past behind and remake himself into someone who was cool, hip, sophisticated, cultured, in the know. He wanted to be "L.A.," which was the antithesis of "Nashville."

When Roger Miller achieved his initial success during the 1964-1966 period, country music had to have "crossovers" in order to achieve big success; Roger Miller could never have been as big a star as he was if he had only been played on country music stations. Roger, like Eddy Arnold, had to achieve success on rock/pop stations—and he did.

The top artist in 1966, in terms of album sales, was Herb Alpert and the Tijuana Brass, followed by the Beatles, Frank Sinatra, Barbra Streisand, The Rolling Stones, Bill Cosby, the Mamas and Papas, The Supremes, The Beach Boys and Andy Williams. Roger Miller was at number 26 and Eddy Arnold was at number 19.

In terms of singles, the top artist for 1966 was the Beatles, followed by the Rolling Stones, Lovin' Spoonful, Beach Boys, Mamas and Papas, Herb Alpert and the Tijuana Brass, Paul Revere and the Raiders, Simon & Garfunkle, Herman's Hermits and Gary Lewis and the Playboys; Roger Miller came in at number 73.

For Country Albums, Roger's *Golden Hits* came in at number six; number one was Eddy Arnold, who had three of the top ten country LPs that year, then Buck Owens, Sonny James, Jim Reeves, Loretta Lynn, Connie Smith and Ray Price. The top country single that year was "Swinging Doors" by Merle Haggard, followed by "Almost Persuaded" by David Houston, "I Love You Drops" by Bill Anderson, "You Ain't Woman Enough" by Loretta Lynn, "Think of Me" by Buck Owens, "Tippy Toeing" by the Harden Trio, "Take Good Care of Her" by Sonny James, "Don't Touch Me" by Jeannie Seeley, "Distant Drums" by Jim Reeves and "Would You Hold It Against Me" by Dottie West. "Husbands and Wives" finished at number 52 and "The Last Word in Lonesome is Me," a song written by Roger that was a hit for Eddy Arnold, was at number 32.

The top "Easy Listening" single in 1966 was "Born Free" by Roger Williams; "Husbands and Wives" finished at number 26 while "The Last Word in Lonesome is Me" by Eddy Arnold finished at number 83.

Chapter 16
Me and Bobby McGee

In 1967 Roger Miller had a top ten country hit with "Walking in the Sunshine"; it reached number 37 on the pop charts. He had another country chart record with "The Ballad of Waterhole #3 (Code of the West)," which did not make the pop charts. The movie *Waterhole #3* starred James Coburn, Carroll O'Connor, Bruce Dern, Joan Blondell, Claude Akins and James Whitmore and premiered on October 10.

The soundtrack to *The Ballad of Waterhole #3* consisted of a series of songs sung by Roger that carried the plot. Those songs—and pieces of songs—were not written by Roger—the music was by Dave Grusin and the lyrics by Robert Wells—although they fit him well and many thought he had written the soundtrack.

Roger's success continued—he was a popular guest on TV shows like "The Tonight Show" and performed in Las Vegas but, increasingly, he was burning bridges with his self-destructive behavior.

Road manager Doug Gilmore remembered an opening night in Reno where lightning hit the casino and blew out all of Roger's amplifiers. "Roger was on stage when that happened and he had no choice but to walk to the front of the stage and say, 'I can continue without the amps but it won't be any good. I'm sure that Harrah's will give you a free pass to come back to another show and I'll be happy to do it,'" remembered Gilmore. "That went well until we got off the stage and then the dope started hitting him wrong. It was a Saturday night and he told me, 'I want you to get all new equipment' and I said, 'Roger, it's ten o'clock on a Saturday night. Where am I going to get all new equipment?' He said, 'I don't care but I want it now.' Fortunately, the bass player at the time was from Reno and knew somebody from a music store who came down, opened up the place and got us all new equipment for the second show. We started the second show but Roger got angry because somebody yelled out 'King of the Road' and he said to the customer 'Get out of here.' Then he stormed off the stage and about an hour later a guy with no neck came to my door and said, 'We need to talk.'"

"We went down to the bowels of this building and there were a bunch of guys there—they were goons, there's no question about that—and there was no question that they were down there to scare me into scaring Roger. They said, 'We have a clock in the floor. We contract with you to play 50 minute shows. Not 52 or 55, not 61—50 minute shows. We've got this all figured out. 50 minute shows. During the last five minutes the clock turns red so you know where you are at all times. And that's how it's going to be so you tell Mr. Miller that if he can't do that then he's fired and he'll probably never work again in Nevada. Ever."

"So I went back to Roger and he's in his bed and he's got like a thousand bennies in his bed and he's playing with them like they're gold pieces. He said, 'What happened?' I said, 'They scared the hell out of me.' And I told him, 'Roger, if they beat me up, I'm coming after you!' So he said, 'We don't need this shit. To hell with 'em!' I said, 'Wait, let's do some math here real quick. You're doing 18 weeks here at 25 grand a week—that's $450,000.' He said, 'Well, I've got a hit record.' I said, 'How much do you make on a hit record, Roger? You ever figured that out?' He was stumped, he didn't know, so I said, '50 grand and the songwriting might be a little bit more. But you're making a whole lot more money here.' 'Well,' he said, 'I never really thought of it that way.' I said, 'Well, Roger, you've got to start thinking about it that way!'"

"He thought he needed the pills to be Roger Miller," said Gilmore. "And they were a great combination because when the dope was hitting him right he was the funniest man who ever lived. But when it hit him wrong, he was lower than whale shit."[1]

In January, 1968 Roger came to Nashville to record but had not written any songs and did not have any he wished to record, but then he found "Little Green Apples."

"We were leaving for Germany with some other dates in Europe," said Doug Gilmore. "It was incredibly cold and Roger hadn't been writing so he spent a lot of time entertaining the musicians because they were old friends. We spent four or five hours in the studio that day and Jerry Kennedy decided to cancel the rest of the session. I believe we were going to spend one more night and then leave for Germany. I called Buzz Cason, who was Bobby Russell's partner in a publishing company and said, 'We don't have anything for Roger and we're looking for songs. Do you or

Russell have anything for Roger?' Buzz said he would call Russell and ask and Bobby called me and said, 'I've got a song or two I'm working on but I don't have anything demoed. When can I play it for you?' I said, 'How about nine o'clock in the morning?'"

They were staying at the Capitol Park Inn and "I ended up with a lady back in my hotel room that night," continued Gilmore. "At nine the next morning there was a knock on the door and it was Russell with his guitar. He saw the girl and asked, 'Is this a bad time?' and I said, 'No, this is the only time we have.' I was still hung over when he sat down and played 'Little Green Apples' and 'Honey' back to back. I was just dumbstruck—I didn't know what to think because I'm thinking 'Am I still so screwed up that this sounds that good or is it really that good?' I asked, 'Have you got a demo?' and he said, 'No' so I said, 'Can you go and make a demo of it?' He and I had both worked with Bill Justis so I said, 'Go to Bill's office and put that down just like you played it—with just a guitar and vocal and bring it back.' He came back around noon with it on a seven and a half inch reel—we didn't have cassettes or anything like that so we always carried a little TEAC with us on the road. I called and had breakfast sent to Roger's room—steak and eggs—because I wanted him to be awake to listen to this. I went to Roger's room and after he ate I played 'Little Green Apples' and 'Honey.' 'Little Green Apples' was the first one on the tape and he listened and said, 'Shut it off,' then he said, 'Is it that good?' and I said 'I think so. I think it's a smash and it sounds like you wrote it.' So he said, 'Well, let's go cut it.'"

"So we called Jerry Kennedy and it was now about three or four o'clock in the afternoon. We said, 'We want to come out and play you a song—we think we've found something.' So we went out to Kennedy's office and played it for him and got the same response, 'Is it really that good?' And we said, 'Yeah, we think so.' So he said, 'Well, let's go cut it.' So he called over to Columbia and we got the big studio, Studio A."

Kennedy called around but couldn't find any musicians. Finally, he decided to play guitar but as they walked across the street to the studio they ran into bass player Bob Moore, who wasn't booked, so he joined the session.

They recorded "Little Green Apples" with Moore on stand up bass and Kennedy on acoustic guitar, then Roger sang harmony on the chorus.

Both Gilmore and Kennedy wanted him to cut "Honey" too but Roger said, "I'm like a bicycle—too tired" and left the studio. Gilmore then gave "Honey" to Bobby Goldsboro, who recorded it; it became a number one on the pop chart for five consecutive weeks. Roger's version of "Little Green Apples," where he sounds rather sleepy and tired, reached number 39 on the pop chart and number six on the country chart. O.C. Smith covered Roger's record and had the big pop hit on that song, which won the Grammy for "Song of the Year" in 1968.

Roger finished recording "Little Green Apples" around ten or eleven that evening, then he and Gilmore went to Bill Justis's studio where they played the recording for Bobby Russell. After that, the group went down to Printer's Alley, collected an entourage and ended up in Roger's room. According to Gilmore, Hank Williams' widow, Audrey Williams "was in that group and she made the comment, 'I was married to the greatest songwriter who ever lived'" and Roger replied, "Yes, and he'd still be alive today if you hadn't driven him nuts." With that, she left.[2]

In September, 1968, plans were announced for a chain of "King of the Road Motor Inns." The first would be built in Nashville. Roger Miller was credited with conceiving the idea.

The parent company was named "Roger Miller's King of the Road Enterprises" and Roger was "Honorary Chairman of the Board." The architectural firm designed the hotel in a style reminiscent of a "medieval Romantic Period," which followed the "King concept." The company planned to have the motel opened by October, 1969 when the Country Music DJ Convention was scheduled and the construction company was set to build the first one for $1.5 million, but a site had not been selected.[3]

In 1968, Roger Miller came to his home in Los Angeles one day and discovered everything in his house was gone; Leah had moved everything out and Roger had no idea she intended to do that or where she was. Some friends took Roger to George Lindsay's house, a few blocks away, where he stayed.

George, who starred as "Goober" on "The Andy Griffith Show," met Roger at a Country Music Association Awards show and discovered they both lived in Woodland Hills so one day back in California, George dropped by, chatted with Roger and they became friends. Roger's cook made white beans and cornbread and Lindsay often stopped in for dinner. Roger had a partial dental plate and was in Las Vegas for a show when he discovered that he had left the dental plate behind. Roger called Lindsay and asked him to go to his house and look for it. George looked around the house and found himself in the kitchen. Seeing a box of oatmeal on a shelf in the cabinet he took it down and looked in it—"I don't know why it struck me to look into it," said Lindsey—and that's where he found the dental plate. Roger flew him to Las Vegas to bring the plate.

The vast quantity of uppers that Roger consumed made him "jumpy" and Lindsay recalled walking with him "and Roger would be looking all around, thinking somebody was following him."[4]

On one of his trips to Nashville, Roger ran into Mel Tillis and invited him to his home in Los Angeles. The two went to the airport and Roger bought Tillis a ticket. "There was a train running through the house," said Tillis, "and there were toys all over the place. Roger said he'd never had any of that when he was a kid."

In L.A., Tillis was exhausted and went to sleep but Roger kept going. When Tillis awoke Roger was nowhere around; finally, after a number of phone calls Tillis found Doug Gilmore, who got him back to the airport.[5]

Doug Gilmore "started fading out with Roger in '68," he said. "We were like brothers. We stayed up nights, telling stories and crying on each other's shoulders. I really cared about Roger and he really cared about me, but he was killing himself, doing fifty uppers a day. Fifty! And I said, 'You can't keep doing that. At some point your body is going to give out. Some day you're going to drive a car through something. In fact, he would be driving down a road watching a TV in the floor board of the car that wasn't there and laughing his ass off at something that was not going on and I'd say, 'Roger, pull this car over. You're crazy!'"

"Well, that happened too many times," continued Gilmore. "And about that time Bernard and Williams came to me with an offer to make me a partner if I would move back to Nashville and find more Roger Millers. We thought they were growing on trees. Well, I came back and signed Ray Stevens, Joe South and some other artists, but my heart really wasn't into management. My heart was into Roger. When Roger wasn't the focus of my attention, I didn't want to do it. I started writing and producing at that time and I wound up getting a lot of jobs, probably because of my relationship with Roger. I did some work for the Dean Martin TV shows and I was music director and consultant on John Denver's TV show and the Mary Tyler Moore Show. Mary Tyler Moore was handled out of our office by Arthur Price."

"When Roger and I split up, it wasn't amicable," said Gilmore. "I told Roger that Don Williams had offered me a partnership if I would move back to Nashville and he said, 'Well, that's a wonderful opportunity for you. How are you going to not turn that down?' and I said, 'I can't turn that down.' He said, 'Well, I want you to go on one more trip with me. We're going to Hawaii for a week and from there to Australia for three weeks. Sit down gig—you go to a club and you're there for two shows a night.' I said 'That sounds like fun.' But what that was about was that nobody ever quit Roger—he fired 'em. So when we got to Hawaii he fired me and it just struck me, 'How could I not see that coming?' That was what that whole trip was about—to get me out of there and let me know that he was the boss. So I said, 'O.K., I get it.'"[6]

On April 15, 1969, Kris Kristofferson was fired from his job of flying helicopters in the Gulf of Mexico after he was caught sitting in a helicopter fast asleep with the blades going full speed above the roof. His double speed lifestyle had caught up with him and he had not allowed enough time "between the bottle and the throttle."

He went back to his room at the Evangeline Motel in Lafayette, Louisiana where "it looked spooky, with a neon Jesus out front, no TV, nothing but a dirty floor. I knew I was going to get sent to jail for non-support or something because I owed $500 a month child support to my wife. My kid was in the hospital with a bill that seemed astronomical at the time—$10,000."[7]

Kristofferson drove his Opel to the New Orleans airport, went in and caught a plane to Nashville. He never went back for that car. After he landed in Nashville, he called Mickey Newbury, who told him to come down to the Ramada Inn on James Robertson Parkway where he had a room. There were two television shows taping—"The Johnny Cash Show" and "Hee Haw" so "we can pitch songs to artists on both shows," said Newbury.

"The Johnny Cash Show" premiered on ABC on June 7, 1969; "Hee Haw" premiered a week later, on June 15, on CBS. Both were variety shows that featured a number of guest artists. At the end of April, both shows were in production.

Kristofferson spoke to Fred Foster and Bob Beckham with his new publishing company, Combine, and they agreed to give him enough money to send to his wife for back-payments and cover the insurance for his young son's hospital bill. Kristofferson's brother flew in to talk to Kris; Kris had told him when he moved to Nashville that he was "going to give it a year." That "year" had been used up several years back, so didn't he think it was time to give up chasing this dream and come back to his senses and his family? Kris demurred and told his brother he was going to stick with it a while longer.

Mickey Newbury told Roger Miller he needed to hear "Me and Bobby McGee," a song that Kristofferson had written after Fred Foster had given him the title. Kristofferson told Fred that he felt he was "dry" and didn't have any songs left in him. Legendary songwriters Boudleaux and Felice Bryant, who'd written classics such as "Rocky Top" and the Everly Brothers hits "Wake Up Little Susie" and "Bye Bye Love" had an office in the same building as Monument. Their secretary was named "Bobby McKee" and Foster told Kris, who was getting ready to leave for one of his trips to New Orleans, about the musical name and "she was a girl!" Foster gave Kris some extra money and said "See if you can write a song 'Me and Bobby McKee.'"

Kristofferson mulled over the idea for several months before the song started to come together while he was flying helicopters down in the Gulf. He had misunderstood Foster's title and thought it was "Me and Bobby McGee."[8]

Kristofferson had been humming Mickey Newbury's song, "Why You Been Gone So Long," which has a thigh-slapping jaunty feel about it. He was also thinking about a young lady he had spent time with hitch-hiking around Europe one summer. He also remembered a Felini movie, *La Strada*, he had seen where the young man gets his freedom from a girl, but ends up crying on the beach; freedom is a double-edged sword.

And he was down in Louisiana so "Baton Rouge" and "New Orleans" played into the picture. As he put the song together the line "with them windshield wipers slapping time" seemed to pull everything together; that was a rhythm and image that fit Newbury's song as well the one he was working on.[9]

As for "freedom's just another word for nothing left to lose," well that came fairly easy to a man who had lost his family, the respect of his parents and former peers and his future as a well-respected man about town. He'd also had his apartment broken into and some things had been stolen. Kris Kristofferson was certainly "free" but that, too, was a two-edged sword. At this point, what did he have to lose?

When Kristofferson played "Me and Bobby McGee" for his song-writing buddies he quickly noticed the song received a different reaction than his other songs.

One friend, Vince Matthews, suggested he cut out the line "Freedom's just another word for nothin' left to lose" because it took away from the concise, colorful narrative that Kristofferson had built in the verse. "He told me, 'God you've got all these concrete images and then all of a sudden you come out with this abstract philosophy,'" remembered Kristofferson. "But I decided to keep it. I thought it worked. And, looking back on it, that was the moment I really began to trust myself. In my mind, I had become good enough, and I decided I could go my own way."

Newbury loved the song and communicated that to Roger Miller. Living the fast lane life doesn't leave you much time for introspective songwriter contemplation, so Roger hadn't been writing any songs. Still, he had a record contract and an obligation to record an album and release some singles.

Newbury found Roger at the Ryman, where he was taping Cash's TV show. Roger liked Newbury's songs and Newbury recommended Kristofferson's song, "Me and Bobby McGee." Miller wanted to hear the song but had to get to Los Angeles to tape an appearance on the TV series "Daniel Boone."

Newbury and Kristofferson connected on the telephone, with New-bury asking, "How quick can you get down here? Roger wants to fly us back to L.A."

It was "the craziest ride to the airport I've ever seen," remembered

Kristofferson. Roger "literally was riding on the sidewalks! We made it to the plane, but I don't know how we ever did. He flew us out there first class and we spent like three or four days and he never listened to a song. He would go do the work on the TV show and then go to bed."

Finally, on their last day in L.A., just before they left Roger's house for the airport, Roger asked Kris to play "Bobby McGee." Kris did, Roger liked the song and when he got back to Nashville, he recorded it.

Roger's recollection of finding "Me and Bobby McGee" was that "I had come back to town from Los Angeles to record. I was just doing television out there because there was no TV in Nashville at that time. I came back here and was looking for songs and I ran into a songwriter, Mickey Newbury, a new guy in town who was just setting everybody on fire. I listened to some Newbury songs and he said to me, 'If you think this is good, you ought to hear this ole boy who's over at the studio. He's working as a clean-up man and set-up guy. Kris Kristofferson.' I thought he should change his name because that was a tough name. I took Mickey and Kris back to my house in Los Angeles to visit with me for a week and Kris sang me songs and he sung me 'Me and Bobby McGee,' which I thought was just a glorious movie. I saw the glory of the song. I ran right back to Nashville the next week and recorded it."

Roger's first impression of Kristofferson was that "he was a different kind of a guy. I didn't see a future, see a lot of what happened to him, but I heard a lot of literate writing. There was something very literate in his lyrics, they were different. He created sharper images. He wasn't writing just heartbreak songs, honky tonk songs. I mean, 'windshield wipers slappin' time' and 'we sang up every song that driver knew' and 'smell of someone frying chicken' in 'Sunday Morning Coming Down.' There's something very literate about that."

"He was very much different from other individuals I had met," remembered Roger. "I knew that women were attracted to him and there was just something about him. He told me that he'd been signing my autograph for years because people used to ask him if he was Roger Miller and he'd say 'Yeah' and sign my autograph."[10]

Roger was so impressed with Kris's writing that he recorded "Darby's Castle" and "The Best of All Possible Worlds" for his album in addition to Mickey Newbury's "Swiss Cottage Place." Roger recorded two versions of "Me and Bobby McGee," one had a long fadeout and another had a shorter one. On that long fadeout, singing the "la la la la la la la's" with Roger was Kris Kristofferson, Mickey Newbury and Billy Swan.

When Roger taped his segment of "The Johnny Cash Show" he sang that song; the show was broadcast on August 30. "Me and Bobby Mc-Gee" entered the *Billboard* country chart on July 7—it never made the *Billboard* Hot 100—and peaked at number 12. It made Kris Kristofferson a full-time songwriter; after "Me and Bobby McGee" Kris claimed that he "never had to work again."

Bobby Neuwirth heard Roger's version of "Me and Bobby McGee" on the radio, loved the song and taught it to Janis Joplin, who recorded it shortly before her death.

Chapter 17
Free at Last

On February 21, 1970 "The King of the Road" opened at 211 North First Street in Nashville. Instead of looking like a castle, the hotel was a nine story high rise with 182 rooms that cost $2.75 million to build. Its interior was designed by a firm described as "one of the nation's leading architect-designers."

Inside was "The King's Room," a dining room that seated 210 people, "The Bar" on the first floor, which featured pianist and singer Kay Golden in the early evening, followed by various musicians. Jim Mundy soon established himself there.

The top floor, known as "The Roof" became one of Nashville's top clubs. Holding 225 people, and open from 8 p.m. until 2 a.m., the club featured two floor shows. Early entertainers at "The Roof" included The Four Lads, The Ink Spots, Arthur Prysock, and Henny Youngman.

Roger Miller hosted the opening of the hotel on February 22. It was a black tie affair.

Roger was getting airplay on country radio, and his records made a respectable showing but there were no big hits in 1970; his version of "The Tom Greene County Fair," written by Dennis Linde, reached number 36 and the two sided "South" (written by Bobby Russell) and "Don't We All Have the Right" made it to number 15.

Kris Kristofferson, Dennis Linde and Billy Swan all wrote songs for Combine Publishing and Roger liked their songs; he recorded Linde's "Where Have All the Average People Gone" as well as "Jody and the Kid" by Kristofferson so Roger flew the three of them to Dallas where he was performing at the Fairmont. The three songwriters were dressed as, well, songwriters, so the Fairmont would not allow them into their posh club. Kristofferson managed to borrow a checkered sports coat from a band member that fit fairly well while Swan and Linde ended up with coats several sizes too big. Wearing those sports coats, they were allowed to watch Roger perform at the Fairmont.[1]

Since Roger was not coming up with any new songs, Charlie Fach at

Mercury suggested an album of Roger's country hits for an album titled, *A Trip to the Country*. Roger was amenable to that and in June recorded "Invitation to the Blues," "Tall Tall Trees," "Don't We All Have The Right," "A World So Full of Love" and enough of his early country songs to fill an album.

Roger and Leah's marriage was on-again off-again. The two would argue and Leah would pack and leave for Texas, then they would reconcile and she'd move back to L.A. It was a stormy relationship punctuated by a lot of laughs; Leah could be incredibly funny. Chuck Blore remembered one evening when Leah kept the group laughing by continually asking, "Am I wearing a hat?" (she wasn't!)

When times were good they were oh so good and when times were bad they were not so good. Sometime around Valentine's Day, 1970 things must have been pretty good because on November 16 Roger and Leah's daughter, Shannon Elizabeth was born at Good Samaritan Hospital in Hollywood. Two months earlier, in September, the couple sold their home in Woodland Hills and bought a house in Royal Oaks.

The Roger Miller wit was in full bloom during a dual interview in *Country Song Roundup* in December, 1970 with Bill Anderson. In answer to the question of how they met, Anderson noted that "Roger was stationed at Fort McPherson in Atlanta" and Roger interjected, "as a prisoner of war." Anderson told the story of borrowing Wanda Jackson's guitar to sing each other songs and Roger replied, "Try to picture two skinny kids with a rhinestone guitar strap that had 'Wanda' on it" and laughed. Anderson told of him and Roger at the Tower Theater in Atlanta when Ray Price walked by in a rhinestone studded Cherokee Cowboy outfit and Roger said, "Wouldn't it be great to be something like that."

Bill Anderson talked about Roger's early years in country music, playing for Minnie Pearl and Roger interjected, "And then we invented country music." In answer to the question "How do you feel when someone says you aren't country?" Roger replied "I never say I am country or I ain't country. I'm just what I am and that's legendary." In response to Anderson's statement, "He's just a plain old ordinary everyday legend" Roger rejoined, "Treat me like any other great man." After each statement, Roger laughed.

Roger told William Anderson, the editor of *Country Song Round-Up* that "the two publications I grew up on were *Reader's Digest* and *Country Song Roundup*. I used to read about Hank Williams. I used to read about Hank and they used to write about the fertile mind of Hank Williams. I'd say someday I wanna grow up and have a fertile mind. So I grew up and got plowed."

In answer to the question of "What is country music" Roger replied, "It's a piece of somebody's heart." Roger then turned to Anderson and said, "Remember when we used to worry as we talked about putting a little bit of our heart in each song we'd write. And what if someday there wouldn't be any heart left."

In response to the question of how he became a successful songwriter, Roger replied, "That's one answer I don't have. I think we just wanna be somebody. I never could explain what I've done. I've always had trouble doing that."

Roger noted that "After success you get careful. There's a feeling of abandon when you first get in the business. You write about tote sacks, loafers, tennis shoes and everything and then you get careful because you've had success with writing about loafers and tennis shoes and then you wanna write about boots."

The *Country Song Round-Up* editor asked Roger "Do you consider yourself country?" and Roger replied, "I always said if you got a ten acre field and you build a fence around it all you have is a ten acre field. If you don't fence it in you have a big, open field."

The editor asked Anderson to "evaluate Roger" and Roger interjected "$400!" Anderson mentioned Roger's early songs, like "Sweet Ramona," "Jason Fleming" and "My Pillow" and Roger said, "They could've dropped those on London during the blitz."

After complimenting Bill Anderson and his songwriting, Roger said, "I've always wanted to be more than a star. I always wanted to be a shining example" and laughed. In answer to "What keeps you going" Roger answered "It's greed."

"I've always thought that art in any form was the ability to capture what goes through their heads," Roger told the interviewer. "There are different people that can do different things. Art is the ability to capture and put down what goes through everybody's minds. A hit song is just a way of saying something that anybody when they hear it will say, 'Yeah!'"

The editor asked Roger and Bill if they ever got frustrated and Roger replied, laughing, "My life is one big ball of frustrations. If it wasn't for that I wouldn't be anything. If it wasn't for my insecurity and frustration."[2]

In March, 1971, Roger Miller was in Nashville to help celebrate the first anniversary of the "King of the Road" hotel. It was announced that King of the Road Enterprises, and Recreacres, Inc., a subsidiary of Walt Disney Productions, had plans to build a 17 story, 400 room $7.5 million motor inn at Lake Buena Vista, Florida to serve the new Walt Disney World.

Miller was proud of his involvement in the scheduled chain of King of the Road Motor Inns. "Honestly, it was my idea to begin this thing two years ago in Music City, U.S.A.," he said. "At first, I stayed awake at night having visions of getting the hotel built to resemble a castle, complete with a moat encircling the building. We later got together and decided to construct a bridge over some water to serve as the hotel's main entrance. I guess the health department thought we would attract too many mosquitoes," he added with a grin.[3]

In 1971 Roger Miller gave an interview to Bill Hance of the *Nashville Banner* and announced that he was "off pills." He had made a similar statement the previous November, saying he quit pills when they began to harm his career and when he "began to lose a grip on everything."

Sitting in The Roof Lounge of the King of the Road Motor Inn, Miller said, "Pills sent my entertainment career into decline. Pills helped sink my television show in 1967. Then I finally quit them. One day I made a big decision—on my own. I was going to be a man or a vegetable. Today—I'm a man! If I never do anything else, I want to get across one message to the young people of America. It is simply this: Don't get involved with pills."

Miller dated his pill habit to when he was 20 years old. "I was young and runnin,' broke and starving," he said. "I was wanting to be a GREAT songwriter-singer and I would take a couple of pills—and in a few minutes, feel terrific. And while I was writing and performing those funny lyrical tunes which made me a fortune, I was also consuming a big number of pep pills a day. Not for one minute am I saying that they caused me to keep on writing that string of songs. I do know, though, that when I got off of them, my writing went dry for a short period of time—up until now."

"I began to realize I was turning into a vegetable when the television show fell on its face," continued Roger. "It was my fault. I know it was my fault. It was the pills. There's no doubt in my mind. I thought I was brilliant. I had the idea that everyone connected with the show also thought I was brilliant. I soon came to realize that I wasn't so smart after all. I feel real bad that I affected so many people when I was staying high all of the time [but] I'm ready to bounce back. I want one more real monster of a record—and go on from there. But I may have to wait until the songs begin to flow. The water has stopped for the moment."

Miller concluded, "I'm glad to be out of the snake pit. Pills were all I ever took. I quit when it dawned on me that I was losing my grip on everything that mattered to me. My marriage was beginning to crumble. My music career was fading. Now I've got things turned in my direction...I don't have any great message for anybody. I'm not a preacher. But I plead with the youth of today—simply don't get involved with pills."[4]

In February, 1972, Roger testified before the Oklahoma legislature that he "swallowed so many uppers during a seven-year binge it's a wonder I didn't die."

"They should be outlawed," he continued "They're killers," adding that he was "one of the lucky few who lived" through those years with amphetamines. "I was killing myself mentally, physically and career-wise," he said. "I used to stay up three or four days and then collapse. If they don't kill you in the blood stream, they'll make you fall off or jump off a building. I used to carry them like change in my pocket. I had to take two or three to go to the store or to conduct my business. I was a falling down pillhead."

Miller, who appeared before the House judiciary committee at the request of Oklahoma Governor David Hall, said he first took stimulants when a friend gave him some in the Army. "We ran around glassy-eyed for two or three days. We thought we were having a good time," he said. Later, "a friendly druggist let me have them through the back door. It took me until I was 33 or 34 years old to grow up. I'm not very proud of that."

According to the article, Roger claimed that the last time he took an upper was June 15, 1969.

Chapter 18
I've Been a Long Time Leaving
(But I'll Be a Long Time Gone)

In January, 1972, Roger was in the recording studio; he did "Sunny Side of My Life" and "I Had to Leave Her" on the twelfth, "We Found It In Each Other's Arms" on the thirteenth, "The World Through Children's Eyes" and "Qua La Linta" on the twenty-seventh.

On January 22, Mercury released *The Best of Roger Miller* and the album reached number 19 on the country charts; in March they released "We Found It In Each Other's Arms" b/w "Sunny Side of Life"; "We Found It" rose to number 34 while "Sunny Side" reached number 63 on the country charts.

On February 25, Roger stopped by WSM in Nashville and did an interview with Ralph Emery for his radio show that was divided into five parts so that Roger co-hosted "The Ralph Emery Show" for a week. During this "week" Emery asked Roger where he lived and Roger told him he lived in the Royal Oaks section of Los Angeles and that "Steve Allen lives about two houses down, Roger Williams lives up the street" and Lou Rawls and Julie London also lived in the neighborhood. Emery said, "This must be the high rent district" and Roger replied, "Yeah, with a G.I. loan you can go just about anywhere."

They talked about the King of the Road Hotel and Roger said the hotel "is one of the great prides of my life." There were three King of the Road hotels, "We've built two and bought one in Los Angeles and we'll start expanding soon," said Roger, although "it's a slow process because it takes an awful lot of money to do it right. It's not a franchising organization; we're trying to do company owned things."

Emery asked Roger if he ever got tired of singing "King of the Road" and Roger replied, "I did for awhile. I went through a period when I got tired of singing my songs and then I realized that the people who come to see me and hear me don't hear them every day so I try to do it like I don't sing it every day."

"Do you still write songs?" asked Emery. "No, I don't. I'm in the trucking business," said Roger, laughing, then added, "Well, they're becoming rare. They're collector's items. I got old, you know. I'm in my late 60s now."

Roger then stated he was actually 36 "to clear the record" and said "I'm writing the music for a Walt Disney picture now. I've been writing on it for two years and I've got three songs. I think they're getting impatient with me. They're doing an animated version of Robin Hood and I'm doing the music and the narration for the picture. I hope it's another 'Snow White.'"

"Would you like to write a Broadway musical?" asked Emery. "No," said Roger. "At one time in my life I thought I would but I don't have that kind of discipline."

They talked about Roger's trip to England and Ralph observed "You must have had some kind of reaction there" and Roger said, "Yeah, I had this rash on my right arm and for two or three days I thought I was just going to boil." Emery noted that Faron Young gave Roger a job "when you were destitute" and Roger replied, "Yeah, he did that and, besides, I was out of work."

Emery asked if Roger ever went back to his hometown of Erick to visit and Roger replied that he went back "once or twice a year." He told a story of visiting after he'd had "Dang Me" and "King of the Road" and won his Grammys. He saw "this old fellow who used to drive the school bus that I rode. I walked up and asked him, 'Hey, do you remember me?' He looked at me and said—pause-'Yeah, I remember you. What have you been doing since you got out of the Army?'"

"Did that humble you," asked Emery. "I've never worn a tuxedo downtown since," answered Roger, who added that Erick was so small that "We had a parade one time and there wasn't nobody left to watch. The high school band was a trio."

Roger told of meeting Frank Sinatra when he and Leah joined Vince Edwards and his wife for dinner at a restaurant one night. Vince pointed out Sinatra and Roger said, "Wow!" and Vince beckoned for Sinatra to come over to their table. "This is my wife," Edwards told Sinatra, "and this is Roger Miller" but before he could introduce Leah, Sinatra said, "Wait, wait, wait," looked at Roger and said, "I think you're the greatest thing that ever came around."

"That was a big thrill, a big moment in my life," remembered Roger.[1]

During the radio show, Ralph Emery played Roger's recording of "Tomorrow Night in Baltimore" and observed that "You don't get many songs where a guy is crazy about an exotic dancer and follows her around from town to town. Did this guy ever get the girl?" Roger replied, "He got her, but it was about three minutes after the record was over."

Roger's current record was "The Sunny Side of My Life," which was written "by a boy who lives in San Antonio," said Roger. "My sister-in-law lives there and heard the song and suggested to the boy that he send it to me and he did and I liked it and recorded it."

Ralph pointed out that "You told me that you'd never heard of a song called 'The Sunny Side of My Life' but there is one, I believe, on a Merle Haggard album." "Well, if you're right," said Roger, "I hope you win a barbed wire mad man."

A discussion of copyright followed where Roger noted that "you can't copyright a title." Emery then asked if someone wrote a song called "King of the Road" would Roger sue them. Roger replied "I don't know" then added, "If they did, I hope their dog dies."

When asked about his family, Roger said he had a boy and girl with Leah but "three children by a former marriage that live in Oklahoma."

"Does it place a hardship on a child for his father to be as famous as you are?" asked Emery. "They grow up seeing their Daddy on television and hearing them on hit records."

"I don't know, I hope not," replied Roger. "My little boy just kinda takes it for granted, I think. When people ask 'What does your Daddy do?' he says he sings, he's on TV or whatever. We don't make anything out of it. I just work for a living, like anybody else. And that's kinda the way we treat it around the house."

In answer to the question, "Would you like for your kids to be in show business?" Roger was emphatic. "No, I wouldn't, unless they're really good," he said. "In fact, unless they're really great because good will just get you by. Unless you're great, it's a heart breaking business."

Roger talked about cooking nachos with Dean, his young son, "which is about the only thing I can do in the kitchen." However, "I've got a cook book coming out in about a month, 'Roger Miller's King of the Road cookbook,'" said Roger. "It's a collection of recipes from all around the world." When asked if it would be sold in bookstores, Roger replied, "It's going to be made into a movie. The first reel will be Lobster Cantonese." As he made each of his witty remarks, Roger laughed.

During the show, Emery coaxed him into telling a favorite joke. "Well, I had this dog when I was a kid," began Roger. "He was an awfully good dog but my Dad was cutting hay one summer and the dog got caught in the mowing machine and it cut all four of his legs off. The dog got all right but that left him with a nasty limp so I got him four wooden legs and fitted him with those legs. It took him a while to get used to those legs but, finally, he could really get around. One night the house caught on fire and the dog burned to the ground but he was all right. After that, I got a wheel barrow and put him in the wheelbarrow and pushed him around and it worked fine until one day he got chasing a rabbit and just about run me to death!"[2]

On May 5 and 26 Roger was on "The Tonight Show"; he was back on that show in September when "Rings For Sale" was released. This peppy tune reached number 41 on the country charts.

During the time that Roger and Leah were married, Roger flew his former wife, Barbara, and their three children—Alan, Rhonda and Shari—out to California for a vacation. They visited Universal Studios, Disneyland, hung out at the pool—just a "normal" visit. "I never saw my Dad or Mom argue," said Shari. "They always loved each other. Mom was very pretty, stunning really, and she and Leah became good friends. Dad was a funny, wonderful guy who loved us. They were alike in a lot of ways."[3]

The kids got along, too; Dean and Shannon from Roger and Leah's marriage as well as Alan, Rhonda and Shari all went places together. "Leah was very pleasant and outgoing," remembered Phyllis Forsythe. "And funny."

Those visits continued off and on through the years. Roger's business office always sent checks for child support on time and Roger regularly sent birthday presents, although Barbara generally had to remind him when a birthday was approaching.[4]

"I'll say one thing for Roger," said James Crow. "He always took care of those kids. He never missed a payment."[5]

In June, it was announced that Roger Miller's King of the Road Enterprises, Inc. had acquired two major properties—one in Valdosta, Georgia and the other in Chattanooga—for future hotels. The president of the firm, which was headquartered in Nashville and Memphis, announced this was for the development of a chain of King of the Road Hotels. The Valdosta facility was located off I-75 and had a 350 seat night club; it was scheduled to open in July. Roger Miller, "major stockholder and honorary chairman of the board," was scheduled to appear during their first opening week.

The Chattanooga land acquisition was at I-75 and U.S. Highway 41. The purchase had not been completed but it was called "another excellent property" which "can be a tremendous benefit."[6]

In August, Roger spent a week on "Hollywood Squares" and in October he was back on "The Tonight Show." In November, he did another week on "Hollywood Squares" during the Thanksgiving holiday. In one memorable exchange, the host of "Hollywood Squares" asked the celebrity guests "How do you put a sheep to sleep?" Roger fired back, "You don't have to. Just stick their back feet in your boots."

Roger always enjoyed the songwriter sessions where a guitar was passed around and each writer sang a song he'd written. A group of songwriters were sitting in Roger's suite at the King of the Road, passing the guitar around, when Larry Henley sang "Hoppy's Gone." He was asked to sing it again. About a week later, Chips Moman produced a session for Roger, cutting "Hoppy's Gone" and a song written by Tree writer Red Lane, "The Day I Jumped From Uncle Harvey's Plane."

Roger did his last recording session for Mercury Records on December 19. Roger had four songs on the country charts that year—"We Found It in Each Other's Arms," "Sunny Side of My Life," "Rings for Sale" and "Hoppy's Gone," but none got higher than 34 on the chart; there were no records of Roger's on the pop chart.

The last two songs Roger recorded for Mercury, "Hoppy's Gone" and "The Day I Jumped From Uncle Harvey's Plane," were not written by him. He was struggling to write—the well was running dry—and the songs he did write, he was saving for his debut album on Columbia; he had signed a contract to move to that label in 1973.

Roger's marriage with Leah ended and she moved back to San Antonio for good, although the divorce proceedings continued for another year. Dean remembers that "My parents would split up and then get back together all the time. When they did that, my Mom would move to Texas with us, then they'd get back together and we'd move back to California then move back to Texas. It was a tumultuous childhood. I lost count—but that happened at least four times."

"I only went to one school for two years in a row," said Dean. "Except for that, I never went to the same school for two years in a row. I changed schools constantly because of the split ups and getting back together and the weird decisions. I kept being shuffled between California and Texas. I remember spending a little more time in California, maybe. And then when I was nine we moved to Texas for good."

Dean learned more than just reading and writing in school during the time his parents were together.

"When I was young, Johnny Tillotson's son was a really good friend of mine," said Dean. "All the stars' kids went to the elementary school I went to. Barry White's kids were there. I was friends with Robbie Rist, who was Oliver on 'The Brady Bunch' at that time. Lou Rawls' son rode the bus and he was a bully. He ruined Santa Claus for me. He was older and he would tell the little kids, 'There's no Santa Claus.' The big one was when he said, 'Ask your parents what the f-word means.' So I go home—I'm in the second grade—and ask my parents what the f-word means. I got the 'We'll talk about it later' line and then a little later I got the big birds and bees speech from my Dad. It was pretty traumatic and I ended up crying because I thought, 'Oh, no, some day I'm going to have to do this!' I was like seven years old and I thought, 'This is terrible—I don't want to have to do that,' I was crying while my Dad was pacing around, throwing his arms up in the air and saying 'What the hell? What did I do?'"[7]

Leah had social ambitions and wanted Roger to be in "society"; "she wanted him to be something he wasn't," said Doug Gilmore. Leah had expensive tastes in clothes and accessories. Roger also enjoyed having nice things, but there was a difference.

"Dad always wanted to be impeccably dressed and have nice things and he had expensive taste for sure," said Dean. "He was wearing the equivalent of Armani suits when Porter Wagoner was wearing rhinestones.

That was totally my Dad's thing but my Mom was always putting down his country-ness, putting down country-bumpkins, telling him 'You can't act country,' and 'Don't be a hayseed.' She was always putting him down in that way but being stylish with fine clothes and watches came from him. He never wanted to be a country bumpkin anyway—he was down to earth but he used to hate it when people would refer to him as 'Country and Western' or 'Let's put a hay bale on the set when you go out and sing.' He hated all that stuff. There was a period I remember him saying 'Don't say country music. Just don't say it.'"[8]

Roger often referred to Leah as "my debutante" when talking to friends, making statements like "I'd planned on coming over but my debutante is upset."

On December 26, 1972—the day after Christmas—the King of the Road gained its most exciting performer in the Roof Lounge when Ronnie Milsap began performing there. Milsap was an R&B singer living in Memphis, but celebrated Christmas that year with his family in Georgia. His wife, Joyce, drove him and their baby son, Todd, up to Nashville in time for Milsap's evening performance, which began at 10 p.m.

The man behind Milsap coming to the King of the Road was Don Davis, who booked acts at the Roof. Davis offered Milsap more money than he was making in Memphis to perform five nights a week. Milsap brought his band—a drummer, bass player and guitarist—from Memphis with him.

It didn't take long for Milsap to make a major impression in Nashville. On New Year's Eve the Roof Lounge was packed and on January 3 he signed a management contract with Jack D. Johnson, who also managed Charley Pride and began a career that was launched on RCA Records in 1973 with his first hit, "I Hate You" b/w "(All Together Now) Let's Fall Apart."[9]

In 1973 Roger began recording for Columbia Records; his first album was aptly titled *Dear Folks, Sorry I Haven't Written Lately*.

It's a fairly common experience when singer-songwriters have success that the distractions of being a star overtake the solitude of being a writer; there's booze, drugs and women everywhere, available and willing and it becomes a situation where you sign your name for fans rather than write down lyrics to a song. There's a pressure to perform, to be here, there, with this person, that person, problems at home until the original focus and direction with music is lost. A songwriter has to put on the brakes to stop, get away from the public person and get back to the place of the private person. To stop being a "star" and become a writer again.

The dam burst lose—or at least sprung a mighty leak—when Roger joined Columbia. In July he released his first single. "Open Up Your Heart" was reminiscent of the old Roger with the line "jiggle it a little it'll open," the kind of word play that Roger was so good at. It was his best single in a long time; it reached number 14 on the country charts. In August and November he was on "The Tonight Show." In November, his second single for Columbia, "I Believe in the Sunshine" was released and rose to number 24 on the charts.

The album *Dear Folks, Sorry I Haven't Written Lately* was released in the Fall of 1973 and rose to number 26 on the charts, but only remained on the charts for ten weeks. Songs on the album were "Open Up Your Heart," "Whistle Stop," "Mama Used To Love Me But She Died," "Qua La Linta," "The Day I Jumped From Uncle Harvey's Plane," "The Animal of Man," "What Would My Mama Say," "The 4th of July," "Shannon's Song," and "I Believe in the Sunshine."

"Shannon's Song" was written about his young daughter, who he obviously adored as his "baby lady."

As part of the promotion for his new single and album, Roger went to England in June, 1973, for a tour. An article in the *New Music Express* combined a review of the show with an interview with Miller. Roger insisted to the writer that "It's not a country show" and "confessed that he is trying to get out of country and into other things."

In Roger's band were Gerry Cole on guitar, Buddy Emmons on bass and Marty Orritt on drums. The writer was amazed that Emmons, a legendary steel guitarist, was only given one chance to play some jazzy-rock on steel; the rest of the time he played bass.

Roger played his hits, "Dang Me," "Chug-a-Lug," "Engine Engine Number 9," "King of the Road," and "Little Green Apples," did "Orange Blossom Special" on the fiddle as well as his new single, "Open Up Your Heart."[10]

On November 8, the animated film *Robin Hood* premiered in New York City; on December 21 it premiered in Los Angeles. Roger did the voice for "Alan-a-Dale," a rooster, and wrote "Whistle Stop" for the movie. Other voices in the movie were Phil Harris, Andy Devine, Monica Evans, Peter Ustinov, Pat Buttram, Ken Curtis and Roger's former neighbor, George Lindsay.

In 1974 Roger was on "The Tonight Show" in January, March, and August, was Guest Host on "The Merv Griffin Show" in August, and served as host for "The American Music Awards" as well as a television special, "Roger Miller and Friends."

Chapter 19
Australia and New Zealand

In October, 1974, Roger was scheduled to do a tour of Australia and New Zealand but one of his background singers, Marie Caine could not make it so he needed to hire a singer for that tour to sing with Darlene Bronsky, his other singer.

Marie Caine was friends with Marshall Chapman, a South Carolina debutante who moved to Nashville where she majored in French at Vanderbilt University. After college, Marshall fell into the Nashville songwriter bohemian crowd and set out to become a girl rock singer songwriter, fueled by a vision from seeing Elvis in concert when she was eight years old.

She was "living in a $50 a month apartment and sleeping in a loft bed that these guys had built for me," said Chapman. "I had a feeder chicken named Dudley P. Trout who had gotten to be a teenage chicken and then got hit by a car in front of my apartment, which caused my proper southern upbringing to come out so we decided to have a full on chicken funeral in the front yard. Slick Lawson read from the *Junior League of Nashville Cookbook* for the Eulogy. We bowed our heads and he read the recipe for 'chicken ambassadeur.'" Marie Cain attended the chicken funeral, which was a big hit.

Marie and Marshall had been hanging out together so when Marie told Roger that she could not make the tour Down Under, she suggested he hire Marshall. She also told Roger and his band about the chicken funeral, which may have been an enticement for Roger to tell drummer Marty Allred to call and arrange for Marshall to fly to San Antonio for an audition.

At the show in San Antonio, Marie sang the harmony parts while Marshall watched. Larry Gatlin opened the show and after Roger finished his show he announced "Willie is playing" and the group piled into a limousine and went to John T. Flores place. Willie immortalized Flores in his song "Shotgun Willie" where he sang "John T. Flores was working for the Ku Klux Klan" and he "made a lot of money selling sheets on the family plan."

Willie was on stage and never saw them coming; next thing he knew

Marshall Chapman had picked him up off his feet while Roger sat in, playing the drums.

Marshall Chapman flew back to Nashville, then to Los Angeles where Roger appeared at a fund raiser at the Forum with the Jackson Five, Nancy Wilson, Danny Thomas and Carroll O'Connor. "I had never been west of the Mississippi and here I was, at the pre-show meal sitting next to Carroll O'Connor. It was 'Gidget goes on the road,'" said Chapman. "I watched the Jacksons and saw Michael Jackson turn into Michael Jackson before he walked on stage."

After that show, a large group went back to Roger's place, which had been the aviary on the John Barrymore estate. Candace Bergen and Marlon Brando had been previous occupants. There was no furniture in the place, just a great Persian rug and pillows. Everyone sat on the floor, a guitar was passed around, Roger sang some of his songs and then it was time for everyone to leave.

"We were all saying 'good night' but he just held on to my arm," said Marshall. "He was putting on the full court charm. I was 24 years old, single and he was Roger Miller. What am I gonna do?"

Roger and Marshall spent the night together, then boarded the plane for Australia and New Zealand the next day. The 18 hour flight had one stop, in Hawaii, where they re-fueled and then landed in Auckland, where they were met by promoter Barry Coburn. The tour was 28 shows in New Zealand and Australia and lasted about a month. The venues ranged from 1,500 seat theaters in the smaller cities to 4,500 seaters in Melbourne and Sydney.

Marshall wore a blue suede outfit she had assembled by buying a blue suede leather jacket in Nashville and blue suede pants in Los Angeles with blue zip up high heel boots. "Roger always teased me because that outfit always attracted the press wherever we went," said Marshall. "We'd come down off the stage and the press would be on me while Roger just walked right by. He'd say something like 'Where does it say that the background singer in a blue suede outfit gets more attention than the star?'"[1]

Barry Coburn promoted the tour and remembered that "Marshall Chapman wore two outfits for most of that tour. She is tall and wore boots with at least two inch heels on them. I was young when they did that tour—I was only 23—and she was quite provocative. She wore those pants suits.

One was a royal blue color and the other was a bright brown/tan and they were sort of suede and had fringe down the arms and down the side of the legs and she looked spectacular. She would often come over to the side of the stage while Roger was doing a solo thing and put her arms around me and almost scare me. Marshall was such a vivid personality and we had a provocative relationship where she would flirt with me. I was young and so easily affected and I didn't know what to think about this American woman who was just messing with me. She almost intimidated me. She seemed like such a worldly creature; she was very outgoing."[2]

"The tour was a blur," remembered Marshall. "We drove all over New Zealand—Christchurch, Wellington, we even played Invercargill, which is the southern-most town on the planet, the last stop before Antarctica."

"It was pretty much the same songs every night," said Marshall. "He had that album out, *Dear Folks, Sorry I Haven't Written Lately* with that great song, 'Open Up Your Heart.' It had that great line, 'jiggle it a little it'll open.' He also did 'Our Love' with that chorus 'look at the children, did you ever see such bright, shining faces?'"

"We did a lot of dates, more in New Zealand than we did in Australia. We only did four cities in Australia—Brisbane, where I was amazed they had palm trees, Melbourne, Adelaide and then ended up in Sydney. All the shows were great except for one. There was one show when he was just in a bad mood; it might have been Wellington, but I'm not sure. He was upset about something. Every night he'd knock 'em dead except for that one night. He wouldn't come back for an encore and they booed. But when he was on, there was nothing better."[3]

"At that time I really hadn't promoted many country concerts," said Barry Coburn. "I'd mostly done rock—Led Zeppelin, Elton John, Black Sabbath and also acts like Duke Ellington, Muddy Waters and those sorts of people. On the third night of the tour I went down to the dressing room in the theater to let the band know that show time was fifteen minutes away. I knocked on the dressing room door and the door was locked so I knocked again and somebody said 'Who is it?' I said 'It's Barry' and Marshall Chapman opened the door about an inch and said 'It's Barry' so Roger said 'Let him in' and I went in. In theaters they have those big tall mirrors so you can move and look at yourself when you're dressing and one of those was laying out flat in the middle of the room and there were white lines of cocaine across it. And I was like 'Whoa! Haven't encountered this before!' I was immediately handed a rolled up one hundred dollar U.S. bill—I hadn't seen those very often except when I had to pay Chuck Berry in cash—and they were doing lines and offered me some but I declined. I was working this tour and I never touched it. The funniest part was that I had done all those rock tours but I'd never seen cocaine before. There was marijuana around and there was always plenty of drinking but I'd never seen cocaine before I saw it with Roger Miller."[4]

Roger and Marshall's affair continued throughout the Australia-New Zealand tour "but I always sought to be a band member," said Marshall. "I knew I was a band member. Also, I wasn't doing any drugs and he was always teasing me about that because every night after the show he'd pull out the coke and say 'This is the best shit.' I felt real protective of him because he was very sweet but he could also be mean as a snake. He was like that."[5]

The concert may have ended at a certain time, but the music went on and on. "One night we were in Melbourne and Marshall, Roger and I were up in their room and they were playing and it was like magic," said Barry Coburn. "Roger and Marshall each had their guitars and they were playing, cutting up and having fun. There was a bottle of Jack Daniels and other stuff and I was thinking how lucky I was. It was glorious. Roger said, 'You'll get this song, considering where we are' and he sang 'Boomerang,' which I had never heard before. I asked him 'Where did that come from?' and he said 'Well, I wrote it a long time ago.' I asked him if I could get a copy and he said, 'Yeah, I'll get you a copy' and he scribbled a note on a pad beside the bed. I sorta thought it would never happen but at the end of the tour, about three weeks later, I got a package in the mail and on the outside it said 'Tree Music Publishing' with their green logo. It was a reel-to-reel tape of the original demo of "'Boomerang.' That was just fantastic that half way through the tour I heard that song and he actually followed through and got it for me."[6]

During those evenings in his hotel room after the show "He would sing anything and everything," said Coburn. "Sometimes he would sing his own songs but often he and Marshall would just sing everything. I remember him doing Billy Joe Shaver songs but it was almost like a 'Greatest Hits' of anybody and everybody that he sang."

Roger was notorious for hating early mornings. During that tour there were a number of early morning calls so Coburn could shepherd the group to the airport or on a bus to drive to the next show. "Roger was often the last one downstairs while we were waiting," remembered Coburn. "He was never one of the early ones downstairs. On the bus, he cut up a lot of the time. It was clear that he had a great personality and genuinely liked being around people."

Like many others who remember that Roger was incredibly funny but can't remember exactly what he said, Barry related that he "couldn't remember specifics because he was like an onslaught of hilarity. It went from one thing to another and then he'd just drop a line and you'd go 'What was that?' because it was almost like a stumbling line. It was almost like he was stumbling and then he'd pick up on himself and move on and there'd be some spark and then he'd change subjects immediately and launch on to something else."[7]

"I fancied myself in love with him," said Marshall. "I had a crush on him and maybe he had a crush on me, too. He would tease me a lot because I didn't do cocaine. I was wild but I was already wired; I hated that drug. He was off pills but he had coke in plastic bags and we went through customs with it in plastic bags. It scared me; I was little co-dependent me."

"I knew he was real poor when he was young and he knew I was from South Carolina and came from that 'blue blood' background. I told him that the women in my family were supposed to be in the Junior League and have babies and he laughed. I got the impression that kind of stuff was real important to Leah, like it is to a lot of women."

"He was a charmer and I am easily charmed," continued Marshall. "Roger was always teasing; whatever you were sensitive about, that's what Roger would go for. He was real sweet to me because I think he did that with any beautiful young woman. I've been close to a lot of people, like Jack Clement, Waylon and Willie and I don't use the word 'genius' lightly, but he was a genius. As far as 'smart' and 'quick,' Roger was way up there. He was the cleverest, the quickest person I ever knew. One day we got on an elevator in Sydney and we'd been up all night roaring and we were on the wrong end of the evening and these straight people who had just gotten up were on the elevator and they were backing up against the wall. Roger looks around and says, 'The last word in hideous is us.' He had never said that before; he just made it up on the spot. He did that all the time."

After the tour Down Under, Marshall did not hear from Roger. One night she went to the Troubadour in L.A. to see Willie Nelson perform. In the audience were Bob Dylan, Kris Kristofferson and Roger Miller. During the show, Willie introduced Dylan, Kris and Roger from the stage—as well as Marshall. Earlier that evening, Roger had intentionally called Marshall the wrong name—saying "Marshall Thompson" instead of Chapman. When Willie said Marshall's name, Roger turned to her and said, "Where does it say that the background singer gets a shout-out from the superstar on the stage?"

After the show, a crowd went back to Roger's place where they passed around Roger's Washburn guitar with "Louise" written in mother-of-pearl on the neck. Roger was playing "Lord of the Manor" that evening, trying to get a fire going in the fireplace but wasn't having much luck. As he poked and prodded and pulled unsuccessfully on the vent, Willie said to Roger, "Jiggle it a little it'll open."[8]

Chapter 20
Heartbreak Hotel

In late 1973 Roger Miller came into the Troubadour in Los Angeles with an entourage that included Lee Majors and Farah Fawcett. On the stage singing was Gail Davies, who had moved to L.A. in 1967 with her brother, Ron Davies, and the two signed a recording contract with A&M Records.

Gail was singing with The Midnight Band, a group that closed the club each Friday and Saturday night. It was a happening place; the who's who of young Hollywood and the music business often hung out at the club. Roger invited Gail to sit at their table, then asked her out. They went to dinner a couple of times and then he called and asked if she would sing back-up with his band. Marshall Chapman had left and he needed a replacement.

Davies remembers telling him, "I'm not a background singer; I don't want to sing background" but Roger was persistent and promised "It'll just be for a short while before I find a replacement." Finally, Gail agreed, although another opportunity presented itself at the same time.

"In the Midnight Band I was singing the Randy Newman song 'Guilty' and dropping to my knees and screaming a high C with my four octave range," remembers Gail, "and Frank Zappa came in one night after the show and said 'You're the ballsiest chick I've ever seen on a stage. Would you consider touring Europe with me?'" Gail went to a couple of rehearsals with Zappa and "It was great fun but I could tell I wasn't going to be comfortable singing 'The Illinois Enema Bandit' [one of Zappa's songs that was in the show] and I'd already promised Roger I would sing backup with him so I went on the road with Roger."

During this time, Roger was playing nightclubs and dinner theaters "in really posh hotels," remembered Davies, as well as some appearances in Las Vegas. They also played the Astrodome in Houston on a show that included Andy Williams and Kirk Douglas.

On his personal appearances, Roger "was very intent on making sure everything was first class," said Gail. He told her "I don't ever want to be riding around the country in a purple bus wearing rhinestone suits" so his suits were Italian tailored and his shoes were custom made. "He wasn't a cowboy boot and jeans guy."

Roger generally played weekend dates and spent the rest of the time in L.A. The group always flew to a date—"I don't ever remember riding on a bus with Roger," said Gail—where they were picked up by a limo and taken to the hotel, generally for a three or four night engagement. They would do the show and then "people would show up," said Gail. "Vassar Clements came by a lot of times and John Hartford came sometimes." Since Roger always had a nice suite in the hotel, he often held a jam session after his shows. Mostly, they played old country songs and Roger, who loved to play the fiddle, played a lot of Bob Wills tunes. Roger loved Bob Wills, Hank Williams, the songs of the 1940s and 1950s that he grew up with and had formed his taste in music and he never grew tired of playing them with friends.

At this time Roger was heavily into cocaine, although he also smoked marijuana and even used meth. When the jam sessions ended, Roger would usually go to bed and sleep until two or so the next afternoon, get up, do the show, and then have another jam session.

This was a period when Roger wasn't writing any great songs, although he was always writing. Gail Davies remembers sitting with him while he was trying to write a song and he told her "It's really hard for someone to watch you having puppies." She remembers him sitting on the floor with his guitar, playing a piece of a song over and over, going back and forth, coming up with a line and saying "No, no that doesn't really fit. That's a good idea but it really doesn't fit this song—I'll put that in another song" and then giving up in frustration or writing a song that disappointed him because it wasn't as good as he thought it should be. Gail Davies doesn't remember ever hearing any of the songs from those sessions on a Roger Miller record.[1]

Micheal Smotherman (he always spelled his name "Micheal" instead of the traditional "Michael") came from Roger Miller's hometown of Erick, Oklahoma and played piano in a band in high school, then joined an established band after he graduated. That band recruited some of Micheal's former high school band members to join, then moved to San Diego, where they played for two years and released several albums. After two years in San Diego, Micheal told the band members that he was moving to Los Angeles "to get into the real music business."

"I thought I was going to go to Hollywood and conquer show business by sheer dint of my personality," said Micheal. "Well, I ended up living in a store room over a recording studio for a long time." Gradually, Micheal obtained some session work as a piano player. He was friends with Billy Burnett and one night the two went to the Palomino Club in L.A. where Billy's father, Dorsey Burnett was performing. Roger was a long time buddy of Dorsey and came to the Palomino that same evening.

"I just jumped him in the dressing room," remembered Micheal, "and told him I was from Erick and he knew my folks and he invited me to a gig with his band and then I joined his band. This was in 1974 and Roger "was a major star at that time, flying everywhere and staying in nice rooms and getting paid well. I was receiving, in today's money, about $3,000 a week at the time. Roger liked my playing and my enthusiasm so he asked me to recruit some more band members, so I called Marc Durham, who was also from Erick and was in my high school band, to play bass and then Steve Turner, an old running buddy from Venice Beach, for drums."

"We played a lot in Nevada," remembered Smotherman, "and we did a lot of State Fairs but that grated on him because he'd already seen that movie. He was playing the same places that he had played coming up and now he was playing them again so he was not a happy camper. They were still good gigs and he was still doing major league things, but it wasn't top of the line gigs."

Micheal remembers that he and Roger talked about Erick because "we would be thick as fleas 24/7 for like three weeks and then spring apart. He liked to say he was from a small town and had a couple of anecdotes but he wasn't really crazy about Erick because he had a troubled childhood. He was a crippled youth—unwanted basically—so he didn't have a lot of good memories about that. My Dad told me that when Roger was a kid growing up around Erick, people were not real fond of him because he was in trouble all the time. And Roger used to say, 'Around Erick I was that damn Miller kid until 'Dang Me' hit and then I was 'Ol Rog.'"[2]

The year 1974 was a full of conflict for Roger; it was obvious that his marriage to Leah was over. On October 31, he was a guest on "The

Tonight Show" with host Johnny Carson. Wearing a brown suit with a tuxedo shirt, Roger said he "hated endings" and was going to sing a song about "endings." He sang, "Our Love," a song obviously about his marriage to Leah, noting that "sometimes it was no damned good" but, in the end "we could be proud of" our love.

On June 15, 1975 a newspaper article announced that the King of the Road hotel was "held in default" by its lender. Cousins Mortgage and Equity Investments, Inc. of Atlanta gave the hotel ten days to cure the default. If the hotel could not pay its debt, then foreclosure proceedings would begin.

The president of the management company tried to raise money which, according to the secretary and general counsel, was "in the low six-figure bracket," although he declined to be more specific. The executives expected the 182 room inn to keep operating because "you have reservations, conventions, and all kinds of obligations" so it had to remain open.[3]

Accusations of involvement with "The Mob" echoed throughout explanations of how and why the King of the Road hotels failed. The Rooftop Lounge was one of the most popular night spots in Nashville; it was crowded almost every night until the day the hotel closed. There were whispers about money being skimmed, taxes not paid and the books being cooked. At any rate, and for whatever reason, Roger's King of the Road hotel empire that he was building came crashing down. The building remained standing, but there was a new owner and Roger Miller never lent his name to a hotel chain again.

In January, 1976, Roger Miller's divorce from Leah became final; they sold their house in Royal Oaks in June for $235,000. Leah moved back to San Antonio while Roger moved into a home in Beverly Hills. Reporters noted that he was still seeing Billie Jean Campbell—soon to be the ex-wife of Glen Campbell

In July, 1976 Roger performed at the White House for President Gerald Ford. Also on the program was Tammy Wynette, who had just married real estate executive Michael Tomlin on Sunday but postponed her honeymoon to perform for the President on Tuesday. The Jordanaires and Ella Fitzgerald also performed. In the audience were Secretary of

State Henry Kissinger, Secretary of Agriculture Earl Butz, White House Chief of Protocol Shirley Temple Black, and Secretary of Defense Donald Rumsfeld.

Roger Miller's fame came from writing humorous, novelty songs, songs that made you either smile or laugh. They came natural; Roger was witty, loved a turn of phrase and had a keen sense of humor. Although many of the songs seemed humorous when first heard, they weren't. For example, "Dang Me" is a dead serious song about a failed husband and father that is delivered in a light-hearted vein. Those songs pleased him as well as frustrated him because he wanted to be taken seriously as a songwriter, as a songwriter with depth, but felt trapped into being pegged as a novelty writer.

Many artists with long careers are often frustrated as their careers progress because they want to expand, try something new and different, stretch out beyond where they are. Audiences, who like what they've heard from an artist, want them to stay basically the same and be surprised by the familiar when the artist comes out with something new.

A fan knows what he or she likes and when they find it, they want it to stay around. If the fan wants to "expand" or, as popular phrases suggest, "push the envelope" or "get outside the box," they'll find that with another artist. And so there is a constant conflict within creative people to either keep doing what they've always done—and which has proven successful—but which they've become tired of and bored with, or try something new and entirely different from what they've already done. Some artists move into a new direction and their career expands; however, in many cases, artists lose their fans and followers when they stray outside the proscribed boundaries.

Roger Miller felt this frustration. He did not want to keep writing new versions of "You Can't Roller Skate in a Buffalo Herd" or "Do-Wacka-Do" over and over, and yet people paid good money to see the Roger Miller who did "You Can't Roller Skate in a Buffalo Herd" and "Do-Wacka-Do."

The essential problem was that Roger was a funny, entertaining person who loved a crowd to watch him be funny and entertaining, but funny and entertaining people get trapped into being funny and entertaining even when they don't feel like it. Actually, Roger could entertain himself as much as he could entertain a crowd. Jerry Kennedy remembers Roger in a hotel room standing before a mirror, making faces and saying "Cod P. Whistle" over and over and laughing.[4]

Roger Miller loved being Roger Miller. He loved being the center of attention, loved performing for a group of people, whether it was a paying crowd in a club to watch his show or just a roomful of people watching him be a show. The essential problem was that Roger Miller disliked doing the same thing night after night, show after show. He was creative, easily bored, and liked doing different things on different nights. He learned that audiences expected him to do "King of the Road," "Dang Me," "Husbands and Wives," to be funny and he knew that's why they paid to see him. As long as he put on a good show, he had a good income—and Roger liked to spend money. So Roger reined himself in and learned to do a regular show, but he didn't always like it.

"I think he felt pressured to be entertaining," said Gail Davies. "I think he felt like he had created his own demise, that he had created a situation he had to live up to. Every time he went into a place he knew he had to be 'Roger Miller' and be what people thought Roger Miller was and so he lived up to that."

"He had to have people around him all the time, he didn't like being alone" remembered Gail Davies. "I think that had something to do with that feeling of being abandoned as a child."[5]

Chapter 21
Mary

In L.A., Roger often got on the phone and called his friends to go "swarm," or descend on a club or house where they would "roar" or party the night away. He loved the L.A. and Las Vegas life; "He very much liked to hang out with the who's who of Hollywood," said Gail Davies. "He didn't want to be thought of as a country bumpkin. He was slick, he was cool, and he wanted to be with the Hollywood stars."[1]

People were naturally drawn to Roger and his son Dean remembers that he "had this really close relationship with James Cagney. Cagney was much older, and so were all his friends and they had this little crony club of Carroll O'Conner, James Cagney, Ralph Bellamy and my Dad was the young guy in the group and he drove them around. He had this Bentley and was living in Beverly Hills. They would go out to the country club and have lunch and they'd do all this stuff together and my Dad was the entertainer. He said that Carroll O'Conner was always taking pictures of everything. One time they were all sitting around at dinner and Cagney was eating his soup and my Dad said 'It looks like a damn wax museum in here' and Cagney spit up his soup."[2]

Roger and Gail Davies were lovers; she was singing backup in his group and traveling on the road with him. This did not make her popular with the band since they sat in "coach" while she sat with Roger in "First Class" on planes, then rode with him in a limo to the hotel while the rest of the band took a cab or shuttle van. Gail thought she was the one and only but was surprised to discover there were others because "Roger was quite a ladies man."

They were on the road somewhere and Gail was saying how much she loved Roger when someone in the band told her, "Well, you know Roger is engaged." "To who?" she asked. They replied, "You know, the girl singer in Kenny Rogers' band, Mary." That was news to Gail.

Mary came out on the road with Roger "and that's when I quit the band," said Gail. "Mary was so gorgeous, so fabulous and I thought, 'What is going on here?' And that's why I quit the band."[3]

Mary Arnold was born and grew up in Audubon, Iowa, a small town west of Des Moines and just north of the Nebraska border. Her father was a banker, her mother a homemaker, and Mary grew up wanting to be a singer, although "it was extremely difficult because there was no avenue to get out of there." During her senior year, Mary found an avenue; her aunt and uncle lived in California and were friends with actor Buddy Ebsen, who starred in "The Beverly Hillbillies." Mary went out to visit them and met Ebsen, who encouraged her to move out. Mary's Dad had planned on her going to Concordia College in Minnesota but Mary balked; they finally compromised and she attended the Los Angeles Conservatory of Music.

In Los Angeles, Mary became part of the Young Americans, a group of eight young men and eight young women, clean cut and well groomed, who did patriotic programs during the 1960s and 1970s when America was filled with young men and women who were part of the not so clean cut and well groomed counterculture. They appeared on programs with Eddy Arnold, Tennessee Ernie Ford, Eddie Fisher, George Burns and other popular entertainers.

Also in the Young Americans was Mary's best friend, Dawn Herm-ache, who became an original member of the First Edition, whose members included Kenny Rogers. Dawn was leaving the group so a replacement was needed; Mary knew Kenny and when they ran into each other he encouraged her to audition. Ken Kragen, manager of the First Edition, who later became manager for Kenny Rogers and Lionel Richie, held the auditions. After Mary did her song, he asked "Can you leave in the morning?" She said she could and the next day performed with the group in Ohio.

Kenny Rogers left the First Edition, became a solo act and hired a backup group; Mary was a singer in that group. One day Kenny told her that Roger Miller, who was getting divorced, was depressed and could use some cheering up. Roger and Mary had met briefly when he taped Kenny Rogers' TV show, "Rollin' On the River." At the time, Mary "didn't know exactly who he was because I was really young." Kenny arranged for Mary to meet Roger at a birthday party for Kenny's wife, Margo. Mary did not want to do it—she didn't know Roger Miller—but Kenny and Margo came to Mary's apartment and insisted she go.

According to Mary, "I put on this real ugly long dress" and they went to a restaurant called 15AD where the waiters, waitresses, and patrons acted like it was the sixteenth century, yelling "wench wench" to call a waitress and banging on the tables. Roger came in late, stayed a few minutes, then told Kenny he was going over to Pips Backgammon Club and "Why don't you guys come over there later." That didn't set well with Mary, who told Kenny "You're taking me home."

At Pips, Mary and Roger were seated across from each other; finally, he came over and asked Mary, "Can I take you home?" "No," she replied, "I'm going home with Kenny." Roger then asked Kenny if he could take Mary home and Rogers replied, "Sure, that works!" Outside, they got into his car—a yellow Volkswagen Bug—and they drove to the Troubadour where a friend of Roger's was performing. Sitting in the car while parked in front of the Troubadour, Mary "looked over at him and I had this incredible sensation—I'll never forget he had these little glasses on and he looked so familiar, it was really odd—and it took me back. I remember feeling that he was so familiar and I didn't know how or when, but I was going to marry that guy. I absolutely knew it! When I got home that night I called my friend and told her this."[4]

That yellow Volkswagen came about because Roger "was non-materialistic but he would suddenly like one thing—like 'I really like that watch'—and then that watch would become 'the thing' or 'I really like that gadget' and the same with cars," remembered Dean. "He didn't care about cars but once in awhile he'd just say 'I'm going to go out and get that car' but it was always on a whim—it wasn't about the status of it."

"When I was a little kid he had a whole ton of cars," continued Dean. "He collected a bunch of them and then my Mom sold them when he was on the road just to spite him. Some time after that he wanted a VW Bug because Bugs were cool then so we went to a dealership—I was probably seven or eight at the time—and he told me that I could pick the color. So we get there and they have this book of colors and one of them said 'Saturn Yellow' and I was drawn to 'Saturn Yellow' so I said 'Saturn Yellow' and I remember him going 'Are you sure? Are you really sure?' I assured him I was so then he said 'O.K.' That was his sense of honor thing. He had promised I could pick the color so he got that horrible yellow color because I had chosen it and that's the car he picked up Mary in on their first date. She said that gave her a first impression of him that he wasn't pretentious. I really loved that car."[5]

Micheal Smotherman was in Roger's band 1974-1977 and remembers there were numerous parties at Roger's house "three or four times a week. And if you didn't come to laugh, then just get your ass out of there. He didn't want to hear about war, about poverty—none of that stuff. It was get funny or get out. At a lot of those parties, there'd be professional comedians but Roger'd be way funnier than any of them because they did their shtick but Roger was just off the top of his head. Comedians are pretty insecure guys and they would start realizing he was funnier than they were so they'd start pouring it on after awhile until it became obnoxious."

At those parties it "was mainly yee-hawing and flying around the room backwards" and during the L.A. days "the evil Peruvian marching powder." Roger had given up pills and told anyone who offered him amphetamines "Get that away from me." The problem with pills, according to Smotherman, was that "It got to where he was doing so much that it turned on him. Like it always does. He had some dark unpleasant memories about that and he didn't want to know about it. Coming down on speed is kinda rough so Roger and those guys who were true speed guys never came down." Until he did, and then it was on to cocaine and Roger remained a heavy user well into the 1980s.

Those parties also had a lot of music and Roger "liked to play songs in a guitar pull," said Smotherman. "We'd be sitting around with people like Kris Kristofferson, Johnny Cash, Glen Campbell—the cream of the crop—and they'd play each other's songs. They rarely played anything they'd just written, they mainly played songs they were all familiar with."[6]

Chuck Blore and his wife, Judy, would go over to Roger's house "three or four times a month, at least," he said. "People would come in all the time and just sit, playing, laughing and always a ton of marijuana. We'd be over there and it would go on all night long."

"Night after night people would come," continued Chuck. "Mostly country guys you never heard of in your life and they would sit and play. I remember a New Year's Eve at my house and Glen Campbell came by so they started playing around 10 o'clock and they were both enjoying it like crazy, humming and singing and smoking dope. And then about 1:30 someone said 'Hey, guys—it's New Year's.' They'd been going three hours non-stop and we all said, 'Oh, well—happy new year everybody' and then they went back to playing. It was really fun times."

Some nights there was no music, "just funny conversation," said Blore. "He was the funniest man I ever knew in my life, ever, ever and ever. Judy and I still quote things that he said. I wish I could think of a couple. I remember one night he said, 'Well slap my ass and call me junior.' Just tons of things."

Chuck Blore was at Roger's home in Royal Oaks when "he came out of his bedroom and he fell down, kinda tripped," said Blore, "and he had this cocaine in his hand when he fell. He marked a circle around it and put a note to the maid 'Do not clean.'"[7]

Roger still appealed to those booking television shows. "He could do his thing on those shows," remembered Smotherman. "Be a professional show biz guy and get out there and talk to Johnny Carson. But, generally speaking, what you saw was what you got." Roger Miller was always Roger Miller "because he couldn't be anything else."[8]

A bright spot came when a song from Walt Disney's *Robin Hood* movie, "Whistle Stop," reached number 86 on the charts.

Roger's band around 1976 evolved from the group backing Dorsey Burnett at the Palomino. "Roger would come out to the Palomino to see my Dad," said Billy Burnett, "and he'd sit in sometimes. Micheal Smotherman was in the band and he was from Erick, Oklahoma and I told him, 'I've got to hook you up with Roger because nobody is from Erick, Oklahoma. Marc Durham was also from Erick. I introduced them and they were in his band like the next day. Then Craig Fall and Steve Turner joined. One day the guitar player couldn't make it so I played and that's how I got in the band."

"When I started with Roger, we played the Golden Nugget, then the Hilton in Vegas," said Burnett. "That was back when Vegas still had a lot of glamour and it was a great time to be there. You never knew who you'd run into. Johnny Cash came up on stage with us one night. Merle Haggard got on stage and said, 'You boys know any country music?' turned around, hit a chord and sang 'Today I Started Loving You Again.' Willie Nelson got up with us one night with a broken leg—his leg was in a cast."

"We did a long run—about a month—at the Hilton," remembered Burnett. "We only rehearsed the day that we opened at the Hilton, just before the show and that was it. Roger would show us little things in rehearsal, like 'You do this part or this.' I sang the harmony line on 'King of the Road.' But playing with Roger it was pretty much on the spot. He stuck to his basic list of songs most of the time but once in awhile he'd let me do a song or have Micheal Smotherman do one. He'd say, 'Do that song you did the other night' and then introduce me, 'Ladies and gentlemen, Billy Burnett.'"

After the show, "we mostly just hung out," said Burnett. "Back then they had these big houses for the artists—mansions, really—and Roger would go back to his house after the show and we'd pass the guitar around. The parties were great; they were like every night with Roger. And we'd be meeting all those people like Redd Foxx and John Byner, funny guys, and we'd laugh and play music all night long. Roger played a lot of the old country stuff, like Bob Wills, Hank Williams. We played a lot of that on the show, too. We saw the sun come up many times at those parties but that's what folks did in those days. We'd sleep all day or lay out by the pool, then get up and do the gig. It was just an incredible time."[9]

There were usually two shows a night; the first was a dinner show around eight and then a midnight show. Burnett remembers that the management "was quite upset with him once because he wasn't there—he was late. Some lady yelled out 'Where you been, Roger?' and he said, 'I've been watching TV. Where've you been?' Or something like that. We had to work an extra week at the Golden Nugget for free, but generally, he never missed a show, was always professional."

Shortly after Elvis died, Roger played the Hilton and there was a big star painted on the stage where Elvis used to perform. Burnett stood on the star and said, "Wow, Roger—look at this—it's where Elvis stood!" Roger looked at Burnett and replied, "Yeah, but he's dead."[10]

Roger had a song list, taped to his guitar that he usually followed and some stock one liners he said almost every show but "sometimes he'd pull songs out of the hat," remembered Burnett. Micheal Smotherman remembered that "Roger was kinda old school in his shows. It got to where you could tell what time it was without looking at your watch by what joke he told or what song he did. 'O.K., he's doing 'Uncle Harvey's Plane' so we've got 15 more minutes.' He used his stock lines over and over but he was real quick and way out there, he had his own thought processes," said Smotherman. "A lot of times he would come up with those zingers when he was angry or annoyed. That was his funniest stuff. But even his stock jokes were always funny. You can't laugh at something for the thousandth time, but I laughed at it for the four hundredth time because it always struck me funny."[11]

If one of the band members said something funny and Roger incorporated it into his act, he would never attribute the line to the person he got it from "but he'd always look at whoever gave him that line and smile like that was his acknowledgment of 'I haven't forgotten where that came from,'" remembered Smotherman.

Roger did a number of songs he did not write during his show—"Me and Bobby McGee," "Little Green Apples," "The Day I Jumped From Uncle Harvey's Plane"—"but he was always continually not mentioning that," said Smotherman. "For a long time I thought he wrote 'Little Green Apples.' A lot of people thought he'd written those songs because they sounded like him. He never said he wrote 'em, he just played 'em like he wrote 'em," said Smotherman.[12]

It wasn't so funny or pleasant when Billy Burnett decided to leave Roger. "I had a solo deal and my producer, Chips Moman, called and said it was time to make another record. He said, 'You don't need to be doing the sideman stuff. You need to think about yourself and your career.' So that morning Glen Campbell kept me on the phone forever, wanting me to let him help me get things started, so I didn't have a chance to talk to Roger before the show and at the last show the other guitar player pulled him aside and told him. We were on stage at the Hilton and he said, 'You know, I can't hear the rhythm guitar tonight. I guess I'm going to have to play it myself.' It wasn't pleasant; he didn't like me leaving him."[13]

Roger also got angry when Micheal Smotherman decided to leave. "I gave him my two weeks notice when I decided to quit and, all of a sudden, during those two weeks he had a problem hearing the piano and he'd get on me on stage—but he'd said nothing like that for three or four years," said Smotherman. "He could be cruel, but that was just one little facet of him."

Smotherman quit to pursue an individual career after Roger had given him a big break. They were playing in Las Vegas and legendary manager Jerry Weintraub came to see them because he was interested in managing Roger. "Roger had me do one of my songs in his set," said Smotherman, "and afterward, Weintraub told me 'I'll sign you to my label if you want to make a record.' So when I started making that record it conflicted with my band duties so I just told Roger that I was going to try and make a stab at it, like he did. He was rather angry about it. Roger was possessive in a way with a lot of things. Like his band members."[14]

Audiences could be difficult in Las Vegas. "You might be working when there's a teachers convention or something at the dinner show and a completely different group for the midnight show. Or sometimes people from the same convention or whatever but they'd be entirely different—maybe they'd be losing at the tables. Sometimes we had an audience who wasn't really with him and I remember when he got frustrated with an audience he'd tell a joke, then turn around and tell the band the punch line. So we'd all be laughing and the people out front would be straining to hear, saying 'What did he say?' We got a couple of 'flying ovations' on occasion."

People in the audience were always yelling out "King of the Road" while Roger played. Sometimes he held up his guitar so they could see his list of songs taped to the guitar, point to a spot and say "'King of the Road' is here," then he'd move his finger up and say "and we're up here." But sometimes the heckling got to him. One night during his performance a lady yelled out "King of the Road" and Roger said, "Shut up, Grandma." "You could feel the audience draw back," said Billy Burnett. "He tried to make light of it but he never got that audience back with him."[15]

On one occasion, Roger was contacted by a Las Vegas hotel when a scheduled act cancelled and the hotel needed someone to take their place. Roger had taken a copious amount of drugs, knew he was in no condition to perform and begged off, but the hotel booker kept insisting, offered to send a plane, a limo or whatever it took to get him there. Roger finally relented and, in a rush, packed for the trip. When he arrived in Las Vegas, the effects of the drugs were subsiding and Roger was coming down. That's when he opened his suitcase and discovered that what he had packed for the trip was a hammer and a clothes hanger.

Roger and Mary Arnold dated for several years; she was on the road with Kenny Rogers and he was on the road performing, but "we were just connected somehow," remembered Mary. "And I don't know what it was."

Roger would call but Mary wouldn't call him back. "We were working all of the time and I had no intention of being involved with anybody and was extremely independent," said Mary. "I liked him and thought he was really great and he was funny and nice and a real gentleman, but we were both gone all the time."

Mary claims that she doesn't remember their second date or when or where he proposed. "It might have been in January," she said. "I don't know. I know that we got married on February 14, 1978 and my mother was ill. She was not well and I had seen her at Christmas and she thought that we should go ahead and get married so she could be there and see us."

They picked the Presbyterian Church in Santa Monica after they visited with the preacher, Mr. Morrison and looked first at the large area where the full congregation gathered each Sunday. "I don't know this many people," said Roger. "Do you have anything smaller?" Mr. Morrison told them there was a smaller chapel and then told Roger that Will Rogers had given them the money for that chapel, including the stained glass window and, "Well, that was the end of it," said Mary. Roger told her, "This is fate. This is where we're going to be married, right here!"[16]

Roger and Mary went to Reno for their honeymoon; two days after their wedding he opened at Harrah's.

Chapter 22
Santa Fe

At the end of 1977, Randy Hart replaced Micheal Smotherman in Roger's group. Randy grew up in the Washington, D.C. area and was twelve when he first saw Roger Miller perform at the Carter Baron Amphitheater.

About six months after Hart joined the group, guitarist Craig Fall, who was the bandleader, left and the job of bandleader fell to Hart. "We had some extraordinary musicians in that band through the years," said Hart. "I remember David Minor was a bass player early on, David Jackson was a bass player, Craig Fall, Jimmy Hassell, who had been in the First Edition with Mary, was playing rhythm and singing."

Randy had known Danny Gatton, an incredible guitarist back in Maryland, and called him when the group needed a guitarist. Hart told him to come to Los Angeles to audition for Roger so they rented the SIR facility on Santa Monica Boulevard and after they warmed up, Randy called Roger and Mary and said "'OK, you guys can come down now' and when they came in we were either purposely or serendipitously playing 'Orange Blossom Special.' Danny had his own version of that song and Roger had played it for years. Roger walked into the room and Danny was doing what Danny did and it was obvious right then that 'This will work.'"

"We had Danny Gatton and Thumbs Carlille together for awhile," said Hart. "Thumbs came back when we needed a guitar player because Roger called me and said 'Let's try to find Thumbs.' So I started the investigation of 'Where is Thumbs Carlille?' and I remember calling the Union in New York, and that didn't get very far and then one day I was looking at the L.A. Times and Thumbs was playing at the Baked Potato in Studio City. So I called Roger and said 'Thumbs is right here' so he said, 'Well, let's go see him.' So we did. I don't think Thumbs was aware that we were coming. That began an off and on situation—whenever Thumbs could make it—for the next two or three years. We always had great musicianship behind Roger, it was always an incredible band, but the magic, obviously, was always up front."

Hart describes Roger as an "extraordinary" musician. "Melodically, rhythmically, and metrically, he covered a lot of bases. That thought never occurred to me until John Hendricks, a renowned jazz singer with Lambert, Hendricks and Ross, came to see us at a show one time and said to me, 'Do you know that your boss is an incredible jazz singer?' That caught me off guard and I said, 'Well, yeah!'"

On the other hand, "He would slaughter a fiddle most of the time," continued Hart, "but you could hear what he was trying to do and if he'd played in tune it would have been incredible. You would hear him going after extraordinary things on the fiddle but he couldn't execute it in the sense of being an accomplished musician but you could hear the thoughts and you'd go 'Wow, there's some energy there.'"[1]

After they were married, Roger and Mary lived in Beverly Hills. Mary wanted to live by the beach but Roger did not. "He hated the water," said Mary. "He didn't even like to get wet." Still, she knew they had to move. Roger's house was "Party Central" with a constant stream of people in and out, constant parties and activities day and night over and over. There were dope dealers and dope heads and Roger bought a lot of stuff; Mary knew she had to get him away from that. There were people that Mary knew—or at least had met—and there were total strangers. She knew that she could not stand living in this type of situation but Roger loved having people around constantly. Mary also enjoyed having people around—but not constantly. And she did not enjoy having that much dope in the house.

Roger and Mary decided to drive back to Iowa to visit Mary's mother. They drove back in a motor home and Mary remembers that "most people would leave in the morning, but not us—we left at 11 o'clock that night! We had only been on the road about an hour and we had to pull over because we were tired. We were in a motor home, but did we stay in the motor home? Noooo! Roger always wanted to pull in and stay at a hotel."

They traveled "mostly by night," said Mary, "and boy, that was a scenic tour! After we stayed at a hotel, I would get the motor home ready and make him get on it and then I'd start driving and by the time he woke up, we were usually where we were going."

As they drove east, Roger asked Mary, "Have you ever been to Santa Fe?" and Mary admitted "That was one place that I haven't been." Roger said, "Well, I have some old friends there and I think we should stop there and look them up." So when Roger and Mary got to Santa Fe they called Roger's friends and visited, staying in the motor home outside their friends' house.

They liked Santa Fe. "It was a magical place and we kind of looked at houses while we were there but we really didn't see any so we left and thought, 'Well, that's great.'"

That trip "was the first time I had ever experienced CB radios and Roger would get on with those truckers and they just couldn't believe it!," said Mary. "They absolutely did not believe it! And so we would pull over and have coffee with them many, many times and they would tell him about what they liked and what they didn't like about country music. Sometimes they would put us between them—like a sandwich—practically the whole way to Iowa."

On the way back from Iowa to L.A., Roger and Mary picked up John Byner, a comedian and good friend of Roger's. Roger and Byner got on the CB radio "and they were absolutely hysterical," remembered Mary. They stopped at the Grand Canyon and stopped again in Santa Fe "and kind of looked at places again" and then went back to Los Angeles. Roger had a booking in Las Vegas and right after they arrived a friend of their's called and said, "I've found your house!"

Roger had to be in Las Vegas for two weeks "and then we had all this other stuff after that," remembered Mary, "so a good friend of mine flew out to Santa Fe and went to the house and she said, 'You know what, this is an incredible home. I think you need to see it.' So we said 'O.K.' and after Vegas we went down and looked at the house and bought it. And within a month we were living in that place!"[2]

Roger and Mary lived in Tesuque, located about six miles north of Santa Fe. You could not fly into Santa Fe—you had to fly in to Albuquerque and then drive about 60 miles north to get to Santa Fe and "You talk about shock!," said Mary, "We moved from Los Angeles to dirt roads. There was no place to buy anything. If you wanted sheets, you had to go to Albuquerque."

Their home sat on 20 acres and to get there you passed the small, rustic "Tesuque Market," which was a combination general store and restaurant. The "restaurant" was primitive, with a wooden screen door and low ceiling; it served mainly Mexican food. The area was dry, desert like and the ground was hard dirt. The houses in the area were made of adobe and there was a big gate in front of Roger's place with a long driveway. The property sat next to a field by an elementary school and was surrounded by a wooden rail fence.

"Typically, with Roger, this is the way things happened," said Mary. "Before you can even realize what's happening, you're already there and we've moved in and I remember thinking, 'What in the world?!!?' I loved living in Los Angeles. I was fine there. And then, all of a sudden, we lived in Santa Fe. But he loved it and he told me it was the only home that he felt was a real home. He love, love, loved it. He would never have left that place because he loved that place absolutely."[3]

On their property were Indian artifacts. "I don't have to hunt for 'em," Roger told an interviewer. "They're all over my property. They were the original Pueblo people, the cliff-dwelling people. I find pottery. Not whole pots but big chunks, big shards of pottery. I keep 'em in a big bowl in the house. It's just great pieces of old, painted pottery. The painting is still brilliant on some of 'em. Some of 'em have been underground and just washed up in rains...I found two pieces of an Indian corn grinder. You know, they were here, and it's an amazing thing to look down and there's sort of a message from the past. Somebody made that sucker and fired it and boy oh boy, there's almost fingerprints on there, you know."[4]

The marriage to Mary and the move to Santa Fe were major turning points in Roger Miller's life. Before he settled in with Mary, he needed to have people around him constantly. He needed an audience to entertain and he needed a place like Los Angeles where there was something going on all the time.

Roger was comfortable with Mary; she was secure and devoted to him. After Mary, Roger no longer needed to have a crowd around him and when that need of a constant audience was gone, Roger became comfortable just being himself. He left the frenzied world of L.A. and retreated to a quiet, secluded home in Santa Fe.

That doesn't mean that Roger became a hermit. He still went out and performed and kept his toe in show business. And he often got with friends in Santa Fe, like Don Meredith, and hung out.

Roger took Mary to Erick, Oklahoma to meet his family and friends. "I think we picked up a mobile home because there was no place to stay and so we stayed in this mobile home," said Mary. "And we woke up and people were peeking through the window and there were people outside and I went 'Oh, my God!' Everyone just wanted to be there and wanted to welcome us. They were really nice to me. I was his third wife, so some were pretty attached to the second one and hadn't really gotten over that and I understood that but they were such lovely and simple people and they were always glad to see me."

Roger had not told Mary about any of the people she might meet because "Roger's thing, pretty much his whole life, was that you experienced things through him, just being with him," said Mary. "He did not pick anyone out to say anything about them, like 'Oh, you're going to meet so and so and this is what it's like.' He never would have done that. You experienced things with him and so as I met these people, he would say who they were or what they had done—maybe he had written a song about them or used them in a song. He had a huge amount of conflict with Erick and the people there and being from there. He had really mixed up feelings about Erick his whole life."[5]

During that trip, Roger performed at the high school in a benefit for the Senior Citizens Center. Also on the show was Bill Mack, who sang a song. That evening was recorded and Roger reminisced about growing up in Erick. He started by saying, "I've entertained all over the world, sat and talked to two Presidents, but how do you talk to the people who taught you how to talk?" After a couple of songs he called out some names and talked a bit about them. He noted that "Miss Kelly told me one time that I had talent and that's the first person who ever said that word to me," then added "It don't matter where you come from you can go anywhere—it's all out there."

He performed "This Here Town," a new song which he said he wrote about Erick. The lyrics state that "this here town is home to someone but this here town ain't home to me."

In their home in Santa Fe they had "a lot of clocks," said Mary. "Roger loved to work on clocks—to take them apart and put them back together, fix them, oil them or whatever."

On his nightstand by the bed he had a picture of his Mom and Dad, a basket that had some Indian artifacts in it. There were, of course, pieces of paper—mostly scraps—where he'd written down an idea for a song or a piece of a song. There were probably some tools and things that he used because "Roger loved to tinker, he was always tinkering," said Mary. "We had a horse barn and on the side of it was a little room and that was the place he did wood burning, tooling and stuff like that."

Roger "constantly doodled, like artists do, because things were constantly coming out," said Mary. "Like he would make up a song out of his head, it would be totally inside his head. And he had his little quirks. One thing was 'You have got to stop cleaning ash trays!' So I said, 'What do you mean?' and he said, 'Practically every time I get up and go to the bathroom that ash tray is clean. I want those back. That's what I smoke!' So he made an invention that was a little piece of wood and he hollowed it out on the inside so, when he finished a cigarette, he stuck it down in there and it would go out and nobody would touch it. Otherwise we would throw them out."

Living a more settled life in Santa Fe meant that Mary invited family to their home. It also allowed her to know Roger's mother, Laudene.

"Roger's brother, Dwayne, came to visit us," remembered Mary, "and they were talking about their Mom and I said, 'Why didn't you ask her about what happened? Why don't you know about that?' And they were like 'Well, because you don't ask her' and I said, 'Why? She's your mother.' Roger had no relationship with his mother—none whatsoever, so I invited her and her husband to spend Christmas with us one year. I'm really family oriented. So they came—they were happy to come—although it was odd and uncomfortable because Roger really didn't know them. Even though he loved his mother, he didn't know her. She and I were in the kitchen doing the dishes while Roger was upstairs and I said, 'You don't have to answer this if you don't want to, but I'm just curious about what happened?' And she said, 'Well, what do you mean?' And I said, 'You know Dwayne and Roger are here and they're talking and they don't know why you gave them away or why or what happened.' And she said, 'I didn't want to. It was such a horrible time when my children were taken away from me. I was very young and had never left Arkansas and then I was living in Fort Worth, Texas and my husband's dead and I have three small children, it's the Depression and I have no skills. And so they came to take them temporarily but they never brought them back. I had no money or anything to get them back.'"

"Laudene's life was a book in itself," continued Mary. "She was this incredible woman, she had such a rich life and Roger didn't know anything about it and he was very much like her. They were very similar with their sense of humor. Both were very quick witted. I remember one story where she worked at a bank and told her co-workers, 'I'm just letting you know that I'm Roger Miller's mother' and they said 'Who?' and she said, 'Mother!' That was her in a nutshell. She was so smart. We had a long, long talk about what happened and she said that her mother was disabled. I asked, 'Why?' and she said, 'Well, because she had her leg amputated.' And I said, 'Well, why?' and she said, 'Well, you didn't ask questions like that!' And I looked at her and said, 'Well, what do you mean? You don't know why your mother lost her leg?' And she said, 'Well, no.' That may explain the breakdown in communication in that family. Then again, it was just a different time. It was amazing how much Roger and his mother were alike."[6]

Laudene divorced Claude "Pinky" Sims around 1957. Sims worked for the telephone company and reportedly made "a lot of promises" about helping her get her boys back when they married in 1940 but nothing came of those promises. Laudene then married C.B. Burdine on September 10, 1959. Her two daughters with Pinky were teenagers but Joni died in a car wreck on September 5—Laudene's birthday—in 1965. The other daughter, Elizabeth, known as "Bitsy," was mentally handicapped and blind and was placed in an institution.

C.B. Burdine was an entrepreneur; he owned pawn shops, raised cattle and "continually had new schemes and dreams. They moved a lot because C.B. always saw greener pastures," remembered Martha Holt Nichols, "but he idolized her and those years with him were her happiest years." Laudene obtained a job in a bank "and became a computer guru," said Nichols. She worked at that bank until she retired. C.B. died on September 3, 1986 while they were living in Rogers, Arkansas.[7]

After Laudene's husband passed away, Mary included her in everything they did. "I think we went on a cruise or something right after her husband died and I just made her go. I thought it was sad for Roger not to know her and she was such an incredible woman. So, in the end, he did get to know her and enjoyed her immensely.

"Laudene traveled with us until she just couldn't do it any more and her children got to know her," said Mary. "She was with us every holiday and especially each Christmas. Roger's birthday was on the second of January and so while she was there we always started planning his birthday party and he would always say, 'I don't want a birthday party. I hate birthday parties.' So I'd say, 'Well, okay, we're just going to have some friends over and have a little birthday party.' It was impossible to buy anything for him. He had to hate something first before he could like it. One year we got him these really fabulous custom made cowboy boots and he opened them and we were so excited about them but he just looked at them and said, 'Hmmpf.' And we said, 'You don't like those boots?' And he said, 'Not really.' And we thought, 'Well, okay.' We didn't say anything but Laudene and I just looked at each other. Later on that day Roger tried them on and then he never took them off. They were his favorite boots and he absolutely adored them. I said to him, 'You just had to hate them first before you could like them.' We would plan his birthday party every year and he would be mad at us because we would do that. And every year at his birthday party he had a fabulous time. Every single time. He would forget how much fun he had the year before and how much he loved it. That was Roger!"[8]

After Roger and Mary moved to Santa Fe, Chuck and Linda Blore came out to visit for Roger's birthday. On one New Year's Eve, Chuck and Linda's young daughter became sick and had to be taken to the hospital. "We spent that New Year's Eve at the hospital," remembered Blore. "And everybody recognized Roger so he went out to the car and got a guitar. We were in the Emergency Room and he came in and started entertaining all these people. It was funny because all these people were sick, with bandages and stuff and Roger was singing 'Dang Me.'"

During another visit, there was snow on the ground and the Blore's daughter and Roger's son, Dean, were lying in the yard making snow angels. Roger stormed out "and told the kids they didn't know how to do this, then laid down in the snow and started making snow angels," said Blore. "It was important to him that they do it right. That was one of the great things about Roger. It could be something as small as losing a penny or something really big but they were all equal value in terms of his heart and soul."

"We had so much fun," remembered Blore. "You couldn't be in a room with him without laughing out loud. And he had a depth to him."[9]

Chapter 23
Open Up Your Heart

During the late 1970s and early 1980s, Roger Miller felt like the music business had passed him by. He could still get booked in Las Vegas, in supper clubs and at Fairs, but his records weren't heard much on the radio. In 1975 he had one record on the country chart, "I Love a Rodeo," which reached number 57; in 1976 there were no Roger Miller records on the charts and in 1977 his "Baby Me Baby" only reached number 68. There were no Roger Miller records on the charts again in 1978 and then in 1979 "The Hat" barely made the country chart, reaching number 98 and staying two weeks.

In April, 1978, Roger came to Nashville to be on an ABC TV special, "Country Night of Stars." During his time there, he played the Exit/In, a listening club, with his seven piece band. The club, which seated about 200, was not full but in the audience were some old friends, including Chet Atkins. Roger wore "an immaculate summer suit [and] seemed the picture of devilish charm." He started his set with "In the Summertime," then did a medley of "You Can't Roller Skate in a Buffalo Herd" and "Chug-a-Lug."

Tennessean reporter Laura Eipper noted that "Miller at times seemed not so much relaxed as uncaring about his performance" and that his "well-known, off the cuff humor from time to time came off as arrogance and disregard, although at times his sincerity as a performer shone through as in a quiet rendition of 'Old Friends' toward the end of the evening."[1]

Most of his set consisted of songs from his new album, *Off The Wall* on the Windsong label. Miller told a reporter "It's a serious piece of work. There's not a funny song on it" and added, alluding to the not-full audience, that "There are lots of people around here who don't know what I do for a living."[2]

The *Tennessean* reviewed the first of the two shows and concluded their review with "Miller has got a terrific show in there somewhere. Hopefully the home folks will get a chance to see it tonight."[3]

The *Off The Wall* album was released in 1977 on Windsong and came during the time when Jerry Weintraub managed Roger. The label was originally founded by John Denver, who Weintraub managed. The album was produced by Milt Okun, who produced Denver, and Micheal Smotherman described Okun as "one of those real old school guys who didn't really do much of anything, to be honest. I mean, he'd show up at the session but he wasn't one of those producers who'd say, 'Hey, I got an idea, let's try this.' It was 'O.K., that sounds good. What's next?'"

Smotherman noted that "by the time he did the Windsong Record, he had money and a life outside of hanging out with songwriters. A lot of times, when you get into comfort, it takes a little of the edge off."

On that album were two songs that Roger and Smotherman co-wrote. "Roll Away" came "about four in the morning when I was just messing around on the piano and he was in the bedroom watching TV and then he just came out after awhile with a verse he'd written while watching TV." The other song was "I've Gotten Used to the Cryin'" and Smotherman stated that song came about roughly the same way. "The songs we wrote together were primarily songs that I had started and had quite a bit done on and he just came up with some lyrics bam bam bam right off the top of his head. He gave me the words—it was words from him. He didn't have anything to do with the music at all. It was all lyrics."

Smotherman noted that their songs came "when he just happened to be in the mood a couple of times. We never said 'Let's sit down and write a song.' He'd rather ride a unicycle to Memphis."[4]

There were no chart records for Roger Miller in 1980.

In country music, this was the heyday of the "Outlaw" movement and two of Roger's friends, Waylon Jennings and Willie Nelson, were riding high. Roger remembered when he was the big star and Waylon and Willie were scuffling along; now their roles were reversed and Roger didn't even have a record deal most of the time.

In 1980, Roger taped an appearance on "A Tribute to Chet Atkins" TV special. In an interview with Red O'Donnell, Roger said that he still performed "about 18 or 20 weeks a year on the Las Vegas-Lake Tahoe casino circuit" and that "I put songs I write on the shelf, so to speak. I suppose I should do something about it. I've had some serious talks with Buddy Killen at Tree...about returning there."

Discussing his career, Roger said, "Success came so suddenly—and in abundance. One day I was nothing; the next week I am a star. Well, at least a celebrity. Let me tell you something about success. It can take you places you never dreamed you would be. Man, when success falls on you it's dangerous to run with it. You should walk."[5]

Around 1980 Roger was honored during a special event at the Smithsonian Institute in Washington. "There were only about 300 people there," said Randy Hart. "It was some of their biggest benefactors and I'd never seen Roger this nervous. It was a very high society type thing and we did a set, took an intermission and then came back and closed. We were doing 'Old Friends' the way we always did, in 6/8 time—we would do the introduction and Roger would talk—well, we get into the song and Roger forgot the lyrics. I can just hear him trying his best to remember and he walks back and says 'Let me go to the closest one first' to get the lyrics and that's Mary, who sat in the curve of the piano. She can't remember the lyrics so he comes to me at the piano and I can't remember the lyrics so he says, 'I've got a very tight unit. When I blank out, they all blank out' and there was this nervous laughter. He's really trying to maintain his composure, trying to be cool about it and hoping the lyrics will come to him. Nobody can remember the lyrics and he finally gets so frustrated he turns around, off mike at this black tie big deal and says 'Ain't nobody thought of that sonovabitch yet?' And then he remembers the lyrics but gets a gnat in his throat so he starts to sing and then he coughs and says, 'I've got a gnat in my throat. Gnat. G-N-A-T.'"[6]

On January 3, 1981, Roger recorded a live album that contained his biggest hits, "Chug-A-Lug," "Dang Me," "Engine Engine #9," "England Swings," "Fraulein," "Husbands and Wives," "In the Summertime," "King of the Road," "Me and Bobby McGee," "Old Friends," "That's When the Loving's Done," and "You Can't Roller Skate in a Buffalo Herd." In 1981 he had "Everyone Gets Crazy Now and Then," which reached number 36 on the country chart in *Billboard* and in 1982 "Old Friends," a record he recorded with Willie Nelson and Ray Price, reached number 19 on the country charts and stayed on radio playlists for 16 weeks.

The *Old Friends* album was a duet album with Willie Nelson and instigated by Nelson. It was recorded at Willie's studio in Texas over several days. Willie noted that doing the album "wasn't hard. We just sat down and started singing Roger Miller songs. We did ten, but we could have done twenty more."[7] The songs they did were mostly from his early days in Nashville: "When a House is Not a Home," "When Two Worlds Collide," "Half a Mind," "Guess I'll Pick Up My Heart and Go Home," "Husbands and Wives," "Sorry, Willie" and "Invitation to the Blues." They did a new song, "The Best I Can Give Her" and Roger wrote "Old Friends," where Ray Price joined Roger and Willie.

There was a bright spot now and then. In 1981 David Frizzell and Shelly West released their version of "Husbands and Wives," which made top 20 on the Country chart in *Billboard*.

Randy Hart had never heard "Husbands and Wives" before he joined Roger. Hart was knocked out by the song and asked "How can anybody come up with one line that's the whole chorus?" ("It's my belief pride is the chief cause in the decline in the number of husbands and wives") and Roger answered "Oh, I'd been up for about three days."

Roger's life was growing calmer with Mary, but there were still situations that could only happen with Roger. Once, Roger invited Chuck and Judy Blore to join him and Mary at a small night club. The couples were sitting in the audience when the club owner invited Roger up on stage "to say hello to the crowd." Roger went up but said "I won't sing," remembered Blore. "He said, 'Hi, I'm Roger Miller' and some drunk guy yelled something and Roger said, 'Excuse me?' cause he didn't hear him. This drunk came up toward the stage and said, 'Kiss my ass. That's all you are and I'm the sonovabitch who can do it.' He was coming up after Roger but passed out before he got there."[8]

Stan Moress got his start in the entertainment industry in the mail room of the powerful public relations firm, Rogers and Cowan because his third cousin, Henry Rogers, was a principal in the firm. Moress moved up to the television department and met Jay Bernstein, a junior PR agent and the two formed a public relations firm that handled Burt Bacharach, Dionne Warwick, Petula Clark, Roy Clark and a number of other major artists. After about five years, he joined MGM and represented Mike Curb and the Mike Curb Congregation during the late 1960s when Curb became president of MGM Records. Moress worked for the MGM label for five years, then joined the Scotti Brothers when they set up a management company.

The Scotti Brothers represented the Bellamy Brothers, who had just released "Let Your Love Flow" and the Hager Twins, who were on the country music TV show "Hee Haw." The Scotti Brothers and Moress then signed and worked with Eddie Rabbitt, Gloria Stefan (then known as the Miami Sound Machine) and Donna Summer.

In the very early 80s (1982 or 83) Moress decided to pursue Roger Miller as a client. Moress had known Mary Miller when she was with Kenny Rogers. "I always thought she was a phenomenal artist and great personality and very funny," said Moress. "I would see Roger once in a while and was always fascinated with how unusual and unique he was—his personality would just shine and he was incredibly funny."

Moress and his partner, Herb Nanos, contacted Mary Miller and arranged to go to Santa Fe and meet with Roger to discuss management. "We met and had a few drinks and everything was great," remembered Moress, "and Roger and Mary drove us back to the hotel where we were staying. It was freezing cold when we got out of the car and as we left Herbie said, 'Well, good night, Jimmie!' And I said, 'Where did you get Jimmie from?' Well, Herbie had a fixation on Jimmie Rodgers, the great country artist back in the 1920s and 30s. So the next day we called Mary and she answered with her great wit, saying 'When are you guys coming to Santa Fe to meet with Roger?'"

Stan and Herb talked with Roger and Mary and Roger agreed to let them manage him. There was no big plan set or contract to sign. "Roger wasn't big on written proposals," said Moress. "He went more on his gut and on personality and whether we could get along. At that time he needed someone to guide him and make things a bit easier for him so he didn't have to be in the middle of it all. His bookings were from William Morris and some were very good and some of the dates, like with every artist, weren't so good. We knew all along that we weren't going to have a hit record but the uniqueness of Roger, just being around Roger, was worth it to me."[9]

One of the things that Moress did was get the Nashville booking agency, Buddy Lee Attractions, involved in Roger's bookings. He played primarily fairs and festivals at this time and it was mostly "soft ticket" dates where a customer paid a single ticket price to an event—perhaps a state fair or the San Diego Wild Animal Park—and, as an added feature, the attendee could also see a concert by an artist.

On each of his shows, Roger opened with "My name's Roger Miller and I've written 800 songs and I'm going to play them all tonight." That always brought a round of laughter as Roger started his show.

After Stan Moress became his manager, Roger then acquired a new booking agent, Tony Conway with Buddy Lee Attractions. Conway was Willie Nelson's booking agent and Willie told Roger about Conway and Conway about Roger so when Willie introduced Roger and Tony one night, Roger said, "'I'd like to talk with you' and the next thing I knew I got a call and we met and I became Roger Miller's agent," said Conway.

"He had been doing a few casinos—he wasn't working a lot at that time—but he wanted to," said Conway. "He wanted to go back out on the road and work as much as he could. He had a great band, a big group, like nine or ten pieces. I used to complain to him and Stan that the band was eating up all of the profits. When he went on the road he'd have to get 'x' amount of hotel rooms and 'x' amount of airfares. We started booking Roger and tried to put him in a lot of different situations that he hadn't played in for years and did some colleges. We put him in some festivals, fairs and performing arts centers. We did a lot of those theaters and casinos. That's the time when the casinos were really starting to open up. He also did some symphonies. He had a great symphony show with charts for the whole orchestra."[10]

In June, 1982, Roger Miller played at the Lone Star Café in New York. In the audience was Rocco Landesman, a former professor at the Yale School of Drama. In 1977 Landesman started a private investment firm and in 1982, about four months before he met Roger, the production of the musical *Pump Boys and Dinettes* premiered on Broadway. The story is about four men who work at a gas station and two waitresses at the Double Cupp Diner; the music leans towards country and country/rock. Landesman played a part in getting that musical off the ground and on the stage.

Rocco Landesman was born and grew up in St. Louis. In 1964 and 1965, Rocco was in high school when Roger was hitting big with "Dang Me," "Chug-a-Lug" and "King of the Road." He has been a lifelong Roger Miller fan ever since.

Landesman graduated from the University of Wisconsin, then went to the Yale School of Drama, where he received a Ph.D. and taught for several years before he left the academic world and started a hedge fund and invested in race horses. Some friends he'd known at Yale, Ed Strong and Michael David, wanted to start a theatrical production company so Landesman "gave them some money to set up an office, have a telephone line and so forth" and they founded Dodger Productions. Their first production was *Pump Boys and Dinettes*, and Landesman had a "small investment" in the production. It was difficult to call yourself a Broadway producer with such a small credit, but Landesman dreamed big.

When Roger Miller made his rare appearance in New York at the Lone Star Café on lower Fifth Avenue, Rocco Landesman knew he was going to see the show and also knew he was going to ask Roger about writing a Broadway musical based on Rocco's favorite novel, *Huckleberry Finn* by Mark Twain. Rocco thought that Roger "had the same kind of impish humor that Twain did and the same kind of exuberance."

Rocco and his wife, Heidi Ettinger, a fellow Yale alumn, introduced themselves to Roger and Landesman asked "if he would do the score for a Broadway show and he looked at me like 'What are you talking about?'" remembered Landesman. Roger had never read *Huckleberry Finn* and had only seen one musical on stage—*How to Succeed in Business Without Really Trying*. He saw *Oklahoma* on television but in his entire 46 year life those were the only musicals he had seen.

When he stood in front of Roger and Mary with the proposal to write a Broadway show, Roger's response was along the lines of "'What is that' and 'Who are you?'" said Landesman. "But Mary picked up on it. She immediately said, 'I'd like to hear more about this. Contact us.' She was the one who saw right away that there might be something in this, that it may have a possibility."[11]

Like most stars, Roger had a number of projects continually presented to him. There had been TV shows in the works and tours and projects of one type or another that for whatever reason had not worked out. Roger had learned to be skeptical of opportunities that came out of left field.

Mary put Landesman in touch with Roger's managers, Stan Moress and Herb Nanos and he "was back and forth with them for quite a while," said Landesman. "They said, basically, 'Write a letter saying what you want to do.'" So Landesman wrote a letter and sent it to Roger, who did not respond, so Landesman sent him another letter, and again no response but "I was kinda persistent about this," said Landesman, "and one day I got a call from Stan Moress saying, 'If you're really serious about this and want to meet with Roger, he's doing a concert at Sparks Casino in Reno and you can talk to him about this a little more.'"

According to Moress, they did not tell Roger that Rocco was coming.

"Of course I jumped at the chance," said Landesman. "And I went out and saw his concert and then went backstage and visited with him afterwards, which was a great thrill for me because Roger Miller was my hero; I idolized him and his music." Backstage, Roger sat with his guitar and played some of his songs and "It was funny because a lot of times he wouldn't remember the words, but of course, I knew all the words to all the songs so I would coach him on getting the right lyrics."

At the end of their get-together, Roger said, "If you're serious about this, what do we do? Is there a script?" (A "script" is what you write for a film, but a "book" is what is written for a musical. Roger always called the "book" for the musical a "script.")

"At that time, we didn't have any such thing," said Landesman, "so I went to Bill Hauptman, a Texan who I had known at the Yale School of Drama, and who I also thought had a feel for this kind of language and asked him to write a book based on *Huckleberry Finn* with places for the songs."[12]

Bill worked quickly and, in a couple of months, they had a book and sent it to Roger, who read through it and agreed to do the songs.

Chapter 24
On the Road Again

The early 1980s were a turning point in Roger Miller's life. He no longer needed to have a crowd around him constantly, no longer needed to entertain a traveling circus. The big difference was Mary, who gave him the emotional support he needed.

"Roger and I were together all the time," said Mary. "But we weren't in the same space so we both had plenty of room to work and yet we knew that we were there. So he could be alone." Mary added, "Roger always said that he wasn't really funny but the reason he was funny was because he was afraid that everyone would leave. So he kept everybody entertained."[1]

Manager Stan Moress noted, "Once he got home, he liked to stay home." Moress saw the importance of Mary to Roger. "Mary was a strong, very smart woman who adored Roger and protected him but understood the realities of living in the real world. Roger wanted to live in the real world sometimes and sometimes he didn't—he just wanted to write and hang out and laugh. He was a news junkie—he had the television on all the time to the news stations—and read the *New York Times*. Roger loved the news and was extremely smart. I remember that he would just ramble around the house, watch the news, read the newspapers and laugh."[2]

"He didn't like the travel," said Tony Conway. "He always said, 'If I could just snap my fingers and be on stage it would be great.' He didn't like the travel or being away from home and going through all that rig-a-ma-roll. I know when we put him on tour we'd try to do it in runs so he didn't have to stay out all year long. He'd go out and do a couple of weeks and then go home for a month, that type of thing. He was always like that—I don't think it became something in the last couple of years. He just didn't enjoy the travelling and he flew to a lot of his shows because it was too far to travel by bus. Most of his band was based out of Nashville and a couple of guys were out of L.A. and so they would all have to fly to meet at a certain place. There were times when we did do some bus runs but you had to get up at four in the morning. You couldn't fly out of Santa Fe, you had to fly out of Albuquerque."[3]

Sometimes travel involved early morning flights and "Roger hated getting up in the morning," said Randy Hart. "And when he did, he never drank coffee, it was always Coke. Morning noon and night he drank Coca Cola. He could have been a poster boy for Coke."[4]

Roger and Mary lived comfortably off his song royalties and personal appearances. "They always lived a really good life and never wanted for anything," said Moress. "Mary saw to that. She made sure they didn't spend too much and they were semi-practical, given the nature of the beast."[5]

Mary remembers that "There was a period when I remember consciously thinking that we were married, had an accountant and I didn't know what the bills were. I had no idea what our mortgage payment was and I didn't have any idea about anything because all of these people took care of that."[6]

The problem that Stan Moress and Herb Nanos had to face was how to get Roger's career going again. Roger joked later that his managers showed up one day and asked "Do you want to get back into show business?" and Roger replied, "I thought I was." The truth was that he was still playing shows but had burned a lot of bridges during the 1970s. In 1976 he was fired from the Fairmont in Dallas for being consistently late—the first time they had ever fired an entertainer—and he'd been belligerent and obstinate in Las Vegas to the point where the major venues did not want to book him.

Tony Conway and Buddy Lee Attractions faced a number of angry concert promoters when they signed Roger Miller. "We had to convince them that he wasn't doing drugs or drinking and he was a different person," remembered Conway. "When I got involved with him it was kinda his comeback with some TV appearances. He was a regular on Johnny Carson and all the talk shows. He was talking about how he'd gone through the craziness but he wasn't doing that any more. Our sales pitch was, 'You've got to bring in Roger Miller because it's a completely different show and he's a completely different person than he was in the past.' There were some promoters who wouldn't do it—some held a grudge or whatever—but I had gone through the same thing with George Jones. With Roger, it worked because people wanted to see him. There was plenty of work. He didn't want to work twelve months a year, he'd pick and choose. Also, he was getting pretty good money, at that time."[7]

The traditional way for a singer to get to the top is with a big hit record on radio "but we knew that was probably out," said Moress. They signed him to a label, Scotti Brothers, and recorded an album but nothing charted.

"It was very difficult to book him nationally on a consistent level because radio and records were the driver," said Moress. "We wanted to maintain a certain price so he didn't feel like he was working on the edge of the business because he was still prolific. It was difficult at times, although he always seemed to understand it. He may not have wanted to understand it, but at the end of the day he seemed to understand it and he'd say, 'O.K. we'll do it.'"

Roger was always popular on TV talk shows, so Moress and Nanos thought they could get him a spot on a dramatic show. They sent "pictures, bios and video tapes to the guy who was booking 'Quincy, M.D.'—everything they needed to make a decision about him doing a guest spot" said Moress. "Finally, I went to the guy and he said, 'We're really looking for somebody younger.' Well, I had to call Roger and give him the news as nicely as I could that they were looking for someone younger and he said, 'You tell 'em I'm 28 but I've been up for a couple of days.'"[8]

Stan relayed that to the agent and, despite the initial turn-down, Roger obtained a guest shot on "Quincy, M.D." The show saw Miller play a country superstar who was severely burned while free-basing cocaine. It was eerily similar to the real life story of comedian Richard Pryor.

In an interview promoting the show, Roger was reluctant to answer questions about his own drug use. "I'm so sorry I said I ever had a drug problem," he told the reporter. "I didn't have a drug problem at all—not compared to what people are doing today. This was the '60s. I took some speed and stayed up a few days. That's all the hell I ever did."

When pressed about why he admitted to a drug problem in the past, Roger replied, "Johnny Cash had taken a bunch of stuff and then he got on the Carson show and confessed. Suddenly, he had his own ABC show. So I thought, 'That's for me!" before concluding that he had promised himself "I'm gonna quit this stuff, lay it down. June 17, 1969 was the last piece of dope I ever touched, which was just an upper. Then I went on the Carson show and confessed. So many people have jumped on it. Well, I've got problems, like everyone, but not the kind you can buy."[9]

Roger told another interviewer that "I didn't really walk away from the music business. I just took some time to do what's really important. Dean will be going off to college soon and this is kind of my last shot at the parent thing."

Miller noted that his 11-year old daughter, Shannon, "lives in Texas with her mother, so I don't get to see her too often. I don't hear from her." He paused, then said, "Some things you just can't do anything about."[10]

Roger spent a lot of time playing in Las Vegas, Lake Tahoe, Reno and Atlantic City before casinos proliferated all over the country. After his shows, Roger often called a band member or called Randy Hart and said "Why don't you get the boys together and come on up." "We used to call it 'The Third Show,'" said Hart. "He'd regale us with stories or 'Here's a new song.'"

There were many changes in the band during the late 1970s and early 1980s. "He didn't like anybody quitting on him, but he didn't mind firing somebody. Or having me do it," recalled Hart. Sometimes Roger told Randy to do what Bob Wills used to do, which was 'tell the band member that we need to go have a cup of coffee.'"

"I think my record was Steve Duncan, a drummer," said Hart. "I think I had to let him go three times. It was kind of an 'x factor' of a personality dynamic and his playing ability. You had to be able to read Roger. It was hard to stonewall Roger with the band. You know a lot of people drop bars and you have to do that but Roger's tempos and the whole thing was somewhat like a moving target and you had to be able to move with everybody in the band and with Roger. If you had any resistance it made things difficult and Roger could feel it and know it. And if Roger felt there was a personality mismatch, although he wouldn't say that, then it wouldn't work. Through the years we had to let some of the guys go even though they were great players."

The relationship between Danny Gatton and Roger was both close and volatile. "Danny never tried to upstage Roger but Danny was beginning to get a little bit of a name himself outside of Roger's band and his playing was phenomenal," said Hart. "It was attention getting but not in an overt, purposeful kind of way. I think at times that Roger felt that may have been a little too much of a distraction. And Danny was not one to pull punches. When something was on Danny's mind, and you pushed the right buttons, he'd let you know. So he and Roger got into it a few times and there was one time when I think Danny said 'That's it.' Roger had done something or said something that really really pushed the wrong buttons with Danny and when we came back to the next show—it was in Atlantic City—Danny played like 'O.K. I'll show you' and it was musical fireworks."

Later, Roger cut Danny with a remark on stage about not knowing a song he wanted to play "so it looks like I'll have to do it myself" and that was the final straw for Danny; he quit and never returned.[11]

By the late 1970s, most of Roger's wildest days were behind him but his career was struggling. Randy Hart recalled that "Once a manager or agent pulled me aside and said 'We're kind of in a re-build with Roger.' At a lot of the places that we played I would hear stories because I was logistically setting up the jobs, coordinating various things where you have to deal with management and they would tell me horror stories about Roger in the past, but I never really encountered that when I was with him. Once he was with Mary, she was an anchor for him."

Roger could be pretty touchy when it came to remarks about his career. "I made a comment to him once early on, I mean I was 23 or 24 so I didn't really understand the things you should and shouldn't say," said Randy Hart, "and I said very innocently, 'You need another 'King of the Road'' and he looked at me—I remember the look—and he said, 'Yeah, well, that's what they tell me.' He knew it as well as anybody else, if not better."

There were always audience members yelling out songs, especially "King of the Road" and Roger would either say, "We'll get to that" or "Nah, I'm not going to do that one tonight," said Hart. "He'd pick up his song list sometimes and sigh and say, 'I've written so many hits, it's just so hard to remember them all.'"

Roger was pretty consistent with the songs that he played "if not in terms of order, then in terms of selections," remembered Hart. "Sometimes he'd throw us a bit of a curve in that he would go back to songs that we were not that familiar with, like his early songs. I remember he'd do 'Billy Bayou' or 'When a House is Not a Home' and we'd never heard those but after he'd get through the first verse or so we'd figure it out."

"There were certain anchor points in the show like 'I've written so many hits that I can't remember that one' and some others but when he was on, he was like Lenny Bruce," said Hart. "A lot of his funny lines and comments were like his music in that you could take those things on a couple of different levels. There was a broad, universal 'Ha Ha' level and then there's kind of an afterthought of 'Wow!' It was extraordinary."

Roger attracted a wide variety of people who stopped by his dressing room, "not only his peers in the music business, icons, but people outside the music business as well," said Hart. "He vibrated a lot of people on a very high creative level. There were a few layers of entertainment factor there but the I.Q. of what he put across was higher than the average Joe, if you wanted to tune into that."[12]

Chapter 25
Big River

In January, 1983, Roger was in Austin, Texas to tape "Austin City Limits"; the show was first broadcast on January 24.

Roger wore a black shirt and white pants and opened the show playing a Fender electric guitar and singing "Me and Bobby McGee," then did "Dang Me." The band was led by pianist Randy Hart; band members included Danny Gatton and Lee Rollag on guitars, Ron Shumake on bass; Shannon Ford and Mary Miller sang backing vocals. The band members were dressed in dark pants with a white shirt, all wearing suspenders. There was a Las Vegas Showroom look and sound about the group with Roger wearing a show biz smile and the band had obviously performed this show a number of times.

Roger ended "Dang Me" with some scat singing, then told the audience, "I've been watching 'Austin City Limits' for a long time and I thought 'Boy, I'd like to be on there sometime and now I am'" before introducing himself, saying "My name is Roger Miller and I'm one of the greatest songwriters that ever lived." It was good natured and humorous and the audience chuckled. "Let me humble up a little," continued Roger. "I've written about eight or nine hundred songs in my life and I'd like to do about seven hundred or seven-fifty here tonight—whatever we have time for." He then sang "You Can't Roller Skate in a Buffalo Herd" which morphed into "Chug-a-Lug," then did "England Swings." He introduced his "beautiful wife, Mary" and they did a duet on "Husbands and Wives." As Roger sang "King of the Road" he took off his guitar. It seemed like Roger started a song without first letting the band know what he was going to play, but the band was always quick to catch up with him.

Roger picked up his fiddle and did a Bob Wills number, "I Can't Go On This Way" before he announced, "This is my twenty-fifth year professionally" and introduced the first hit he wrote, "Invitation to the Blues," which Ray Price released in 1958.

The show was fast paced, song after song, which fit into the Las Vegas format. Throughout the show Roger looked like a man who had done thousands of shows and knew exactly how to pull another one off.

Roger introduced Willie Nelson, and they did a duet on "Old Friends." As the song progressed, Roger took off his guitar and handed it to Willie, who played the lead sections. In the end, Roger picked up his fiddle again and he and Willie did "Milk Cow Blues."

In addition to his role on "Quincy," titled "On Dying High" (broadcast on February 9, 1983) and his appearance on "Austin City Limits," Roger had been on the PBS "Jubilees" show, was doing an American Express commercial, and had a song, "They Won't Get Me," on the upcoming *Superman III* soundtrack. His new single, "Days of Our Wives" was released on Scotti Brothers Records.[1]

A review of his show at the Riviera in Las Vegas at the end of 1983 stated that "Miller's forte is comedy, whether in song or standup jokery and audiences come to expect generous helpings of his drawling funnies amid the hit songs...Even his serious songs are planted with humor ... Miller will make a tongue in cheek linguistic farce out of a mock Mexican song, but the only recognizable word is the finale 'Ole!'...There is also his sage advice on bolstering those casino players whose luck has thinned considerably, 'If you lose, there's plenty more where that's goin'...No longer the unpredictable 'bad boy,' where his onstage misadventures led to second billings, he now tends to his programming, yet never makes it one of those formal, square routines. He's still loose, affable and has more hilarious toss-aways than most of the regular funny men. His stories are legends in showbiz along with the high repute of his knowledge about writing enjoyable tunes. Taking to the fiddle, Miller...shakes the room apart with his version of 'Orange Blossom Special.'"[2]

Roger had agreed to write songs for the Broadway musical based on *Huckleberry Finn* "but it was a difficult process to get him started because I don't think he had the confidence he once had and felt he couldn't suddenly write a whole score for a show," remembered Rocco Landesman.

During his initial discussions with Roger, Landesman had "tricked him a little bit. I said, 'We can use some of your old trunk songs. There's a lot of songs we can re-work to fit in the show, so you won't have to do that much—just a few.' And little by little I think I got him increasingly seduced and interested in doing this," said Landesman.[3]

There is a difference between "making up" songs and "writing" songs.

Roger loved to "make up" songs and did it constantly.

"He never gave it a rest," said Mary. "He would be driving along when I first met him and he'd say, 'Do you have anything to write on?' He would just make up this whole thing, this whole song would just come out right there and I couldn't write fast enough. I think that's why I still print today, because my writing wasn't legible and if I printed I could print really fast and that's how he wrote the songs—this stuff would just come out. I mean, you would look at him and go 'God, I'm looking at the mountains or whatever and he's making up songs!'"[4]

But *writing* songs is work; a sustained period of concentration is needed, there are usually re-writes involved, a questioning of each line to make sure it is stronger than the previous line and fits in the song and "Roger hated to write," said Micheal Smotherman. "I don't know if he was tired of it or what but he loved just having fun. That was his deal."[5]

Roger "procrastinated and procrastinated and procrastinated," said Landesman. "He was not known for self discipline. He used to describe himself as a sprinter. He would get a hook for a song or a lyric or something would come into his mind, like 'the last word in lonesome is me,' which was a brilliant flash of genius and then he would frame whatever song he could around that burst. That's the way he tended to work." Landesman noted that "In show writing you have to have extended songs that come back and repeat each other and advance the plot and develop the character but Roger wasn't going to be that guy."[6]

In fact, many of Roger's songs from the "Dang Me" days were written almost as fast as he could sing them. During his early days of Nashville, when he was trying to establish himself as a songwriter, he would spend time on a song because he had to. But, generally, Roger didn't put a lot of work into his songs; they flew out of his head, landed on his guitar, and that was that.

Roger was notoriously lazy, so getting him going was a major challenge. Landesman stayed in touch, made phone calls, but inducing Roger to start writing was like pushing string. Finally, one day Roger called Rocco and played "Hand for the Hog" over the phone and asked, "Is this what you're looking for?" And Rocco said, "That's exactly what I'm looking for." The first new song Roger wrote specifically for the show was "We Are the Boys."[7]

Mary stayed on him to write but Roger resisted. Mary suggested they see some Broadway musicals but he refused; he said he didn't want anybody else—or any other songs—influencing him. He wanted it to be all Roger. In August, 1983, there was a confrontation in Santa Fe when Rocco flew in to apply some pressure on Roger to write. Roger was working on a song, "Eat Your Greens"—which did not make it into the show—and there was the pressure of time because the musical had to have the songs before it could be staged.

Rocco and Mary insisted Roger write a song and Roger "lashed out at us," said Rocco. Earl Schieb was a painter of customized cars and Roger was angry when he told them, "If you want Rembrandt, Rembrandt takes time. If you want Earl Schieb, you can have that in twenty minutes."[8]

They "literally locked him into a room" and Roger wrote "Guv'ment." Roger said he imagined his Dad while writing the song; Elmer Miller would wave his arms and cuss the "guv'ment" during the Roosevelt era of the New Deal. The song is witty and funny, but has an underlying anger in it as well, reflective of the anger felt by Roger because he had to do something he didn't want to do.

The struggle to get Roger to write songs for the musical was ongoing; Mary stayed on him constantly. "We were going to come and visit one time," said Chuck Blore, "and Mary said, 'No, you can't come' and we asked, 'Why not' and she said 'Because I'm standing here with a whip over him day after day.'"

On one visit, Chuck Blore noticed a "huge trunk" in Roger's and Mary's bedroom in Tesuque and asked Roger, "What's in the trunk?" Roger replied, "Oh, just some old songs I never finished." Chuck said "Let's look at them" and Roger reached in the trunk, pulled out some of the sheets of paper and said, "This will work in the musical!" Blore pointed out that songs had to be written for the musical but Roger countered, "I'll make it fit." They were just lyrics on scraps of paper, but Roger remembered the melodies.

Blore used one of the songs in that trunk, "When I'm Down (I Know He's Up There)" for *God and the Other Kids*, a movie he wrote where all the characters in the Bible are played by children who are five and six years old. Another song that was pulled out of that trunk was "Oh, the merry-go-round goes around and around, the ponies go up and the ponies go down/ the children all come and they laugh and they play cause they—" but then Blore could not remember the rest of the lyrics.[9]

Another unfinished song in Roger's trunk was "Cupid shot an arrow in the air/And it fell to earth and hit me in the leg/so now my leg loves you."

Roger's off-the-cuff creativity was legendary. Chuck Blore remembers walking through the apple orchard in Tesuque with Roger and an apple fell from a tree and broke into three pieces. Roger said, "Isn't it wonderful how God works?" and picked up the apple "and made up a song right there, 'The Apple and Me,'" said Blore. "It had a beginning, middle and end. Genius is a word that really belongs with Roger."

Glen Campbell had a religious experience and was telling a group of people that he had been born again. Roger replied, "That must have been tough on your mother."

Roger was also known to be moody. Chuck Blore remembers visiting Roger and Mary at their home in Tesuque "and we'd spend at least five or six days a year living in his house and sometimes Mary would come down and apologize, say 'Roger doesn't want to come down.' We'd be there half a day and then he'd eventually come down. But he'd just go through a funk some times."[10]

Roger sometimes brought in new songs to play during his personal appearances and Randy Hart remembers Roger playing "Leavin's Not the Only Way to Go" before it was part of *Big River*. Randy thought that "You Ought to Be Here With Me" was another song he heard Roger sing before it became part of the musical.

Mostly, Roger just wrote songs for the musical and the production staff figured out a way to make them fit into the plot. Or they altered the story line a bit to bring the song in. Songs like "World's Apart," "You Oughta Be Here With Me" and "Leavin's Not the Only Way to Go" were songs that Roger brought in and the production crew made the songs fit. Songs that Roger wrote directly for the show include "River In the Rain" and "Muddy Water."

Writing the songs for *Big River*, "He would start something and then pull off of that—it would fit into something else," said Mary. "So a lot of it was fragmented, but a lot of it was used. He could pull things from an idea that he had, you know ten years ago, but he hadn't forgotten it, because he didn't work at song writing. It wasn't a business to him. He worked at being creative and during that period when we lived in Los Angeles everyone was just sucking off of him, to put it bluntly, and following him around with tape recorders. Two people—Larry Gatlin and Glen Campbell—definitely did. And I said to him, 'Doesn't that bother you?' And he said, "No, because I can think of more stuff.' It really didn't bother him but a whole song could be written off those things he said."[11]

Roger worked on songs—off and on but mostly off—for *Big River* throughout 1983 and into 1984. Both Rocco and Mary "were trying to push him harder," said Landesman, "and Mary really put her foot down. 'You've got to do this,' she told him—I think we both did. But it wasn't going to happen without Mary insisting that it happen. And little by little, as he started to do it and we started to hear the songs, and they were obviously wonderful, I think he started to get more confident that he could do it."

There were three different productions of the musical; the first was in Cambridge, Massachusetts at the American Repertory Theater in February 1984 because "Bob Brustein, who had been Dean of the Yale Drama School when I was there and was a friend," said Landesman. "I got him interested and he also knew Bill Hauptman." At this point, "the show was really a play with music," said Landesman. "I think it only had seven songs. It was much more a play with some musical interludes."

It was during the rehearsals for the Cambridge production that, for the first time, Roger Miller saw what he was working on and this inspired him. He played songs for the cast and crew as they sat around a table and "it was a big thrill," said Landesman. "Roger sang his songs on the guitar and those people were mesmerized to have a talent like that, a legend, strumming the songs for the show." Roger never fully visualized the musical until he began to interact with the actors, director and musical director and the musical came to life in front of him. One day at rehearsal he brought in a new song, "Free at Last" and, as he played it "everyone's jaw dropped," said Landesman. "Everyone was so moved by this song they'd never heard before. And I started to get very excited because I saw that this was actually gaining traction. He was doing some incredible songs."

That's not to say that he was writing those songs on time. There were times when Landesman or the director told Roger "I need a song but the next day there wouldn't be one and the next day and the next day after that there wouldn't be a song until finally we'd start to get more urgent and angrier about it and eventually he'd do it," said Landesman. "It was a frustrating period. I'm sure it was frustrating for Mary and for everybody else. Roger could be very difficult; he could be a prick. Like a lot of people who had been big stars, he was an odd combination. He could be fun and generous but he could also be incredibly narcissistic, self-involved and childish. He was a mix of all that."[12]

In February, 1984, when the first production was staged, the *Boston Globe* did an interview with Roger, who stated, "I usually don't speak English till two o'clock and my clothes don't fit till mid-afternoon." The reporter noted that Roger was wearing "wildly checkered socks."

A preview was held at the Loeb Theater Drama Center in Cambridge prior to the official opening on February 22. Roger stated that "This theater thing has been so rewarding. I once scored a Disney movie, *Robin Hood*, in the early '70s, but all that was just pre-recording the music in a studio. There's much more of a live edge to the theater and that's been really exciting."

"I've written the greatest music I've ever written for this," continued Roger. "It's just been flowing out of me. And to see a whole company of actors doing it is a thrill I can't describe."

Talking about Rocco Landesman, Roger said, "It was a real thing of his to get Mark Twain and I together. I always loved people like Twain and Will Rogers, and my lyrical work was akin to them, so I said O.K. I'm not a student of Twain or a student of anything, but I felt a great kinship with Twain when I got into this. And I realized I would never want to disturb a 100-year-old piece of work without enhancing it."

"I don't have a burning desire to be on top again," said Roger. "I've lost that surface tremble. I could be pacing around and lighting one cigarette after another but I've been through that. I won every prize, but the really good thing is that I wrote all of my songs, which means I own the well. I'm very comfortable on royalties and concerts."[13]

Rocco Landesman remembered that "Athol Fugart saw the show and thought it was one of the great works in the American theater. He was incredibly moved and affected by it, so I started to feel that we had something. Then we went to La Jolla."

La Jolla was next "because Des McAnuff, who we picked to direct the show, was the artistic director there. So we went out to do a production there and it was because of that production that we were able to raise the money for a Broadway show because that show was good enough to get support."[14]

In La Jolla, Roger wrote "four or five" more songs. His son Dean remembers staying at a hotel in Los Angeles and his Dad coming down one night with a brand new song, "Muddy Water."

Chuck and Linda Blore drove down to La Jolla to see *Big River* and were appalled when, at the end of Act I, the cast mooned the audience.

The show was refined again before it headed for Broadway, but first they went to the Shubert Theater in New Haven, Connecticut, where Yale is located, for a final tune-up. There were some more songs written there—by this time, Roger had caught the vision of what a Broadway musical could be—and the show ended up with seventeen songs.

Throughout the process there was a common challenge. Roger was great at writing one minute and thirty second songs, but the songs in a musical have to be three or four minutes long. "A lot of credit goes to Des McAnuff because it was Des's genius to make those songs work in an integrated Broadway show and I believe they worked very, very well," said Landesman.

Rocco pointed out that the song "You Ought to Be Here With Me" was sung by a character, Mary Jane, to a dead person in a casket which a reviewer, Walter Kerr, said "was a credibly wonderful conceit and joke." Another example is "Leavin's Not the Only Way to Go," which Huck, Mary Jane and the slave Jim sing from different parts of the stage. "It was incredibly effective and worked wonderfully but you needed just the proper staging to make that song work," said Landesman. "Des did that. Also Danny Troob, the musical director, deserves a lot of the credit for that. It was up to Danny Troob and Steve Margoshes to arrange and orchestrate them so they fit into a Broadway framework. Roger didn't read or write music so he would just strum out the basic song and the music department took it from there."[15]

Later, after the show had been a Broadway success, Roger reflected that he "learned a new form of creative discipline" when writing the *Big River* score. According to Roger, "I stopped a lot of the crap I was doin,' runnin' hard and heavy. I sat and really took the writing seriously, and realized that I could dip into a bucket that I hadn't really dipped into before. I'd never written fiddle hoedowns before. Never wrote religious hymns or gospel music."

"I went in my mind and sat on that river, night after night," said Roger. "I asked a bass player from Hannibal, Missouri one day, 'Is there a hill outside of Hannibal?' He said, 'Yeah.' I said, 'Good. I've been settin' on it in my mind.'"[16]

As the show progressed, "Mary's role can't be underestimated," observed Landesman. "She went to all the rehearsals; Roger had no patience for any of that stuff. But Mary would go and sit through tech rehearsals that went on for fourteen hours with people standing on stage while the lights were adjusted. She absorbed all of that, couldn't get enough of it. She was really the one, from day one, who saw the possible payoff."[17]

On July 14, 1984 Barbara Crow Miller died suddenly; she was 45 years old and apparently had a bad heart valve. It took everyone by surprise. Their daughter, Shari, contacted Roger, who did not attend the funeral but sent a "huge bouquet of roses."

Barbara had remarried a couple of years before her death "but loved Roger until her dying day," said her sister, Phyllis. "She never got over him. Nobody ever measured up to him for her."[18]

Some of the family members wanted to move the grave of Roger and Barbara's first child, who died a month after his birth, from Shamrock to Duncan to be buried beside his mother but Roger said "No." "There's a reason he's buried there," Roger told the family members. "And the only way he'd be re-buried is if Barbara wanted that and she's gone."[19]

That settled the issue; Barbara Crow Miller is buried in Duncan while Michael Dean Miller remains buried in Shamrock.

Chapter 26
Dean Miller

Dean was thirteen years old when Roger and Mary moved to Santa Fe. Dean decided he wanted to live with his Dad so his mother said "Go" and he moved to Santa Fe; Dean and his mother did not speak again until he was 26.

Dean loved Santa Fe; this is where he spent his high school years. After he graduated from high school, Dean spent a year at Pepperdine in Santa Monica, then went to the American Academy of Dramatic Arts before transferring to the California Institute of the Arts, where he graduated.

During those high school years Dean saw Roger perform "thousands and thousands of times," he said. "When I was not in school I would go on the road with my parents so I spent the summers going to all these exotic, cool places. I remember being a teenager in Vegas and my Dad would do shows and these show girls would open and I'd find the perfect place to stand backstage. It was pretty wild for a child. You probably couldn't live that childhood now but my step-Mom sang with my Dad so they'd go on stage and I was free for the hour or hour and a half in Vegas which is, you know, not always good. But at that time it was a little different than it is now."

"Many, many times I was the fly on the wall," Dean continued. "I used to call myself the invisible kid cause I just wanted to be part of that, I wanted to see it all so I'd hide around the corner and watch or try to tag along as much as I could so I have many many stories of hanging back while stuff was going on."

Dean remembers that he heard Roger say the same funny lines "many many times. He had stock ones but then he had some that just tumbled out. One of my favorites came when he was doing a show that I must have seen five thousand times so I knew the lines that were stock—and then I knew when a heckler came in and he was just making it up. The best one that just came off the top of his head came one night in Las Vegas when he asked, as he usually did, 'Is there anyone here from Oklahoma? I'm from Oklahoma.' Somebody from way in the back said, 'Yeah,' and Dad said 'When you pull into town you've got to take the mattress off the top of your car and then you'll get better seats.' I mean, how do you think like that?"

Roger Miller "had a really cool way of being with people—he was very humble and approachable and was nice to people and had a way to keep moving," remembers Dean. "It wasn't like being with Elvis—he had a way of turning it on and turning it off. That's why he lived in Santa Fe, because nobody cared. He could put on a ball cap and not care. I don't think my Dad had the same kind of thing when he walked around as some other people. It was different in the 70s when I was really little but he was really cool about it and it just seemed to be part of life."

"My Dad told me one time 'I have two different ways of being,'" continued Dean. "'When I want to be noticed I take the cap off and I stand a little straighter and I walk a little different. When I don't want to be noticed I just turn it off.' He felt like he could turn it on and off. He wasn't a person who tooted his own horn. I think had he done that, had he been a person who pursued more publicity or hired a publicist, he would have had a lot more recognition. But he wasn't interested in all of that. I think he would have been more known and respected had he done all those things but I think that all my Dad was really interested in was having fun. He just wanted to continue the fun, the enjoyment, enjoy every day. He never wanted the party the end. I don't think he cared much about strategizing his career."

Roger "never bought an album by somebody else and listened to it," said Dean. "He didn't want the radio on in the car, didn't put on records, but he did have the television on 24 hours a day. Night and day. At night he slept with it on; that TV never went off. When he was young he was very influenced by other people but I think at a certain point he said 'I want to create and I don't want anyone to say 'You lifted that from him' or whatever. I never saw him buy a record and that was so weird when I was a kid. I never discovered music through my Dad. I didn't even know who the Beatles were when I was a little kid because I think my Dad looked at them as competition or something. It was weird because I discovered all my music through Top 40 radio or through kids at school and then, later, my Dad's friends. I would investigate their music because they were his friends or acts who ended up in a show."

"I never knew him to read a book but he read newspapers and magazines constantly. On airplanes he was always reading anything that fit his short attention span. He'd read those 'bathroom reader' kinds of books. He loved stuff like *Popular Mechanics*, loved gadgets, had a mess of gadgets, fixed clocks for a long time, had a clock fetish. But everything had to fit his short attention span—books with short factual things and TV twenty-four hours a day, especially 'The Price is Right.' That was his favorite show. He'd say, 'I love The Price is Right.' He also got on a 'Wheel of Fortune' kick for awhile. There was a time when we had this big family joke because every night we'd sit down to dinner and my Mom would turn the TV around to watch 'Wheel of Fortune' and one night I just said, 'This is so sad, we don't even talk to each other—we just watch 'Wheel of Fortune.' She said 'You're right' and from that time on she didn't turn the TV around for 'Wheel of Fortune' during dinner."

"I remember that I always thought 'The Price is Right' was the loudest show on television. It's just noise noise, bells and bells and I would hear that in the morning—my Dad would get up at eleven or twelve or two or whatever and he'd have that on and one time I asked him 'Why do you watch this horrendous show? It's the loudest show' and he said, 'Because Bob Barker is a professional. I like to watch him because he's a pro. I love to watch him work.' He loved Bob Barker and he thought Johnny Carson just hung the moon."

"He liked old movies," said Dean. "His favorite western was *The Man Who Shot Liberty Valance*. He had video cassettes. He had the first of everything—the first video recorder. I remember in the 70s we had the big three quarter inch machine and you could get like fifteen minutes of tape or something on it. He had the first brief case telephone and the first phone in the car where you pushed a button. He had every gadget. He had the first big brick phones. He was big on gadgets and he would build little things. He built a door bell system in our house where you walked up and pulled a rope and it rang our door bell. He just loved little gadgety things."

"I know he could write off the top of his head—Mac Davis ripped that off from my Dad. That thing of sitting on the TV show and making up a song."

"He'd watch his friends when they were on TV. I remember that Glen Campbell would always call whenever he was going to do a talk show and he'd talk to my Dad for 20 or 30 minutes and write down everything he said and steal it to say on the show. So when the phone rang and my Mom said, 'Glen's on the phone' Dad would say, 'He must be doing Carson.' Cause that's the only time he called. My Dad was really hip to that."

Once, when Glen Campbell was playing in Albuquerque, he rented a helicopter to visit Roger but got lost and landed in a drug store parking lot about five minutes away. Campbell got out of the helicopter, asked directions to Roger's house, then got back in, followed the road over and landed in the field beside Roger's house.

Roger's close relationship with Mary made him "more secure so he was a different person in his later years," said Dean. "Don Meredith was a close friend and Willie Nelson was someone he confided in. I used to watch him and Willie together and I said to my Dad one day 'There's some bond you guys have because you had this before either of you had success.' They knew each other when there was nothing to gain and they were bonded so when they sat down together I'd see something between the two of them. I felt that no one else could be in that club because they didn't have anyone in either of their lives that knew them way back when. Neither was a star when they first met so they had a bond that was unusual. I know Merle was a good friend. But Willie, I perceived from the exterior, was a close friend."

Roger "had a Bentley that he loved to drive and drove it in California all the time. After we moved to New Mexico he parked it one day and never drove it again. He said 'I just don't like it any more' and the car sat there and rotted; it had rats living in it. After he parked it, he never touched it again, never took care of it. He just walked away from it one day and was done with it. Also, he was hit by a drunk driver and they crushed the back end so he had it re-built. That may have been part of the reason why he didn't want to be in it."

As for the songs themselves, "Sometimes it was about him and sometimes it wasn't about anything at all—it was just word play or goofing around. I think he had no boundaries," said Dean. "From jokes to humor to stuff off the cuff he was constantly creating. It's like he was almost cursed with word play so when someone said something he'd hear it in five different twists. In his head he was always doing this word play."

The genius of a genius always amazes those who are closest; Dean came to know that his Dad was a genius but never understood how that came to be. "He didn't have any formal education," said Dean. "He didn't read or study or anything. It's weird. I don't know where some of that stuff came from. Just born with it, I guess."[1]

Chapter 27
You Oughta Be Here With Me

There were lots of times when we didn't know if we'd be successful, if we'd make it," remembered Rocco Landesman. "There were a lot of leaps of faith along the way. I remember one time before the New York show opened we were all sitting around in Roger's apartment, which he sublet from actress Patty LuPone. I remember as I was standing up to leave—and everybody's nervous and on edge—I was about to open the door to leave and he looked me dead in the eye and said, 'How can we fail? We're so sincere.'"[1]

On February 11, 1985, rehearsals started for *Big River* in New York; on March 26 it opened at the Shubert Theater in New Haven and ran until April 7 for a final tune-up, then it was ready for New York.

John Goodman joined the cast in La Jolla and was the only member of the cast who remained when Landesman moved the show to New York. There had been some significant changes; the musical had seven songs when it was first staged in Boston; in the New York production it had seventeen songs. In La Jolla, the cast mooned the audience as they sang "When the Sun Goes Down in the South"; that was taken out.

Big River opened at the Eugene O'Neill Theater at 230 West 49th Street in New York on April 23. By this time the show had 20 actors playing 65 characters in 45 scenes. The show was directed by Des McAnuff and produced by Rocco Landesman, Heidi Landesman, Richard H. Steiner, M. Anthony Fisher, and Dodger Productions, Inc. (Michael David, Rocco Landesman, Edward Strong, Des McAnuff, Sherman Warner).

The musical came on the One Hundredth anniversary of the publication of *Huckleberry Finn*. Roger did publicity for the musical, doing interviews with key media.

"I've been in show business for 28 years and I never knew much of what went on in the theater," Roger told one interviewer. "In TV or recording, you can capture something, but in theater it's always changing."

The show won the Best Musical Award for the season from the Boston Critics Circle when it was done at Harvard. That was a great start—but it wasn't New York.

Just before the New York premiere, Roger did an interview with David Patrick Stearns for *USA Today*. The article begins, "Roger Miller's phone has been ringing all day. This time it's Johnny Carson's office, wanting to rush Miller onto 'The Tonight Show' before his Broadway composing debut Thursday in 'Big River.'"

"When you're in your 20s and the world comes at you, you can get a little fritzy," said Roger, who was 49 at the time. "But I can handle it now. I've had a lot of experience handling it."

Talking about the music, Roger said, "I didn't realize it until we got [the show) all stood up," he says. "Before, I just wrote record music and wrote it for years. When I turned to do this play, it seemed to be an open window to do just any kind of style and thing I wanted."

Roger related to the character Huckleberry Finn, saying "The people who raised me, my aunt and uncle, were from Arkansas. Country people. We farmed, had cattle and this, that and the other. This particular book was my boyhood. All those things were stirred inside of me and it just started to flow."

Roger remembered his Dad grousing about the government and that became the song "Gov'ment." His family romanticized their home state of Arkansas and that was captured in the song, "Arkansas." The memorable "River in the Rain" is "a mental picture of a rainy night, and the words and sounds just developed," said Roger.

Asked how he would react if the musical was a success, Roger said, "The attention is great and it's good business." The writer noted that Roger believes he can handle success "a lot better than he did the first time around, when he became notorious for marathon parties and amphetamine abuse—a subject he won't discuss now."

The writer observed that Roger "has adjusted well to New York, living in a chic Greenwich Village apartment sublet from Patti LuPone, finishing lyrics while waiting for his wife in Macy's shoe department and indulging in his favorite urban sport, 'fishing for cabs.'" "It is like fishing," said Roger. "'Oh! I've got a big one! It's a Checker!'"[2]

On April 23 Roger was on the Johnny Carson show wearing a suit without a tie. He sat beside Carson, played his guitar and sang three songs from the musical: "Muddy Water," "Leavin's Not the Only Way to Go" and "Hand for the Hog."

During the run in New York, Roger played the role of "Pap" for a number of shows. When Willie Nelson came to town, he was ushered backstage and they visited in Roger's dressing room. Roger loved playing "Pap" although, as Landesman remembers, "He ad libbed. He couldn't remember the lyrics, couldn't remember the lines half the time, so he ad libbed things, but it always worked out."[3]

Randy Hart went to see *Big River* in New York and sat in front of Roger and Mary. When "How Blessed We Are" was sung, Roger leaned forward and whispered to Randy, "We just put this song in."

"We never had the reason or opportunity to discuss any kind of spiritual thoughts or beliefs that he had," said Hart, "but if you listen to that song, you get a sense of what he was aware of from a spiritual perspective and it was profound to me. I thought, 'I worked eight years with this guy and I didn't know that he had that kind of observation.'"

"I thought the play was an excuse for Roger's songs because it was a showcase," said Hart. "Maybe it was my own perspective because I had seen where those songs came from but I thought 'This is kind of strange' because the story line is from A to B to C but the songs bounced around quite a bit. The collection of songs didn't provide a real story like *The Music Man* or *The Sound of Music* where you can get the story from the songs. In his case, you couldn't, but they were incredible songs. I remember that, before the play was on Broadway, we were playing a date in Montana and we had to drive from wherever we were to the airport at Billings. The sound guy was driving and I was in the passenger's seat. It was at night and it was a beautiful sky, just crystal clear and Roger and Mary were in the back seat and Roger took his guitar out and went through all these songs from the play, one after the other, and God, it was magical."[4]

On June 3—about six weeks after *Big River* opened on Broadway—the Tony Awards were held; the musical was nominated for ten awards.

"We knew we were in pretty good shape at that point because the show had started to gain traction and was selling well and popular," said Landesman. "Frank Rich gave us a mixed review, which was the only less than enthusiastic review we got. But Walter Kerr came out that Sunday with a rave for it, which was great and assured us that the show was going to be on Broadway through the Tonys and then we'd take our chances at the Tonys."

The evening of the Tony Awards "Everyone was very anxious but as we started to win for the book and Heidi won for the set, we started to feel pretty good," said Landesman. "And when Roger won, that was a really great moment. On the way to the stage he stopped where I was and gave me a big hug before he went up. And when he received the award he looked at it and said, 'This is a helluva deal.'"[5]

Roger thanked a lot of people but not Mary, the single most important person in getting him to write the songs for that musical. He heard about that later.

Big River won seven awards: "Best Musical," "Best Score" by Roger Miller, "Best Featured Actor" (for Ron Richardson who played Jim, the runaway slave), "Best Adaptation" (for writer William Hauptman), "Best Direction" (for Des McAnuff), "Lighting" (for Richard Riddell) and "Scene Design" (Heidi Landesman). *Biloxi Blues* by Neil Simon won the "Best Play" award that evening.

"That was a great night for all of us," remembered Landesman. "We ended up going to a club and stayed out until nine the next morning. Of all my memories in the theater, that's probably my happiest—the night that *Big River* won all those Tonys. For me it was a great validation that my basic insight was right. My whole career has followed from one idea—that Roger Miller was a genius. I had that single idea and all you need is one idea. My idea was that Roger Miller was a special talent and a genius and could write a Broadway score."

"Of course, it was a tremendous validation for Roger," added Landesman, "because he was the first country artist to cross over into this, in some perspective, high falutin' realm in the tradition of Gershwin, Cole Porter and Sondheim and the great composers over the years."[6]

A newspaper article the next day noted that *Big River* had not been selling out and "One damper on the festivities was New York's hotel strike, which prompted organizers to move the post-awards ball away from the New York Hilton, which is being struck by its employees, to the Grand Hyatt, which has agreed to contract terms."

During the 1985 season, "only 33 new shows opened" while 50 shows opened in 1983.[7]

After the show was a success, Landesman reflected that "Roger took a big leap with *Big River* because I really hadn't done anything like this. For some reason, I don't know why, but he believed that I would deliver. At least I kept delivering what I said I would and things kept happening. If we knew then what we know now, we'd never have tried it. There's a great passage in *The Season*, William Goldman's great book about the 1963 Broadway season and it's very insightful. Goodman said that you can almost always predict the success of a show by looking at the program and seeing the experience of the people who are doing the show. What are their credits, what have they done? Well, in this show, I had never produced a Broadway show, Bill Hauptman had never written a book for a musical, Des McAnuff had never directed a Broadway show, none of the actors, with the exception of Rene Auberjonois had ever been on Broadway, and Roger Miller had never seen a show, much less written a score. You would not have given a nickel for our chances with that show. They were too many novices, too many people who didn't know what they were doing. It all seems too ridiculous, but everybody was a novice and a first timer and we got along because none of us knew better. We didn't know that we were likely to fail. We thought we might succeed but any rational analysis would have told you it was a one in a thousand show."[8]

In June, just after *Big River* won at the Tony Awards, Roger and the cast came to Nashville to record the original cast album. It was the first time an original cast recording of a Broadway musical had been done in Nashville. Jimmy Bowen, head of MCA Records, had lobbied to have the recording done in Nashville and produced the sessions.

Bowen first met Roger in the early 1960s when he was producing Dean Martin. He came to Nashville and "rented a big bedroom in a hotel," said Bowen. "There'd be six or seven or eight songwriters—with just one guitar—who'd gather in the room and play songs. Roger was in one of those pitching sessions when the phone rang and someone answered it and it was for Roger, who said, 'Tell 'em I'll call 'em back. I'm next.' He didn't want to miss his turn to play a song!"[9]

Bowen had received a call from Stan Moress—Roger's manager and formerly Bowen's "right hand man" when they both worked for MGM in Los Angeles—about doing the cast album so Bowen, along with his wife and Moress, went to the show in New York.

"There were three reasons I wanted to do that album," remembered

Bowen. "First, it was Roger Miller and if I could do anything with Roger, I would. Second, I realized a great cast album would last a long time; it could be around 50, 80 or 90 years. And third, I wanted to do a Broadway album."

Bowen cut the rhythm tracks in Nashville, then went to New York where he had the cast come in and sing their parts. "I had them sing their parts over and over and over until it was right," remembered Bowen. "I didn't realize that every time they came in to sing they got a week's pay so that album cost over half a million dollars."[10]

In addition to the Cast recording, Bowen announced that Roger Miller would be signed to MCA Records and record a new album in the fall, which would feature four songs from the *Big River* musical. Roger missed the press conference on June 17 at the BMI office in Nashville announcing the cast recording because his flight from Dallas was delayed.

On September 9, BMI's Nashville head Frances Preston hosted a grand party at her home for Roger Miller. An article by Robert Oermann about that party states, "Gazing at the crowd of stars, executives, songwriters and friends who turned out to salute him, Miller grinned broadly. Did he get tired of smiling so much during the evening of congratulations? 'The grin has just begun!' he said with glee."

Those at the party included Minnie Pearl, Tammy Wynette, Jessi Colter, Waylon Jennings, Ray Stevens, John Hartford, The Oaks' Joe Bonsall, T.G. Sheppard, Hillary Kanter, and Marty Haggard. The party was the same night of the annual Harlan Howard Birthday Bash but Bobby Bare and Harlan both came. So did Nashville Mayor Richard Fulton and songwriters Sonny Curtis, Jack Clement, Bobby Braddock, Curly Putman, Hal Bynum, John D. Loudermilk, Danny Dill, Marijohn Wilkin, and Joe Allison.[11]

The next month Roger was back in Nashville for the release of the original cast album. That event, hosted by MCA on October 21, was held on the General Jackson, the Opryland showboat, which regularly cruised the Cumberland River. About three hundred of "Nashville's elite" were on the boat, along with Rocco Landesman, Ron Richardson, who played the slave "Jim" and Daniel Jenkins, who played "Huck" in the Broadway show.

That same month Roger hosted the Sixteenth Annual Nashville Songwriters Association International Hall of Fame banquet and induction ceremony at the Hyatt Regency in Nashville. Inducted that evening were Carl Perkins and Bob McDill, but the first half of the evening was devoted to Miller, who gave a speech before he was surprised with a special award honoring his Broadway success. After accepting the award, Roger said, "I was asked to do that play. That's my answer to people who ask me how I got into theater. They said, 'Roger, we'd like ya to write a play' and I said, 'Sure'" before adding that he "hadn't read a book since I read Lassie four times."[12]

Miller, who had formed his own publishing company, Roger Miller Music, signed with Tree Publishing again at the end of 1985. He could have signed with a number of other publishers and probably gotten a better deal in terms of a monetary advance, but Roger always remembered that Buddy Killen had given him that five dollars when he had absolutely nothing and Roger stayed loyal to his friends, especially his friends from the early days.

As part of that publishing deal, Roger re-recorded a number of his early hits and Tree released them on a "Greatest Hits" package. This allowed them to control the recordings as well as the songs as they shopped the songs to various ad agencies for use. Donna Hilley, vice president of Tree, called it "one stop shopping" when a company wanted to use one of Roger's songs. If a company wanted the original recording, they had to deal with Mercury, the label where Roger recorded his early hits, in addition to Tree.

It was a big week for Roger in Nashville. He had been honored by the Nashville Songwriters Association International, the Country Music Association, Broadcast Music Inc. (BMI) and MCA Records. Commenting on his new deal with Tree, Roger said, "I've been with them a long time, and they've always taken care of my music. I'm very comfortable there. At this point in life, I don't want to sleep with strangers."[13]

Chapter 28
How Blessed We Are

After *Big River*, Roger was back on top again. He had a different image of himself; he was proud of what he had done and told a number of friends that he was going to write another Broadway play "To prove to those turkeys that this wasn't a fluke." His album for MCA included several songs from *Big River*; "River In The Rain," was released as a single and reached number 26 on the Country Chart in *Billboard*.

"That album just sold a little," said Jimmy Bowen. "At that point Roger would have been an 'old act' and radio and retail were into new acts. It could have worked but we didn't quite capture it, it wasn't quite right. There was a lot of competition out there and it was good but it wasn't right for the times. We didn't hit that niche, didn't quite hit the bell."

"Roger had the most incredible mind of my generation," remembered Bowen. "The things he said were so loose and open; you couldn't believe the things he'd say. He was brilliant, the Will Rogers of our times except he didn't have a newspaper column. I remember he said one time 'The strongest man in the world can stick his thumb up his ass and hold himself at arm's length.' Now how does somebody think of things like that?"[1]

In January, Roger was honored at the sixth annual National Songwriters Awards Show, which was hosted by Roy Clark and actress Barbara Eden.

During the Spring of 1986, Roger decided he would go back on the road again. He encountered a problem because his road manager, Randy Hart, now worked for Steve Wariner, so he hired Larry Richstein. Ron "Iceman" Shumake, who had played bass for him since 1980, re-joined him. Roger also called Micheal and Darlene Smotherman to join his band again. He and Mary invited the Smothermans to visit them at their home in Santa Fe and Micheal noticed that Mary "was definitely a kind of rudder for him" and "Man, she would not take any of his shit."

"Roger could be a brat," said Smotherman. "If he was in a bad mood, he was just a brat. If he didn't like the airport, the food or whatever. I remember that we were at his house and it was three in the morning and we were laughing and playing the piano and doing all kinds of things and

Mary came to us and said, 'O.K. Roger and Micheal, it's time to go to bed now.' She turned around and started to walk off and Roger said, 'Hey, watch it!' and Mary answered, 'Oh, I'm afraid, Roger.' He said, 'You're really skating on thin ice now' and she said, 'Oh, now I'm really afraid, Roger.' I think he liked that because he had a strong personality. It was easy for him to be the Alpha dog. But Mary was a strong woman and she wasn't timid. She stood up to him and he needed that."[2]

Roger was still Roger but a lot of the craziness was gone. He took a lot of cocaine but there were no pills. He was still incredibly witty with a razor sharp mind but the days of hanging off the ceiling behavior were pretty much behind him.

In August, 1986, he released "Some Hearts Get All the Breaks," which only made it to number 81 on the Country chart.

In June, 1987, Roger came to Nashville and talked with Ralph Emery in a hotel room as Ralph taped the conversation to use later on his shows. Talking about Rocco Landesman and *Big River*, Roger said, "He'd been a fan of mine for many years and he would quote me lyrics from my work, from 'Half a Mind' to 'Big Harlan Taylor.' He knew every word of every song that I'd done. I'd never met a scholar of my work. He told me he'd always wanted to get my work together with Mark Twain and I told him, 'It's a little late, because Mark Twain can't defend himself.' He said that he had a great idea that if I'd write music to *Huckleberry Finn* that it would be a great musical."

"I've always had visions for my music but I'd never thought about stuff like that," continued Roger. "Rocco would walk with me and talk about the qualities of lyrics and different levels of things and he said, 'You're the only man who can do this' and I said 'Really?' he said 'If you won't do it then I won't do it' and I thought, 'Well, I wouldn't want to rob you of the opportunity of doing a great musical on Broadway.' He said, 'If you write the songs then I will clear the way. I'll get the book written, I'll get investors together and clear the way.' As we went along, I found that everything he said he'd do, he'd do. He's a man of his word. I said, 'Let me try a couple of things' and, as I started looking at the novel, I realized that the people in the novel were my people. They talk the same language that was in the book."[3]

Emery asked Roger if he was a fan of Mark Twain before the musical and Roger replied, "I was a fan of Mark Twain like I'm a fan of Will Rogers. I'm a fan of people who communicate like that. I wasn't a scholar of it, but I always appreciated it."

Asked if he was going to do it again Roger said, "Well Brother Dave Gardner said 'You can't do nothin' again!' But, yes, I'm going to do it again. I'm trying to get the rights to *The Grapes of Wrath*, which I lived. I came from a town on Route 66 in Oklahoma. *The Grapes of Wrath* is a couple of generations later after *Huckleberry Finn*. My Dad's brother went to California but my Dad and Mother couldn't afford to go to California so they stayed. I remember Dust Storms and I heard a lot of stories about eating split beans and split peas. I've read the Steinbeck story but if I can't get the rights to *Grapes of Wrath* I think I can create my own story about the heartland."

Emery asked about him doing a one man show on Broadway and Roger said, "I have a lot of options. After *Big River* hit, the theater owners and theater guild people in New York talked to me about it. I've watched Lily Tomlin and Jackie Mason do their one person shows and they're very successful. I've been an entertainer and I like to talk to people, so I could come out and play my fiddle and talk about my songs. I could talk about the news and about the President—a little bit of politics but not a lot of politics. I'd say things like 'Selling arms to Iran is like letting Charles Manson out of jail with a map to the stars homes.' Humor stuff. You know I'm into humor."

"It would be 'An Evening With,'" continued Roger. "Some people are talking to me about a project on Will Rogers. They're talking to me about doing that and I can spin a rope and I can slap a horse as good as anybody. I've read a lot about Will in the last few years and Will would just talk and do his rope tricks. So I could talk to people and I've got music too. I've got Ernest Tubb records!"

Roger told Ralph that he lived in Santa Fe after he "absolutely fell in love with it. It's a different city than any other city. It's an adobe town, it's got some dirt streets. Great painters live there." Roger noted that "From the crest of the hill by our house I can see the Santa Fe Opera House. Sometimes, on summer nights when the wind is right, I can hear opera from the roof of my house."

Roger added that "I've got a satellite out there on a hill and I can get the English Channel. I can get Chanel Number Five on a clear night."

Speaking of Mary, Roger said that she's "one of the great women that I've met in my life. I met her when I was on 'Rolling on the River,' the television show hosted by Kenny Rogers and she was this gorgeous woman that everyone just wanted to look at. I was smitten by this woman but we didn't connect until six or eight months later when Kenny Rogers was having a birthday and asked me if I'd like to come to his party. I went and Mary was my gift! We kinda connected there and we've been together ever since."[4]

Roger continued to make regular appearances on "The Tonight Show" but admitted that he didn't know Johnny Carson "other than the show. "I've never visited with him," said Roger. "I've always had a great rapport with Johnny, he's easy to talk with. One night, off camera, I said 'John, I've known you for years but never see you, except on camera' and he said, 'Well, let's keep it that way.'"

On July 31, 1987, his old buddy Thumbs Carlille died.

In September, the Los Angeles *Times* ran an article that stated *Big River* was "still playing full houses at the O'Neill Theater." This led to a phone interview with Roger, who was fifty at this time and in the midst of a week long concert engagement in St. Louis. Asked about the success of *Big River*, Roger stated, "I have to say that it all came as kind of a shock, coming from left field the way it did. It was my first exposure to musicals, my first time with a Broadway producer, and I didn't really see myself as that kind of a person. It was pretty heady stuff…what I can tell you is that I'm sure glad it came by because, looking back, I wouldn't have missed any of it for the world."

Concerning the persuasion used by Rocco Landesman, Roger said, "In the end, it didn't take much convincing; the songs just started coming to me, along with the music, and I realized I could write the production stuff that was needed. The novel got me thinking about my own people and experiences growing up in Oklahoma, working in the cotton fields as a boy, the pain and stuff of living in the country. I found I could use a lot of that in the songs."

"I knew the meat of the story because my people were like the Twain people and I tried to use that to make the songs accessible," said Roger.

"I felt that theatrical people aim at the critics a lot, but I wanted to raise the people out of their seats [with the songs]. The critics can't deny it when you do that."

The article continued that "Things began to slide in the 70s. He admitted to drinking too much and disdaining the record business that launched him. He went through a depressing separation and divorce. He was working—there were concert tours and other songwriting projects—but there was downtime too. Then the 'Big River' project came along opening up 'a new world for my talents.'"

"Right now I'm taking it easy, doing a little touring and spending the lazy life at home," said Roger. "But I'm sure I'll do something else [in the theater]. I'm a theater buff now and don't think I'll be able to stay away for long."[5]

Tony Conway proposed the idea of Roger doing a one man show "but he resisted that, wasn't in favor of doing that because he said he needed the band," remembered Conway. "That was his crutch. But I had seen him and been around him when it was just him and his guitar and I thought 'This will be perfect.' If he did a one man show, I thought we could get a lot of dates and the money would either stay the same or go up and he would make so much more because he wouldn't have that entourage on the road with him. He did not like the idea; he was nervous about it but I kept on him about it, kept on and on and kept on Stan about it until Roger finally said, 'Well, we'll do one and see how it works.'"

"We booked him at the DuQuoin State Fair in Illinois," said Conway, "which is probably one of the nicest outdoor venues in the country. It's like a park and we booked it as 'An Evening with Roger Miller.' It was in the 8,000 seat grandstand and we sold about 6,000 tickets. You had to buy an extra ticket to that show, it wasn't included in the regular Fair ticket."

At that point in his career, Roger could usually sell 2,500 to 3,000 tickets for a show.

"I picked him up at the airport, I think it was St. Louis and drove him up there," said Conway. "At the DuQuoin State Fair the stage is in front of the racetrack and butts up against the grandstand. At most fairs, the stage is behind the race track, which makes it harder for a performer to connect with an audience. We drove up to the stage and I remember him getting out of the car and he was hobbling around, said his back had gone out and it was killing him. He had to go down about four or five steps to get to the backstage area and he had to hold on to the railing. I was like 'uh oh' because he was really in pain. I went down to the dressing room and he's sitting there and tells me 'I don't know if I can do this show tonight because I can hardly even stand up.' I said 'We'll get you a stool with a back on it' because I'd worked with Don Williams and I knew what that was like. I asked, 'Can you walk out to the stool?' and he said 'Yeah, but' and then he started getting nervous because he'd never done a show without his band. He said 'There's a lot of people out there. I don't know if I can do this by myself' so I said, 'Yeah, you can do it, you can do it. Just tell some stories between songs and you'll be fine.'"

Roger walked out on stage, sat down "and after about the first song I could tell he was completely at ease. He wasn't nervous anymore," said Conway. "He was a nervous wreck before he went on the stage. The crowd just loved it and laughed and he got a standing ovation. It was an unbelievable night. When he came off the stage that night he told me 'Let's go set a bunch of these up' so that's what we did. We kinda went back and forth. We'd do Roger Miller with the full band set-up or Roger Miller by himself. It was really great because I think it gave him confidence that he could go out and do this after all those years."

Roger and Tony developed a close working relationship. "He was one of the funniest guys you'd ever met in your life," said Tony. "I remember him calling me up all the time from the road or from the house. It wasn't about 'What have to you done for me today,' it was just to talk and tell me stories and just keeping the relationship going. It was great. I had a lot of respect for him."[6]

In July of 1987, Roger and Mary adopted Margaret Taylor Miller, a baby girl they called "Taylor." Roger thought he was doing that for Mary—he already had kids that were grown—but he told a friend, "The minute I put that little girl in my arms the other day, I was a goner." They also adopted a boy, Adam. The Millers were incredibly happy raising those kids and this was another turning point in Roger's life, a settling down and embracing the value of "family."[7]

Chapter 29
Walkin' in the Sunshine

The year 1988 began with *Big River* playing in Nashville at the Tennessee Performing Arts Center. Roger Miller played "Pap" during the week-long run.

The show opened on Tuesday, January 5 and finished Sunday night. On opening night there was a champagne celebration hosted by BMI, MCA and Tree Publishing with proceeds going to the Metro Arts Commission. The city proclaimed "Roger Miller Week" and he was toasted and hosted for his "return" to Nashville. The weather wasn't very cooperative; there was a huge snowfall and freezing cold, but the crowds came out to see *Big River*. A review of the opening night in the Nashville *Tennessean* noted that when Roger "made his appearance as Huck's comic but reprobate Pap, the response was immediate and warm."

There was a bit of criticism about the performances, with the reviewer stating "If the play itself gets off to a slow start it's because Huck and the others over act, yielding to an indulgent tendency to broaden the humor and turn the story into a cartoon. Happily, as the work progresses, the actors grow into the roles and put warmth into the humor to create memorable characters and scenes with the power to touch deeply."[1]

Commenting on Miller's performance, the reviewer stated "As for Miller, what a ball he has singing his sassy tirade about the 'Dad Gum Gov'ment' and making Huck laugh in spite of himself."

There was a great deal of irony in Roger Miller's performance at the Tennessee Performance Arts Center because it stood on the site where the Andrew Jackson Hotel formerly stood. That hotel is where Roger Miller got his first job—as a bellhop—when he came to Nashville in 1957.

In 1988 the Academy of Country Music presented Roger with their "Pioneer Award." In presenting the award, Roy Clark said, "When they made him, they threw away the gyroscope." Roger countered with "When they made me, they smoked the mold."

He was making money from radio commercials; he was the spokesman for Hardy's, did a Car Quest commercial and did ads for AT&T and McDonalds. "I've sold a lot of food over the last few years," said Roger.

"I've been selling a lot of lunch meat in Texas and the Southwest, Decker Meats. Still touring. On 'Nashville Now' and TNN." About his home in New Mexico, he said it's the "only one with a Bentley and a tractor in the front yard."

He rented an apartment in Nashville, hoping to stay close to the songwriting community. [2]

In June, at the Summer Lights Festival in Nashville, Roger wore a tuxedo and performed in front of a large orchestra at the Metro Courthouse stage. As he stood in front of the elegantly dressed symphony, Miller asked, "What's this band called, anyway? Let's just call them 'The Roadhogs.'"

During the show he talked about his early days in Nashville and said, "I can see the L&C tower from here," as he looked towards the National Life and Casualty high rise. "When I first saw that, I thought Loretta (Lynn) and Conway (Twitty) must be doing really great."[3]

The National Public Radio Show, "The Prairie Home Companion," hosted by Garrison Keillor, came to the Ryman Auditorium in Nashville and Roger was a guest. As he walked in the back door, carrying a "satchel and a cased guitar" he stopped, looked at those assembled, and said, "Well, I just got my second wind—I broke my first one." The group laughed and Roger then turned to the closest person and said "My Daddy had that Midas touch—everything he touched turned to mufflers." Roger was on a roll so he continued, "I asked this old boy for a rough estimate; he kicked me real hard in the balls and said, 'Four hunnerd dollars!'"

According to Russ Ringsak, who was there, Roger "must have gone through twenty zingers and when he finally went to his dressing room and we put ourselves back together I was grateful to be able to remember even those three. You grinned for days after an encounter with Roger Miller. Or years."[4]

Mickey Raphael, who plays harmonica in Willie Nelson's band, remembers riding in a car with Roger when he said, "I'd give my right arm to be ambidextrous."[5]

Bill Anderson remembered that Roger once said "I once knew a guy who lied so much he had to get someone else to call his dog" and "I caught him in the truth one time, but he lied his way out of it."[6]

Ray Stevens had not seen Roger in quite a while when he ran into him at the Nashville airport. "Hey, Rog—where you been?" asked Stevens. "Played Kansas City last night," replied Roger. "Beat 'em six to two."[7]

During his regular shows, Roger came out with his acoustic guitar, sat on a stool, sang his songs and talked with the crowd. He took requests, answered hecklers and provided witty asides and observations.

In October, 1988, "The Roger Miller Special," a TV show done for The Nashville Network (TNN) was broadcast. The show, filmed on the Mississippi Queen river boat while cruising down the Tennessee River, featured Roger singing some of his songs, including "River in the Rain" and "Muddy Water" from *Big River*—and guests Tanya Tucker, Lyle Lovett, Libby Hurley and comedians Williams and Ree. Miller saw the show as a "pilot" for a regular talk/variety show but it never developed.

Roger was still talking about doing another Broadway show. "I've got about three different groups approaching me about another Broadway show," he said, and stated that one of the groups included author Larry King, who wrote *Best Little Whorehouse in Texas*. It was noted that his next musical probably would not be based on a literary classic because "The classics, interestingly enough, are almost all tied up. People have options on a whole lot of them for shows. I may have to do one about Cowboy Copas," said Miller.[8]

The idea he came back to time and again was a Broadway musical for the classic western *Shane* but Rocco Landesman never came up with a book for the musical, although Landesman admits, "I don't know whether *Shane* would have been the right one but I think there could have been another one. But right after *Big River*, I didn't have the patience to crank up this process again because I remembered how arduous it was to get him to write the first show. Still, when Frank Rich collected his reviews in a book, *Hot Seat*, he said the really tragic thing was that the two of us never got to do another show together because Roger would have been great."[9]

A story about Roger by Bob Claypool in the *Houston Post* quoted Roger saying that his high school class had "37 students; me and 36 Indians. During recess we used to play cowboys and Indians and things got pretty wild from my standpoint." Another line he often used was that the school held a dance "and it rained for three days."

Commenting on the "Pioneer Award" he received from the Academy of Country Music, Roger said he was unaware that he would receive it. "Oh no, no idea at all. I was supposed to give a speech and I didn't have any idea what to say. No, everybody kept it a secret from me—I didn't know it until they announced my name. No telling what else is goin' on behind my back!"

"I hate those award shows, really," said Roger. "You sit there all night and then when they call your name, your pants are so wrinkled it looks like you're smuggling cantaloupes."

"I didn't even know I was old enough to get an award like that. I mean, when you get those awards for career achievement, you have to look out. It tends to put a halo on everything you do, and, if you take it too seriously, it will put an end to your work."

Commenting on *Big River* he said, "I was looking for new avenues and new ways of writing anyway. You have to—you don't want to be playing Gilley's when you're 64. That alternative wasn't too attractive to me, so I had to find somethin'!"[10]

Some of his old songs came back on the radio through recordings by new country artists. Ricky Van Shelton had "Don't We All Have the Right," which was number one on the country charts in 1988 and led to Van Shelton winning the CMA's "Horizon Award" that year.

In 1989 the Bear Family group in Germany released a CD of Roger's material. The liner notes were done by Otto Kittsinger, who interviewed Roger who admitted he "routinely buys the many books by country music stars to see what they say about him."

He referred to himself as a "Jekyll and Hammerstein" and his music as "depressive jazz," then admitted that the phrase was "just something to say. Not that I'm a big jazz buff; I like jazz, I like the idea of jazz, free form thought association, free form. I like that, it makes a colorful sound, a peacock sound, a flourish of color—peacock pickin.'"

Roger said of his songwriting that it "seems to be a talent I've always had. I think that way. As a boy I tried to think about words and phrases and things and it just comes out. It seems like when I'm talking to people or people are talking to me I'm under a certain pressure and sometimes under that pressure I say things I'd never say if I were just sitting around by myself, but of course you don't talk out loud when you're by yourself.

It's just part of my good humor and wit. I don't know; I have no explanation for it."

He continued that "I start with a catch phrase or an idea and then sometimes the bridge of the song will come first before I even know what the idea's about, other times the song is halfway through before I know what the song's about, and sometimes the story will change halfway through. I'll take the first line and I'll sing it, like running up to a wall, and just before I hit that wall the second line will come to me, by forcing myself to sing it. Eventually I find I've gotten the wall to move enough to show me the whole song."

"I thought 'Your Cheating Heart' was the ideal song, simplicity," said Roger. "I admired that and tried to follow that [although} I like complex rhythms." In answer to the question of what he wanted to be remembered for, he replied, "I just want to be remembered for what I did, a writer who tried to be creative and tried to further his music by experimenting. I always took a great deal of pride in being original. When somebody said 'My God, where did that come from?' that was the big payoff to me," before adding, "I figure when I'm too old to be Roger Miller, I can be in television."[11]

A phone interview with Roger by Rick Nelson of the Tacoma *News Tribune* before Roger performed with Mel Tillis at the Opera House there noted that Roger "answered every question fully but sounded like he could doze off at any minute."

He noted that TNN was talking with him about hosting a show. "They're talkin' to me about doing a series of shows," said Roger. "I'm ready to do about anything. I'm usually doing something new each year, so maybe I'm ready for that. I've got no regrets. My life has been a great adventure. The singing and songwriting has been great, and the Broadway thing sort of topped it off."

Talking about his act Roger said, "It's just a hell of a show. I do old songs, talk about new songs. I do my show. It's just Roger Miller, whatever that is, and I do it good. I play my guitar. I play my fiddle. I talk. I'm busy with the audience. It's a lot of entertainment. I've never seen my show, but I understand it's great." Roger concluded that "It's easier to open. You go home early."[12]

"My Dad at that period of his life was pretty cantankerous, wanted to be alone, isolated and spend all of his time with his little kids," said Dean. "If you talked to any of his agents at the time the big joke was that he was the only artist they had that did not want work."

"Stan Moress was telling him, 'You know, Roger, you ought to start writing with these young, hot writers—they're really good. And that's how you get on records, you write with new artists' and my Dad said 'Did Picasso co-paint? No!' He was actually mad, he wasn't being funny. He was saying 'Leave me alone, I don't want to do that.' My Dad didn't really like to sit down and co-write with another person; he did it with Dwight Yoakam and he did it a few times for some reason but he always said 'I wanted to write by myself.'"[13]

Roger noted that "I lost interest in recording several years ago, and I just haven't hardly got it back. I've never done a video. I never have been offered one....it takes a lot out of you to concentrate on recording all the time. That's a lot of pressure to compete and try to stay Number One."[14] Although Roger said that to a number of people, it was just a bluff. Actually, he was extremely frustrated that he no longer had hit records on the radio, that there was no consumer demand for his albums and thus no incentive for a major record label to invest in him. It was hard for him to accept that, as an artist, his time had passed. Now it was Clint Black, Garth Brooks, Vince Gill, Alan Jackson and other hot young hunks who were on the airwaves. Roger was admired but seen as a relic of the past.

"I've probably had a strange career," said Roger. "I've sort of lived at my own pace. I'm always trying to grow in music, and music is still my passion. I've never concentrated in the last few years on just making a record that other people concentrate on. I'm either thinking about television or something else."

On his songwriting he said, "I ain't bad. I write Americana. I just try to appeal to everybody. I think I've got a sense of what people like. I never try to aim at the men or the women. I just try to aim so people will go 'Oh, I like that.'"

"Some people feel the rain, and some just get wet," said Roger. "I don't know. I say a lot of things. Some people are sensitive. Some people are not...God's house is the heart of a child...They used to ask me things and I'd say something. I think children are closer to God than we are.

They just came from Him. Then there's old people and I guess in-between are watermelon feasts."

"I'm always interested in kids," continued Roger. "Kids, looking at life, trying to be somebody and making it. I'm into that a lot. I'm into kids getting second chances. We all screw up the first time...I've done a lot of stupid things in my life. Luckily some of them didn't get out. I've never hurt anybody, though."

In answer to the question, "Why not write a book?" Roger answered, "I never felt like the last chapter. I've always felt like I'm working on another chapter. I've been approached by it, but I don't know, I'm in everybody else's book."[15]

Someone should have taken Roger Miller into a studio, turned on the tape machine, and let him make up songs, tell stories and sing whatever crossed his mind, like producer Rick Rubin did with Johnny Cash. It would have captured the essence of Roger Miller, revealed him as a great wit and great songwriter, made him commercially successful and been a valuable historic document of one of the most important songwriters and performers in American music. The great American public would have truly appreciated Roger Miller if that had happened. But no one did that.

Chapter 30
Old Friends

In 1989 Roger and his band went to Japan for a show. Traveling with Roger was his wife, Mary, and mother, Laudene.

"On that trip, they consistently wanted your passport," said Mary, "so we'd get to the head of the line and someone would say, 'Can I see your passport?' and Laudene would start going through her purse.'Oh, yeah,' she'd say, 'I have it but it's just not accessible.' And each time she pulled out a pair of pink pajamas and we'd ask her, 'What are you doing with those? Why didn't you pack your pajamas?' And she'd say, 'Well, what if my bag doesn't come?' It just panicked her to think what would happen so she kept those pink pajamas in her purse for a good month while we were gone."[1]

In November, 1989, Roger came to Nashville to perform with the Nashville Symphony. The show, held at the Tennessee Performing Arts Center before a crowd of about 1,400, saw Miller sing "In the Summertime," "England Swings," "I'm a Fool for You," "Dang Me," "Husbands and Wives," "You Can't Roller Skate in a Buffalo Herd" and "Billy Bayou" as well as several songs from the *Big River* musical, "Muddy Water," "Hand for the Hog," "Arkansas" and "World's Apart." He played fiddle on "Moanin' Low," "Faded Love" and "Devil's Dream" and did a song he wrote that would have been a classic if it had ever been released: "If You Won't Be My Number One, Then Number Two on You."

Prior to Roger's appearance, the Symphony played selections from Irving Berlin, Bedrich Smetana and Leonard Bernstein. Roger was backed by Marty Stuart on guitar, Buddy Skipworth on piano, Larry Marr on bass, drummer Joe Daugherty and Mary, who sang backup.

Reviewer Henry Arnold noted that "In spite of his 'good ol' boy' demeanor, Miller's music is a sophisticated blend of country and pop, with a hearty sprinkling of jazz and blues. At the same time, some of his songs have such a ring of folk music to them, you might think he had learned them at his grandmother's knee."[2]

Reviewer Tommy Goldsmith noted that early in the evening Roger announced, "My name is Roger Miller, one of the greatest songwriters that ever lived. I've written so many hits it's hard to keep up." The reviewer noted that "These boasts were delivered with such innocent pride that they were accepted with great good humor. Miller's just a funny guy, that's all, and he's all the funnier because he so clearly thinks he's so funny—he follows all his own bits with infectious laughter."

During this period, Roger and Jerry Kennedy talked about getting together again to record. They planned to do "If You Won't Be My Number One, Then Number Two On You," but plans fell through, although Miller confessed "Other interests have taken me other directions in the past few years, but it's like dancing with the one that brung you—we want to make some records. I've been doing other things and I haven't paid close attention to my recording career."[3]

By this point, *Big River* was touring all over the world; in addition to the United States, it was a hit in Australia, London and Tokyo.

In his personal life, Roger was increasingly frustrated because he wasn't feeling well. It was something that he couldn't quite put his finger on. At a date in Colorado, he played an outdoor festival and could hardly walk up the stairs because his back hurt so bad. At the end of the show he was taken to the hospital in an ambulance. He was having trouble with his voice as well; it was getting increasingly difficult to sing.

At the end of 1989, Roger was interviewed on the phone by an old friend, Joe Allison, for the BMI archives. He said that, with writing songs, "I learned that you have to take a bigger bite, a stronger bite out of a subject than just saying it...I learned what temperature you had to write a song for it to make a difference. And so I started to take a bigger bite."

"I started really looking at myself and bouncing things off myself and learning that I could throw ideas in my own melting pot and it would kind of come out different," said Roger about his early days in Nashville. "And I had that incredible energy. I was at it night and day." Joe Allison pointed out that those were wild, crazy times and Roger said, "Oh, I was doing laps where there weren't tracks. I was excited and I knew that I was on to something. And it took me years to get settled down into it. But I knew what I was doing. It was going too fast. I was going too fast for me after a while."

Talking about writing the songs for *Big River*, Roger said, "I just really slaved over these songs and I found..I was writing on a different level and I found that I could do things in there that I didn't know I could do before. I've always been surprising myself ... I knew from the start—I said I'm going to write it my way and I believe I can put people music up there. I said I know about music—I know what it takes to stand in front of people and raise them out of their seats. And I said I think I can do that."

"It was pretty heady stuff," continued Roger. "I knew where I was, I knew what I was doing and I said, 'Lord, Lord.' Somebody in Nashville asked me what I was doing up there in New York writing a play. I said I'm coming from the floor. I said this is going to come from the floor. And I knew I was hitting the Big League and I was at all the rehearsals and we re-shaped the play and I got into actors and their motivations and things like that. And I just learned a whole lot."

Writing songs for a Broadway musical, Roger said, "I look for them. I walk around and scratch for them and I look for—I usually know what temperature of a song I want and I look for that and then when I get the hook on it I know I'm right. I got a little signal that tells me when I'm right. When I'm trying to put it with the book. I like to write—I learned another word in New York. I like to write ethereally ... I told Rocco I'd like to take reality and hit it a glancing blow ... That makes the music kind of move along with it like smoke."[4]

Dean Miller moved to Nashville in 1990 to pursue a career in songwriting. Soon after he moved, he met Shawn Camp, another aspiring songwriter, at the Bluebird and they began writing songs together. Shortly after their meeting, Roger, along with Cowboy Jack Clement, Don Everly and Brenda Lee were scheduled to go to Belmont University for a panel discussion for students. Roger, Mary and their two children stayed at the Vanderbilt Plaza and Shawn remembers going with Dean to their room and walking to the door of the bathroom where Roger, wearing a nice suit, was combing his hair. Seeing Dean and Shawn dressed in rather shabby clothes with bolo ties, Roger observed, "You boys dressed way up tonight, didn't you?"

On the way over to Belmont in the limo, Roger asked Shawn where he was from and when Shawn said "Arkansas," Roger launched immediately into the song "Arkansas" from *Big River*.

Later, Shawn landed a job playing guitar for Trisha Yearwood and when they played Albuquerque, Shawn rented a car and invited Dean to join him as he headed to California. But first they went to Santa Fe for dinner with Roger, Mary and the children.

At Roger's house "I was in such awe of him that all I could eat was a baked potato," said Camp, "and Roger gave me a lot of grief over that." After dinner, they passed the guitar around and sang some songs, told some stories and laughed. When Roger went outside to smoke a cigarette, Shawn went outside with him and, as they stood on the porch, Shawn asked Roger, "When are you going to come back to Nashville and make another record?" Shawn remembers that "it got really dark all of a sudden and Roger said, 'They don't care anything about what I do.' I said, 'Well, everybody I know cares because we love what you do.' But it was a strange sensation to see Roger be covered with instant darkness. I never knew that side of him until that moment."

Trisha Yearwood was opening for Garth Brooks in Calgary, Canada and Shawn and Dean were on the phone when Dean told him that Roger and the family were also in Calgary and encouraged him to call. Shawn did and invited them to the show. "They were all over that," said Shawn, "so I got them all passes and we hung out backstage and sat on amp cases while Garth played. Roger was just shocked at the whole scene; the huge crowd and Garth's extravaganza of a show."

Shawn told Roger he was trying to leave Trisha's band and Roger invited him "to come play with me." "I'm on for that," replied Shawn, "That's a deal. That was in August and I think he got sick in September and I never saw him again."[5]

In February, 1990, one of his songs, "Walkin' Talkin' Cryin' Barely Beating Broken Heart" was a hit for Highway 101. The song, written with Justin Tubb back in the early 1960s, reached number four on the country chart and Roger was featured in the video.

In 1990 Roger cancelled some dates because he had trouble singing. He thought it was nodes on his vocal cords—or maybe throat cancer. Actually, it was a tumor on his spine pushing into his throat. That's why he thought there was something wrong with his throat.

Roger would clear his throat but still couldn't sing; he complained about his voice but didn't know what was wrong. The problem continued to nag him.

During a tribute to Willie Nelson at the Pantages Theatre in Hollywood, Dwight Yoakam and Roger each sang a Willie song. Dwight told Roger how much he admired him as a writer and that he had an idea for a song, "It Only Hurts When I Cry" and Roger's "eyes lit up and he said, 'Now I like that.'" Dwight then asked if Roger would be interested in writing with him and Roger agreed, after telling Dwight that "I've never co-written with anybody," explaining that "there's been some people's names on some of my songs but I never actually co-wrote."

About a month later, in Dwight's house in L.A., the two got together "and just started swapping lines." They basically finished the song that day although they "talked on the phone one other time and just kind of batted back and forth," said Yoakam.

When asked what it was like to write a song with Roger Miller, Yoakam replied, "Staying up with his wit and how his mind worked and the speed of his mind would be like trying to ride a bicycle alongside a taxiing Lear jet and keeping up. It felt like that at times. Interestingly enough, we were literally trading line for line. He'd say "the only time I feel the pain," which started that melodic approach on that first line, and I'd answer him. That set the pattern for the rhyme scheme of the song and how we were going to play off each other...kind of posing comments, the juxtaposition. The irony being that the only time is all the time, right?"

On the recording, Roger sang harmony with Yoakam. The musicians union required that each person on a session needed to supply positive identification before the paperwork could be completed. The session leader had forgotten to ask Roger for his driver's license so when he came into the control room after singing, someone said, "Roger, we need to see your driver's license." Roger immediately replied, "Well, how fast was I singing, officer?"[7]

On December 21, 1991 "It Only Hurts When I Cry" entered the country chart and went to number seven.

In 1991 Roger appeared on the Statler Brothers TV show and was host of the "Country Music Spectacular Concert" in St. Petersburg, Florida in January. On the show were Alabama, the Judds, K.T. Oslin, Garth Brooks, Sawyer Brown and Restless Heart.

"I always fit in," said Roger in a phone interview about the show. "I'm never over the hill. I come from the flat country, so I can't go over the hill. I'm always on call to do something, whether it's a Broadway show or whatever. I always just try to rise to the occasion, so in this case, it's just one more occasion."

Roger continued, "I never get to see my shows because I'm always working. But I do everything but dance. I've got some jokes, some witticism. I guess I just come out and entertain."

Roger noted that "There's talk of me doing a one-man show on Broadway. And they also have an idea to do a show about my life, so that's in the works. I wouldn't want to do both of them, though. I wouldn't want to have a play about my life and then me going and doing my own one-man show because it's autobiographical anyway; my one man show is. But I don't know. My life is sort of TBA at this point. Everything is 'To Be Announced.'"

Talking about his early days of Nashville, Roger said, "I was just everywhere at once and just wanted to make a name for myself in this business. I guess opportunities were a little different then, so I came up through every path. I started out at the same time that Mel Tillis did, so we all just sort of plowed our way through."

Roger first met Willie Nelson at a club in Fort Worth. "We became friends there and talked about songwriting and hung out," remembered Roger. "And then later on he came to Nashville and I loaned him a car. And so we've been friends for about 35 years."

"I still approach this business like I did when I first started out," said Roger. "I like to amaze people with what I can do. I'll try to do anything and I thought, 'Well, maybe I can amaze them a little bit by acting in my own play.' And it came off well. I just like to do interesting things and be good at it. If I can't be good at it, I don't want to do it."

Roger had gone to see Dr. Robert Ossoff at Vanderbilt in October, 1991 and "was stunned to learn he had cancer." Roger reportedly confided to a friend "That doctor might as well have hit me in the head with a two-by-four when he told me I had a lump growing below my vocal cords and it was cancerous, I went numb."

Marty Stuart stopped by Roger's hotel room to visit with him and Mary and asked "How do you feel?" Roger replied, "I feel like a shotgun that's been in a corner for twenty years that hasn't gone off and it just went off today and the shotgun wonders what the hell's going on."[6]

Roger stayed in Nashville during his treatments at the end of 1991. In April, Roger taped a "Tribute To Minnie Pearl" for a television special. Bill Anderson knew of Roger's problems with cancer but thought it was in remission when they stopped in the hallway to talk. "Have you got a good doctor?" Anderson asked. "The best," said Roger, "Dr. Ossoff." After a short pause, Roger continued, "I think his first name is Frazier so it's no wonder his office is so cold with a name like Frazier Ossoff."[8]

Chapter 31
Leavin's Not the Only Way to Go

The last show that Roger Miller did was at the Renaissance Hotel in Nashville at the Country Music Association's SRO Road Convention for talent buyers, bookers and promoters in the Fall of 1991.

"Months before the show, Stan and I talked about how Roger really wanted to do something so all the buyers could see him in a variety of settings," said Tony Conway. "He could do a one man performance and a full band performance. They had an orchestra at the convention that year and Roger was set to be the headliner and play with the orchestra, play with his band and do some stuff by himself. It was like 'Here's all three ways that you can buy Roger Miller.'"[1]

Barry Coburn moved to Nashville in 1984 and was involved in the SRO organization. He remembered that Roger was "great and flippant, entertaining, just magic" that evening. Coburn managed Alan Jackson at that time and Alan won the award for "Best New Touring Act," which was the first big award he won. Since Jackson was on the road, Barry accepted the award "and gave a little speech on behalf of Alan and thanked everyone involved. When I finished, Roger stepped up to the microphone and said, 'Boy, that was a great speech! That's the sort of guy we need in the White House. Let's push him in that direction!' It was a thrill to hear him say that."[2]

"He did a great show—he was wearing a tux—and he was a class act, like Ray Price or Eddy Arnold," remembered Conway. "He was like the pinnacle of class and it was a packed ballroom. He was the host so he introduced the people who presented the awards but when it came time for the 'Agent of the Year' award instead of introducing a presenter he said, 'And now I'd like to present the Agent of the Year Award.' I wondered, 'Why is he doing that?' Then he said, 'My agent, Tony Conway' so I went up and he presented me with the award and that was really one of the highlights of my life."

After the show there was a reception in the suite at the top of the hotel where key buyers and promoters had a chance to meet Roger. Stan Moress and Mary were with Roger when Tony went backstage after the show and thanked him for presenting the award. Roger said, "Come here, we need to take a little walk" and that's when Roger told Tony, "I've got some news. You're not going to like it but we're going to have to cancel the next six month's worth of dates."

Tony was flabbergasted.

"I've been diagnosed with cancer and I've noticed my voice isn't right," said Roger.

"I couldn't tell tonight," said Tony.

"I'm going to have treatment," said Roger.

The small crew then went upstairs to the reception and nobody there knew they'd seen Roger Miller perform his last concert.

"All these people wanted to get their pictures taken with him," said Conway. "It was a great night for everybody—for Roger and for me and for all the buyers. But the next day I started cancelling the shows."

In Nashville Roger had lunch with Chet Atkins and Steve Wariner. At this point, he was going through cancer treatments and had trouble speaking; in fact it was mostly a whisper. Chet asked Roger how he was feeling and Roger answered, "Let me put it this way, Chet: I've taken 'Cattle Call' out of my show."[3]

"When I got involved with Roger I think that he was—I don't want to use the word 'depressed'—but he was down," remembered Conway. "I was a huge fan of Roger Miller and I thought he was such a great talent that he needed to get out there so people could see what he was all about. They needed to appreciate his sense of humor and songwriting. He was an icon to me and I've had that relationship with a few artists through the years. Once he trusted me, he followed my suggestions or leads and once I knew that he was doing what he said he was going to do then I felt the same about him."

"I never ever in all my years with Roger Miller had any problems with him at all," continued Conway. "He never cancelled shows and the buyers were always happy with everything. It was a good time in his career. I convinced him to try different things, which allowed him to work more and opened him up to a freedom to express himself."

"He was always a gentleman to me. If he told me he was going to do something, he'd do it; he was a class act from start to finish. It was really sad because I felt that at that point in his career he was making this big comeback and he was happy and was looking forward to doing shows. We had a lot of shows on the books that we had to cancel and then obviously we never re-scheduled them or continued the tour. But before that, it was a happy time for Roger Miller."[4]

When Roger was diagnosed with cancer, "I dropped my whole life basically that last year to help take care of my Dad," said Dean. "I had just moved to Nashville when my Dad got sick and I was trying to start something here but I just had to say 'forget it' and devote all my time to him."

"It was a tough time for us all but in our family you just pretended things weren't happening so I was the only one going 'Dude, maybe you shouldn't be smoking while this is going on.' He never smoked a lot but he would smoke two or three cigarettes a day and I distinctly remember him standing there with that raspy voice, clearing his throat at some event they had in downtown Nashville and smoking a cigarette and me thinking 'What in the hell?' On the other hand, at that point not smoking wasn't going to change anything."[5]

Roger and Mary Miller, with their two children, Taylor and Adam, and their nanny stayed in Nashville while Roger received treatments at Vanderbilt Hospital. They did not want to stay in a hotel room so they asked Stan Moress if they could stay at his house.

Stan had a 4,000 square foot, four bedroom house on Lynnwood Boulevard in the Belle Meade section of Nashville. The house was spacious so there was plenty of room to spread out. Stan would come home from the office around six or seven in the evening and the Millers and their nanny would be cooking dinner. "One time the kids bought rubber spiders and snakes," remembered Moress, "and the kids would put them in my cereal and I'd always act surprised and they would laugh."[6]

"Stan has always been like an uncle, he's always been like a family member," said Dean. "He has always been open and good hearted to our family. Stan always made everyone comfortable, like it's your house."[7]

Roger had chemo treatments and lost his hair but gained weight—he was rather puffed up. But despite the seriousness of what was happening with Roger, it was a fun time with lots of laughter. "We didn't go out a whole lot," said Moress. "We mostly stayed home and watched TV and decorated the house. People would come over to visit Roger. K.T. Oslin came over."

"Roger re-decorated my living room," continued Stan. "And he hung a gigantic mirror—about three hundred pounds—that fell down in the middle of the night. It could have killed one of those kids if it had fallen on them. And he said 'no air conditioning' so he closed up all the vents in his bedroom and the bathroom with cardboard. He wasn't feeling well and he just wanted to be comfortable."

Roger fought against death. He told Stan Moress "I just can't leave these babies!" "That was his biggest concern," said Stan. "Those two kids, Adam and Taylor with Mary."[8]

Dean remembers him saying, "I just have too much fun and there's too much more fun to have and I'm not willing to give it up yet. He always wanted the party to go on and on and on," said Dean. "He just wanted to have more fun. I think he was scared but I think he lost that fear as he lost that sense of reality because I can remember a lot of smiling and laughing even when he wasn't making sense. I don't remember him being in a lot of pain. He gained weight as opposed to losing weight."[9]

By June, the doctors had told Roger and Mary that the chemo treatments weren't working but Mary refused to accept that there was no hope, so she rented a tour bus like country stars travel in and arranged to go to California to see a faith healer. Roger, Mary, Taylor, Adam, the nanny, Stan and Herb Nanos and a bus driver all piled in for the trip across the country.

The cancer was spreading to Roger's brain by this time and "I don't know that he was fully able to grasp totally all that was going on," said Dean. "I think the sense of reality came and went by then."

"They had a driver and drove slowly but straight through to California," said Dean. "She was just trying to get him there in as peaceful a way as possible. They didn't want to fly him because there would be pressure on his brain. Also, he was in no condition to fly commercially with people around him—he was not well enough for that."[10]

"It was like the Beverly Hillbillies crossing the country," remembered Moress. "It was one of the craziest trips I've ever taken. As serious as it was with Roger's health, it was hysterically funny. I give Roger a lot of credit because he was still able to pull off a joke or two when it was obvious that he wasn't feeling well.

"Herb Nanos just howled most of the way there. I was on a health kick and I wouldn't eat any fast food so Roger made fun of me all the way. Actually, Roger, Mary and Herb made fun of me all the way to Los Angeles."

"I can remember Mary calling me one day when they had rented a place in Malibu on the beach," continued Moress. "She said, 'You won't believe what Roger just said.' As they came over the hill and saw the ocean, Roger said, 'Mary, they put in a pool!'"[11]

Mary had rented "a really beautiful house so he could have a beautiful, peaceful place to stay while we were doing these healing treatments but he deteriorated pretty rapidly once he got to California," said Dean. "My Mom didn't have a care giver or help for a long time. It was just me and Mom and those two little kids and the nanny. It was like herding cats with my Dad. Had to take care of him constantly—some days were better than others and some days were easier than others. After about two months there we had gotten desperate so she hired people to come in round the clock to be with him."[12]

During his final days Roger didn't really want to see people because he looked and felt so bad; in fact, he even had the mirrors taken out of his room so he couldn't see himself. Johnny Cash called and asked how he was doing; Roger replied, "My luck is running bad. I need a new liver and California refused to repeal the helmet law."[13]

By this time the cancer on his spine had spread to his brain.

Rocco Landesman stopped by to see him and "He didn't look like himself [but] was still making jokes. His head was swollen and it was hard to deal with. My wife and I knew it would be the last time we'd ever see him."[14]

Waylon Jennings came by while Roger was lying in bed with both eyes closed. When Waylon walked into the room he gasped; Roger opened one eye a bit and said, "You look like hell, Waylon. Go home." Waylon left.

Roger would not talk about his illness to Chuck Blore, even in the later stages. "We talked on the phone all the time," said Blore. "He just liked to talk, to entertain. He'd had chemo and lost all his hair and sometimes he was there and sometimes he wasn't. Mary told me that Roger didn't want me to see him like that. But we'd get on the phone and Roger would say, 'Come over Saturday.' I didn't ever go over there. Judy went all the time because she and Mary were great friends."

The night before he died, he came out on the balcony overlooking the Pacific Ocean to join Judy and Mary and said, "Mary, say hello to Nancy." Mary said, "Say hello to who?" "My angel, Nancy. Say hello to my angel." "Roger, nobody's there." "Mary, don't be rude. Say hello to Nancy."[15]

As his final days approached "you could see that he was rapidly declining," said Dean. "It was at night and I went to the store and by the time I came back he was in a coma so we rushed him to the hospital. He died later that morning, probably five or six hours later. But for days before he lost consciousness, he was not there."[16]

Roger Miller died on Sunday, October 25, 1992 in Century City Hospital in Los Angeles.

Epilogue

In 2004 the town of Erick, Oklahoma paid tribute to Roger by establishing a Roger Miller Museum and "Roger Miller Days." Each year, in late October—around the anniversary of Roger's death—the town puts on a street festival in honor of Roger. Former Roger Miller cohorts Marty Stuart, Shawn Camp and Bill Anderson have performed on the Saturday night concert at Erick High School. Dean Miller always performs, singing a mixture of his songs and his Dad's.

In July, 2003, a production of *Big River* was performed by the Roundabout Theater Company and Deaf West Theater at the American Airlines Theater in New York. It was remarkable that 18 years after the original production was staged in New York it continues to be staged; it is even more remarkable that the play was performed by deaf actors!

Rocco Landesman wrote an article, "Roger Miller: King of the Rhyme" in the *New York Times* for this occasion and noted that he first heard of Roger Miller when "Dang Me" came on his radio in 1964 and his first thoughts were "What the hell was that? Is this guy crazy?" The answer, Rocco said, came 20 years later when he worked with Roger on *Big River* and the answer "was, more or less, 'Yes.'"

Landesman recounted the challenges he faced in working with Roger, stating "Miller had written very little new work in 10 years and as I spent time with him it was easy to guess the reason. His notion of being straight was to drink, snort and smoke sequentially. A three minute song can be daunting when your attention span is 20 to 30 seconds. And even if the gift was still there, the confidence wasn't."

Landesman pointed out that most of Roger's best work "was not really 'country' (a term he despised—I never saw him with a cowboy hat), but what we might now recognize as an amalgam of country, jazz and rap. While he always wrote strong and simple melodies, lyrics would tumble pell-mell into seemingly spontaneous, unpredictable arrangements. Odd words would be suddenly inserted so a line wouldn't scan; rhymes could be four to a line or nonexistent."

Roger's "genius had always been to see everything on the bias, off-kilter, and in doing so, he made it new," observed Landesman.

"Peace of mind is not a term I would readily apply to a sensibility as restless and crooked as Roger Miller's," continued Landesman, "but in the five or so years between the success of 'Big River' and his death, he seemed to me to be taking more satisfaction from his life...his ever present hint of a smile began to convey some pleasure as well as the more usual sardonic bemusement."[1]

In 2010, the twenty-fifth anniversary of *Big River,* there was a production staged in Nashville at the Tennessee Performing Arts Center—the same place the traveling Broadway production was staged in 1988 and the former site of the Andrew Jackson Hotel, where Roger worked as a bellboy when he first arrived in Nashville.

Big River was presented in the small theater with the audience up close. The songs really stood out in this intimate setting. The show was so popular that several extra performances were scheduled.

Roger Miller is still held in awe in Nashville. Dean Miller remembers that he really became aware of the importance of his father when he moved to Nashville and found him to be a revered figure in the songwriting and music community.

"When I moved to Nashville, having an association with Roger was like a secret handshake," said former band member Randy Hart. "It doesn't take much to have somebody who knew Roger start to roll with stories. It's like you strike a match when you mention his name and somebody will light up. It's like a passport to incredible stories because everybody has their own recollections, their own magical moments."

"When Roger was around people, he had to be performing," remembered Randy Hart. "Roger did not feel comfortable sitting back and being part of a group. He had to perform because that was who he was. He was Roger, so naturally he was going to be the center of attention."[2]

In Nashville there is a constant schedule of showcases by young performers hoping to get signed to a label or booked into shows but, as Barry Coburn noted, "For most of those acts, there's nothing that makes you feel good; many of them never make eye contact with the audience. When Roger Miller walked out on stage there was a spark immediately.

He really had a good time and he was a great, amiable guy who genuinely liked people. It was wonderful. I frequently look at young entertainers now and there is no entertainment value. There's a deer-in-the-headlights look about them and I often wish that people had the opportunity to see great entertainers like Roger Miller, who could really connect. It should be magic and that's what Roger had. He had that magic."[3]

Mary Miller moved to Nashville with their two children, Taylor and Adam, and continues to promote Roger's legacy. She is active in perpetuating Roger's career and has written a musical based on Roger's life. Roger's mother, Laudene, died on October 10, 2001 and is buried in Fort Worth beside Jean Miller and C.B. Burdine. Roger's daughter, Rhonda, died on October 22, 2008 in Duncan, Oklahoma.

Amongst the songwriting community, one song—"The Last Word in Lonesome Is Me"—is proof of Roger Miller's genius. Songwriters continue to be amazed that they had all seen the word "lonesome" but never noticed that the last word was "me." It says a lot when a song written in 1965 is still held in awe and amazement by songwriters old and new. And it says a lot that Roger Miller remains a songwriter for songwriters.

Songwriter Bobby Braddock came close to capturing Roger's genius one day as he sat in his car outside a Kroger Grocery store and realized "The last word in Kroger is Roger."[4]

Roger would have loved that.

Appendix

Sources

Chapter 1: The Millers and the Holts

1. Martha Holt Nichols. Personal interview, March 12, 2012
2. Ibid
3. Wendall Miller. Personal interview, March 8, 2007
4. Martha Holt Nichols interview
5. Ibid
6. Style, Lyle E. "Sheb Wooley" in *Ain't Got No Cigarettes: Memories of Music Legend Roger Miller.* Great Plains, Publications, 2005. p. 118
7. Pat Henry. Personal interview March 8, 2007
8. Joy Brookshire. Personal interview, March 9, 2007
9. Hugh Prather, personal interview, March 9, 2007
10. Kittsinger, Otto. Liner notes on boxed set *King of the Road: The Genius of Roger Miller,* released August 22, 1995 on Mercury Nashville.
11. Mary Miller. Personal interview, February 8, 2008
12. Gail Davies. Personal interview, November 13, 2010
13. Roger Miller Museum display
14. Ibid

Chapter 2: Erick, Oklahoma

1. Eldon Hendrix. Personal interview March 8, 2007
2. Pat Henry interview
3. Eldon Hendrix interview
4. Joy Brookshire interview
5. Style, Lyle E., "Bill Mack," p. 272
6. Phyllis Forsythe. Personal interview, January 3, 2011.
7. James Crow. Personal interview, December 8, 2010.
8. Lago, Don. "King of the Road," The Ol' Pioneer, The biannual magazine of the *Grand Canyon Historical Society.* Fall, 2008; Volume 20; Number 2, pp 4-6.
9. Bud Keathley. Personal interview, March 9, 2007
10. Ibid

Sources

Chapter 3: Private John Q.

1. Mary Miller interview
2. Phyllis Forsythe interview
3. Diekman, Diane. *Live Fast Love Hard: The Faron Young Story*. Urbana: University of Illinois Press, 2007 pp 26-32
4. Ralph Emery interview with Roger Miller February 25, 1972
5. Anderson, Bill. *Whisperin' Bill: An Autobiography*. Atlanta: Longstreet Press, 1989 p. 74.
6. Atkins, Chet and Bill Neely. *Country Gentleman*. Chicago, Henry Regnery Co, 1974 pp 146-147.
7. Atkins, Chet. *Me and My Guitars*. Milwaukee: Hal Leonard, 2001, 2003 p 21.
8. Kittsinger liner notes.

Chapter 4: Them Was the Good Old Days

1. Escott, Colin. "Don Pierce: Inside Starday Records" in *Journal of Country Music* Vol 17, No. 1.
2. Ibid.
3. Mel Tillis, personal interview February 23, 2011.
4. Ibid
5. Ralph Emery, interview with Roger Miller, June, 1987.

Chapter 5: Invitation to the Blues

1. Joy Brookshire interview
2. James Crow interview
3. Ray Price. Personal interviews August 4, 2006 and October 2, 2009.
4. Anderson, Bill in *Whisperin' Bill,* p. 75-76
5. Buddy Killen. Personal interview, October 16, 1976, published in *Record World* Magazine, p. 8.
6. "Tree Signs Miller." *Music Reporter*, May 19, 1958, p. 11.
7. James Crow interview
8. Harold Bradley. Personal interview, February 1, 2008.
9. Pugh, Ronnie. *Ernest Tubb: The Texas Troubadour*. Durham: Duke University Press, 1996. P. 230-231
10. Pugh, p. 231

Sources

11. "Country Clippin's" in The *Music Reporter*, November 10, 1958, p. 15
12. Phyllis Forsythe interview
13. Buddy Killen interview
14. Bill Anderson. Personal interview December 27, 2010.
15. Jimmy Key. Personal interview, February 27, 2010.
16. Diekman, p. 62-63.

Chapter 6: When Two Worlds Collide

1. Diekman p. 63
2. Diekman p. 65
3. Style, Lyle E. "Buddy Killen," pp 84-85
4. John D. Loudermilk. Personal interview March 21, 2012
5. George Hamilton IV. Personal interview October 18, 2010.
6. Bill Anderson interview
7. Bob Moore. Personal interview, February 17, 2010.
8. Bobby Bare. Personal interview, March 21, 2012

Chapter 7: A House is Not a Home

1. Jan Howard. Personal interview March 21, 2012
2. Jerry Kennedy. Personal interview, February 25, 2009
3. Kittsinger liner notes
4. Fourth Circuit Court: Davidson County, TN:
   BILL FOR SEPARATE MAINTENANCE, November 20, 1961.
5. Bobby Bare interview
6. Bayron Binkley. Personal interview May 19, 2012
7. Ibid
8. Ibid
9. Ray Stevens, personal conversation, March 26, 2011
10. Ralph Emery interview, June, 1987
11. Ibid
12. Bayron Binkley interview

Sources

Chapter 8: Smash

1. Charlie Dick, personal interview October 19, 2010.
2. Nelson, Rick, "King of the Road Roger Miller a homebody these days." Tacoma, WA *News-Tribune*. Jan 26, 1989.
3. Charlie Dick interview
4. Phyllis Forsythe interview
5. Doug Gilmore, personal interview, February 11, 2010.
6. Turner, Steve. *The Man Called Cash: The Life, Love, and faith of an American Legend.* Nashville: W Publishing Group, 2004, p. 103.
7. May, Carl. "1st Hootenanny Gets Wild Cheers." *Nashville Tennessean,* September 11, 1963 and "1st Hootenanny," "Reserve Tuesday for Hootenanny" and "Hootennay Here Tonight")
8. Fourth Circuit and Probate Courts: Davidson County, TN: Barbara Miller filed against Roger Miller. BILL FOR SEPARATE MAINTENANCE, September 27, 1963.
9. Jerry Kennedy interview, February 25, 2009
10. Ralph Emery. Personal interview, August 28, 2010
11. Bobby Bare interview
12. Charlie Fach, personal interview, October 15, 2009.
13. "Wright Agency Signs RCA Victor's Miller," *Music Reporter,* October 5, 1963, p. 15.
14. Broven, John. *Record Makers and Breakers: Voices of the Independent Rock'n'Roll Pioneers.* Urbana and Chicago: University of Illinois Press, 2009, p. 290.
15. Shelby Singleton. Personal interview, February 16, 2009
16. "Dateline Music City," *Music Reporter,* November 16, 1963, p. 4.
17. Phyllis Forsythe interview

Chapter 9: Dang Me

1. "Country Clippings, *Music Reporter* January 11, 1964, p. 23.
2. Jerry Kennedy interview
3. Bob Moore. Person interview, February 17, 2010
4. Ralph Emery interview June, 1987.
5. Bobby Bare interview
6. Harold Bradley interview

Sources

7. Charlie Fach interview
8. James Best, email to author
9. Phyllis Forsythe interview
10. Fong-Torres, Ben. *The Hits Just Keep On Coming*:
    The History of Top 40 Radio. San Francisco:
    Miller Freeman Books, 1998. P. 47
11. Chuck Blore. Personal interview, June 1, 2010
12. "Country Music Spotlight." Dang Me singles review, *Billboard*,
    May 16, 1964.
13. Charlie Fach interview
14. Billy Strange. Personal interview, August 11, 2011
15. Lou Dennis. Personal interview, March 22, 2010
16. Pop Singles: "Breakout Singles": Dang Me" (Seattle, Houston),
    Billboard, June 6, 1964.
17. Jan Howard interview
18. Bobby Bare interview
19. Don Williams. Personal interview June 2, 2009
20. "The 'Jimmy Dean Show' Back—In (Country) Style."
    Billboard, September 26, 1964, p. 3

Chapter 10: King of the Road

1. Kittsinger liner notes
2. Bob Moore interview
3. "Record Review," *Billboard*, November 21, 1964.
4. "Pop Single Review: King of the Road," *Billboard*, January 23, 1965.
5. Album Review: *The Return of Roger Miller*, *Billboard*,
   February 13, 1965.
6. Portis, Charles, "That New Sound From Nashville"
   Saturday Evening Post, February 12, 1965.
7. Doug Gilmore. Personal interview, February 11, 2010
8. Chuck Blore interview,
9. Don Williams interview
10. Ibid

Sources

Chapter 11: The Grammys

1. O'Donnell, Red, "Miller Gets 5 Grammy Awards,"
   Nashville Banner, April 14, 1965.
2. Daughtrey, Larry. King of Grammys Says Wit Not All."
   Nashville Tennessean, April 15, 1965.
3. Biro, Nick. "CMA's Show Draws Plaudits,"
   Billboard, June 19, 1965, p. 1.
4. Biro, Nick, "CMA to Stage Country Show in Chicago,"
   Billboard, May 15, 1965, p. 4.
5. Doug Gilmore interview

Chapter 12: England Swings

1. "WCMS Files a Suit Against Roger Miller," *Billboard*, July 10, 1965.
2. Charlie Dick interview
3. Doug Gilmore interview
4. "Miller Wins MOA Awards," *Billboard*, September 11, 1965.
5. "Miller Date Out," *Billboard*, October 2, 1965.
6. Whisenhunt, Elton. "Miller & Reeves Country Kings;
   Craig Man of Year," *Billboard*, October 23, 1965.
7. Ackerman, Paul. "Great Writer Tradition Lives in C&W Music:
   Roger Miller," in "The World of Country Music,"
   Billboard, October 30, 1965.
8. Whisenhunt, Elton, "Nash. NARAS Starts Campaign,"
   Billboard, October 9, 1965.
9. New Pop LPs: Welcome to the World of Pop, "Roger Miller
   —an updated Stan Freeberg." *NME*, June 12, 1965, p. 16.
10. Review: "Hits Most Likely," May 27, 1965, *Record Retailer* p. 3.
11. Blind Date: Dave Clark: Roger Miller: "Can't Stop Loving You,"
    Melody Maker, August 7, 1965 (Stateside).
12. "Album Reviews: "The Return of Roger Miller: *Record Retailer*,
    September 9, 1965, p. 12..
13. Singles Reviews: Hit! "Kansas City Star/One Dyin' and a-Buryin'",
    Record Retailer, September 30, 1965, p. 2.
14. Blind Date: Brian Epstein: Roger Miller: "Kansas City Star,"
    Melody Maker, October 2, 1965.

Sources

15. Singles Review: HIT! "England" b/w "The Good Old Days,"
    Record Retailer, December 2, 1965.
16. Blind Date: George Harrison. Roger Miller: "England Swings,"
    Melody Maker, p. 9.
17. Escott, Colin. "Don Pierce: Inside Starday Records" in
    Journal of Country Music Vol 17, No. 1.

Chapter 13: Husbands and Wives

1. Emery, Ralph, video tape of TV show, March 8, 1966.
2. Jerry Kennedy interview
3. Harold Bradley interview
4. "Smash Giving Smash Push to Miller TV-er,"
   Billboard, January 15, 1966.
5. "C&W History Made At Astrodome Show,"
   Billboard, January 22, 1966.
6. Single Review. Hit!, *Billboard*, March 3, 1966, p. 2.
7. Hedda Hopper's Syndicated Column, January 9, 1965.
8. Curly Putnam. Personal interview, December 21, 2010
9. Ralph Emery, video of TV show, March 8, 1966.
10. "CARTridge Takes Play At Biggest NARM Parley," and "Mercury
    Department to Handle Affiliates."*Billboard*, March 19, 1966
11. "Shows Mark Country Fete on W. Coast," *Billboard*, February 26,
    1966 and "Owens, Miller Top Calif. Honors,"
    Billboard, March 12, 1966

Chapter 14: It Happened Just That Way

1. O'Neil, Thomas. *The Grammys: For the Record*. New York:
   Penguin, 1993, p. 99.
2. Ibid, p. 101.
3. Welch, Pat. "Grammy King Keeps Throne,"
   Nashville Tennessean, March 16, 1966.
4. Schipper, Henry. *Broken Record: The Inside Story of the Grammy
   Awards*. New York: Birch Lane, 1992 and O'Neil, Thomas.
   The Grammys: For the Record. New York: Penguin, 1993.
5. "Miller Sings in Rainstorm," *Billboard*, May 13, 1966, p. 85.

Sources

6. Hall, Claude. "Grammy Awards TVer: Million $ Worth of Talent,"
   Billboard, May 28, 1966, p. 26; "Miller Set for Grammy Special,"
   Billboard, April 9, 1966, p. 10; and "Grammy TV'er Backing Urged,"
   Billboard, May 14, 1966, p. 4.
7. Marijohn Wilkins and Roger Schutt, personal conversations c. 1998.
8. "Top Singles of the Week" "My Uncle Used To Love Me,"
   Variety, September 7, 1966, p. 42.
9. "NARAS' Nashville Unit Gets 200 New Members,"
   Billboard, September 17, 1966, p. 6; "NARAS Revamps Grammy
   Awards Format; Fewer Prizes, Wider Scope." *Variety*, September 21,
   1966, p. 53; and "NARAS Puts Grammy Wheels in Motion With
   'Eligibility' Forms." *Billboard*, January 29, 1966, p. 4.
10. Harris, Frank. "The Many Successes of Roger Miller."
   Country Music Life, November, 1965, pp 10-13, 29.

Chapter 15: "The Roger Miller Show"

1. "ABC Sweeps 1st All-Competitive Evening (Mon.) in O'night
   Ratings; CBS Wins Couple, NBC Goes Blank,"
   Variety, September 14, 1966.
2. "ABC Wins Second Monday Arbitrons (Trendex Sez NBC,"
   Variety, September 21, 1966, p. 23.
3. Sobel, Robert. "Miller Is Off and Singing In New Weekly TV Show,"
   Billboard, September 24, 1966, p. 26. Robert Sobel.)
4. "TV's New Top 40," Variety, October 12, 1966.
5. "Popsters Swamped the WSM Scene," *Billboard*, November 5,1966,
   p. 6; "Minnie Pearl *Billboard*'s Country Man of Year,"
   Billboard, October 29, 1966, p. 1; and Wood, Herb. "4,500 Are
   Pouring Into WSM's Giant Spread," *Billboard*, October 22, 1966, p. 1.
6. "CMA Banquet Hails New Hall of Famers,"
   Billboard, November 5, 1966, p. 60.
7. "Miller, Tree Top BMI Awards," *Billboard*, October 22, 1966, p. 3.
8. O'Donnell, "Round the Clock: It Was Just Him,"
   Nashville Banner, October 21, 1966.
9. Jan Howard interview
10. Fox, William Price, Jr. "Dang Him!: Roger Miller can't roller skate in
   a buffalo herd, but he swings like a pendulum do," *TV Guide*,
   November 12, 1966.

Sources

11. Style, "Roy Clark," p. 37
12. Kittsinger liner notes
13. Jimmy Dean. Personal interview, September 28, 2009

Chapter 16: Me and Bobby McGee

1. Doug Gilmore interview
2. Ibid
3. "King of the Road's' Motel Idea: 1st Unit in National Chain Planned Here." *Nashville Banner,* September 9, 1968
4. George Lindsay. Personal conversation, March 27, 2010
5. Mel Tillis. Personal interview, February 23,2011
6. Doug Gilmore interview
7. Fred Foster. Personal interview, May 22, 2009
8. Kris Kristofferson. Personal interview, June 28, 2006
9. Style, "Kris Kristofferson," p. 135.
10. Ralph Emery, interview of Roger Miller, June, 1987

Chapter 17: Free at Last

1. Billy Swan. Personal interview, September 3, 2010
2. Roger Miller & Bill Anderson interview in *Country Song Round-up*, 14-17, 46.
3. "King of Road Unit Marks First Year." *Nashville Banner*, March 5, 1971.
4. Hance, Bill. "Roger Miller: Off Pills, Heads King of the Road." *Nashville Banner*, N.D., 1971

Chapter 18: I've Been a Long Times Leaving (But I'll Be a Long Time Gone)

1. Emery interview of Roger Miller, June, 1987
2. Ibid
3. Shari Miller Standridge. Personal interview, January 6, 2011
4. Phyllis Forsythe interview
5. James Crow interview
6. Stewart, Elmer. "King of Road Group Acquires 2 Big Properties."

Sources

Nashville Banner, January 13, 1972.
7. Dean Miller. Personal interview, March 10, 2010
8. Ibid
9. Cooper, Peter. "Milsap's Story: How hotel owner helped Ronnie Milsap reinvent himself in 1972. *Nashville Tennessean*, December 26, 2011, Section D, pp 1,3
10. Redshaw, David. "Roger Miller," *New Music Express,* June 16, 1973, p. 30.

Chapter 19: Australia and New Zealand

1. Chapman, Marshall. Personal interview, June 28, 2010
2. Barry Coburn. Personal interview, June 1, 2012
3. Chapman interview
4. Coburn interview
5. Chapman interview
6. Coburn interview
7. Coburn interview
8. Chapman interview

Chapter 20: Heartbreak Hotel

1. Gail Davies. Personal interview, November 13, 2010
2. Micheal Smotherman. Personal interview, April 22, 2010
3. Cason, Albert. "King of the Road' Inn Held In Default." *Nashville Tennessean*, January 15, 1975.
4. Jerry Kennedy interview
5. Gail Davies interview

Chapter 21: Mary

1. Gail Davies interview
2. Dean Miller, interview
3. Gail Davies, interview
4. Mary Miller, interview
5. Dean Miller, interview
6. Micheal Smotherman, interview

Sources

7. Chuck Blore interview
8. Micheal Smotherman interview
9. Billy Burnett. Personal interview, April 7, 2010
10. Ibid
11. Micheal Smotherman, interview
12. Ibid
13. Billy Burnett, interview
14. Micheal Smotherman, interview
15. Billy Burnett, interview
16. Mary Miller, interview

Chapter 22: Santa Fe

1. Randy Hart. Personal interview, July 1, 2010
2. Mary Miller interview
3. Ibid
4. Rhodes, Don, "Ramblin Rhodes," January 8, 1989.
5. Mary Miller interview
6. Ibid
7. Martha Holt Nichols interview
8. Mary Miller interview
9. Chuck Blore interview

Chapter 23: Open Up Your Heart

1. Eipper, Laura. "Miller's 'First' Not His Best." *Nashville Tennessean*, April 5, 1978.
2. Carter, Walter. Roger Miller Roadside 'Exit'" *Nashville Tennessean*, no date, 1978.
3. Eipper, "Miller's 'First' Not.."
4. Smotherman interview
5. O'Donnell, Red. "Miller To Sing On Atkins Special." *Nashville Banner*, May 13, 1980.
6. Randy Hart interview
7. Style, "Willie Nelson," p. 209
8. Chuck Blore interview
9. Stan Moress. Personal interview, February 26, 2010

Sources

10. Tony Conway. Personal interview, June 29, 2010
11. Rocco Landesman. Personal interview, May 4, 2010
12. Ibid

Chapter 24: On the Road Again

1. Mary Miller interview
2. Stan Moress interview
3. Tony Conway interview
4. Randy Hart interview
5. Stan Moress interview
6. Mary Miller interview
7. Tony Conway interview
8. Stan Moress interview
9. Smith, Stacy Jenel. "Roger Miller 'Burned' In 'Quincy' Episode." *Nashville Tennessean*, Feb 6, 1983.
10. Nelson, Rick, "King of the Road Roger Miller a homebody these days." *Tacoma, WA News-Tribune*. Jan 26, 1989.
11. Randy Hart interview
12. Ibid

Chapter 25: Big River

1. Oermann, Robert. "Roger Miller Back, Sticks to Favorites," *Nashville Tennessean*, April 9, 1983.
2. Willard, Bill. "'Country card' Roger Miller is at Riviera," *N.P.*, December 2, 1983.
3. Rocco Landesman interview
4. Mary Miller interview
5. Micheal Smotherman interview
6. Rocco Landesman interview
7. Ibid
8. Ibid
9. Chuck Blore interview
10. Ibid
11. Mary Miller interview
12. Rocco Landesman interview

Sources

13. Morse, Steve. "King of the Road Tunes up for the stage,"
    Boston Globe, February 12, 1984.
14. Rocco Landesman interview
15. Ibid
16. Oermann, Robert K. "Roger Miller Returns 'Home' On Crest of
    'Big River' Wave." *Nashville Tennessean*, June 23, 1985.
17. Rocco Landesman interview
18. Phyllis Forsythe
19. Shari Miller Standridge interview

Chapter 26: Dean Miller

1. Dean Miller interview

Chapter 27: You Oughta Be Here With Me

1. Rocco Landesman interview
2. Stearns, David Patrick, "Dang me! Roger Miller is on Broadway"
   USA Today, March, 1985.
3. Rocco Landesman interview
4. Randy Hart interview
5. Rocco Landesman interview
6. Ibid
7. "Big River Wins Big at Lean Tony Awards" From Wire Reports.
   Nashville Tennessean, June 3, 1985.
8. Rocco Landesman interview
9. Jimmy Bowen. Personal interview, October 18, 2010
10. Ibid
11. Oermann, Robert K. and Clara Hieronymus, "Music Row Elite's
    Party Applauds Roger Miller's 'Big River' Triumph"
    Nashville Tennessean, September 5, 1985.
12. McCall, Michael. "An emotional Carl Perkins honored."
    Nashville Banner October 4, 1985.
13. McCall, Michael. Roger Miller won't be 'leaf'-ing Tree."
    Nashville Banner, October 25, 1985

Sources

Chapter 28: How Blessd We Are

1. Jimmy Bowen interview
2. Micheal Smotherman interview
3. Ralph Emery interview June, 1987.
4. Ibid
5. *Los Angeles Times* article, *N.D.*; in vertical file at Country Music Foundation.
6. Tony Conway interview
7. Nelson, Rick. "King of the Road Roger Miller a homebody these days. by Rick Nelson. *Tacoma, WA News-Tribune*, January 26, 1989.

Chapter 29: Walkin' in the Sunshine

1. Hieronymus, Clara. "TPAC audience embraces Roger Miller, 'Big River'". *Nashville Tennessean*. January 6, 1988.
2. Kittsinger liner notes
3. McCall, Michael. "Miller is a symbol of city, its music." *Nashville Banner*, June 6, 1988
4. Ringsak, Russ. "Small Diversions in the Southwest." www.publicradio.org/columns/prairiehome. May 1, 2003.
5. Raphael, Mickey. Personal conversation, May 23, 2011.
6. Anderson, *I Hope You're Living As High on the Hog...*, p. 146.
7. Ray Stevens. Personal conversation
8. Oermann, Robert K. "Roger Miller special could be a series." *Nashville Tennessean*, October 4, 1988.
9. Rocco Landesman interview
10. Claypool, Bob. "A disciplined Roger Miller became king of the 'River'" *Houston Post*, April 24, 1988.
11. Kittsinger liner notes
12. Nelson, Rick. "King of the Road Roger Miller a homebody these days. by Rick Nelson. *Tacoma, WA News-Tribune*, January 26, 1989.
13. Dean Miller interview
14. Rhodes, "Ramblin Rhodes."
15. Ibid

Sources

Chapter 30: Old Friends

1. Mary Miller interview
2. Arnold, Henry." "'King of the Road' Roger Miller rules symphony stage." *Nashville Banner*, November 4, 1989.
3. Goldsmith, Thomas. "Roger Miller rolls on 'Big River' tide." *Nashville Tennessean*, October 29, 1989.
4. Allison, Joe. Interview with Roger Miller on December 7, 1989.
5. Shawn Camp. Personal interview, April 7, 2010
6. Style, "Marty Stuart," p. 96
7. Style, "Dwight Yoakam," p. 295
8. Anderson, Bill. *I Hope You're Living As High On the Hog as the Pig You Turned Out To Be*. Hermitage, TN: *TWI, Inc*, 1994, p. 152.

Chapter 31: Leavin's Not the Only Way to Go

1. Tony Conway interview
2. Barry Coburn interview
3. Style, "Steve Wariner," p. 278
4. Tony Conway interview
5. Dean Miller interview
6. Stan Moress interview
7. Dean Miller interview
8. Stan Moress interview
9. Dean Miller interview
10. Ibid
11. Stan Moress interview
12. Dean Miller interview
13. Style, Lyle, "Jim Owen," p. 53
14. Rocco Landesman interview
15. Chuck Blore interview
16. Dean Miller interview

Epilogue

1. Landesman, Rocco. "Roger Miller; King of the Rhyme." New York Times, Arts & Leisure," Sunday, July 20, 2003. Section 2, pp 1, 21)
2. Randy Hart interview
3. Barry Coburn interview
4. Bobby Braddock. Personal interview, October 19, 2010

Bibliography

"A musical Sunday." *Nashville Banner*, October 11, 1985 (picture & cutline)

"A Solid Beginning For CMA Building," *Billboard*, January 1, 1966.

"ABC Sweeps 1st All-Competitive Evening (Mon.) in O'night Ratings; CBS Wins Couple, NBC Goes Blank," *Variety*, September 14, 1966.

"ABC Wins Second Monday Arbitrons (Trendex Sez NBC)," *Variety*, September 21, 1966, p. 23.

Ackerman, Paul. "Great Writer Tradition Lives in C&W Music: Roger Miller" in "The World of Country Music, *Billboard*, October 30, 1965.

Advertisement. "RCA Victor" that lists Roger Miller as an artist, *Music Reporter*, November 1, 1963.

Albert, George and Frank Hoffmann. The *Cash Box* Country Singles Charts, 1958-1982. Metuchen, N.J.: *The Scarecrow Press*, 1984.

Album Review. "Roger and Out." *New Music Express*, June 12, 1965.

Album Review: "Hits Most Likely." *Record Retailer*, May 27, 1965.

Album Review: The Return of Roger Miller, *Billboard*, February 13, 1965.

Album Review. "The Return of Roger Miller," *Record Retailer*, September 9, 1965.

Album Review. "The Return of Roger Miller," *Billboard*, February 13, 1965.

Album Review. "Roger and Out." *NME*, June 12, 1965.Allen, Bob. George Jones: *The Life and Times of A Honky Tonk Legend*. New York: A *Birch Lane Press* Book published by *Carol Publishing Group*, 1984, 1994.

Anderson, Bill. *I Hope You're Living As High On the Hog as the Pig You Turned Out To Be*. Hermitage, TN: TWI, Inc, 1994

Anderson, Bill. *Whisperin' Bill: An Autobiography: A Life of Music, Love, Tragedy and Triumph*. Atlanta: *Longstreet Press*, 1989.

"Anderson, Miller, Owens BMI Awards Winners." *Nashville Tennessean*, October 22, 1966.

Anderson, Omer. "Army Drops Bomb on 'Protests," *Billboard*, January 15, 1966.

Arnold, Henry." "'King of the Road' Roger Miller rules symphony stage." *Nashville Banner*, November 4, 1989.

Atkins, Chet with Bill Neely. *Country Gentleman*. Chicago: Henry Regnery Company, 1974.

Ayres, Tom. "Ray Price Remembers Hank Williams: Or, How Old Hungry Gave Ray Price His Start." *Country Music*. Volume Five, Number Twelve, September, 1977. pp 41-44, 56.

Bailey, Jerry. Roger Miller Will Host TV Documentary Series." *Nashville Tennessean*, June 20, 1973.

Bibliography

"Big River Wins Big at Lean Tony Awards" From Wire Reports. *Nashville Tennessean*, June 3, 1985.

Blind Date: Brian Epstein: Roger Miller: "Kansas City Star," *Melody Maker*, October 2, 1965.

Blind Date: Dave Clark. Roger Miller: "Can't Stop Loving You." *Melody Maker*, August 7, 1965.

Blind Date: George Harrison. Roger Miller: "England Swings," *Melody Maker*.

Bowen, Jimmy with Jim Jerome. *Rough Mix*: An Unapologetic Look at the Music Business and How It Got That Way—*A Lifetime in the World of Rock, Pop, and Country as Told by One of the Industry's Most Powerful Players*. New York: Simon and Schuster, 1997.

Bowman, David. "Kris Kristofferson: The Great Gravel-Voiced One talks of films, beautiful actresses, the importance of Dylan and chillin' with the Sandinistas." http://www.salon.com.people. September 24, 1999.

Bradley, Andy and Roger Wood. *House of Hits: The Story of Houston's Gold Star/Sugarhill Recording Studios*. Austin: *University of Texas Press*, 2010.

Brady, James. "In Step With: Kris Kristofferson." *Parade Magazine*, July 10, 1994, p. 18.

Breakout Singles," "Dang Me" in *Billboard*, June 6, 1964.

Brooks, Tim and Earle Marsh. *The Complete Directory to Prime Time Network and Cable TV Shows 1946-Present*. Eighth Edition. New York: Ballantine, 2003.

Broven, John. *Record Makers and Breakers: Voices of the Independent Rock'n'Roll Pioneers*. Urbana and Chicago: *University of Illinois Press*, 2009.

"C&W History Made At Astrodome Show," *Billboard*, January 22, 1966.

Campbell, Glen with Tom Carter. Rhinestone Cowboy: An Autobiography. New York: *Villard Books,* 1994.

Carey, Bill. *Fortunes, Fiddles & Fried Chicken: A Nashville Business History.* Franklin, TN: *Hillsboro Press*, 2000.

Carter, Walter. "Roger Miller Roadside 'Exit'" *Nashville Tennessean*, no date, 1978.

"CARTridge Takes Play At Biggest NARM Parley," and "Mercury Department to Handle Affiliates."*Billboard*, March 19, 1966

Cash, Johnny with Patrick Carr. *Cash: The Autobiography.* San Francisco: *HarperSanFrancisco*, 1997.

Bibliography

Cason, Albert. "King of the Road' Inn Held In Default."
  Nashville Tennessean, January 15, 1975.
"Cerebral Palsy Telethon To Be Aided by Cash."
  Nashville Tennessean, March, 3, 1970.
Clark, Roy with Marc Eliot. *My Life: In Spite of Myself!* New York:
  Simon and Schuster, 1994
Claypool, Bob. "A disciplined Roger Miller became king of the
  'River'" *Houston Post*, April 24, 1988.
"CMA Banquet Hails New Hall of Famers," *Billboard*, November 5, 1966,
  p. 60.
Cooper, Daniel. "Being Ray Price Means Never Having to Say You're Sorry.
  The Journal of Country Music, Vol 14, No. 3, 1992. pp pp 22-31.
Cooper, Peter. Liner Notes, "The Pilgrim: A Celebration of Kris
  Kristofferson." *American Roots Publishing*, 2006.
"Country Clippings," *Music Reporter*, January 11, 1964.
"Country Clippings," *Music Reporter*, November 10, 1958.
"Country Music Spotlights," *Billboard*: single reviews, "Dang Me,"
  May 16, 1964.
Cusic, Don. *Discovering Country Music. New York: Praeger*, 2008.
Cusic, Don. *Eddy Arnold: I'll Hold You in My Heart. Nashville:*
  Rutledge Hill, 1997.
"Dateline Music City," *Music Reporter*, November 16, 1963.
Daughtrey, Larry. "King of Grammys Says Wit Not All."
  Nashville Tennessean, April 15, 1965.
Dean, Jimmy and Donna Meade Dean. *Thirty Years of Sausage, Fifty Years of
  Ham*: Jimmy Dean's Own Story. New York: *Berkley Books*, 2004
Dickerson, Deke. Liner notes, A Man Like Me: The Early Years of Roger
  Miller, *Bear Family Records*, BCD 16760 AH.
Diekman, Diane. *Live Fast Love Hard: The Faron Young Story*. Urbana:
  University of Illinois Press, 2007.
"Does Roger Miller Know What He Wants?" by Eva Dolin. *Country Song
  Round-up*, 1964.
Doyle, Don H. *Nashville Since the 1920s*. Knoxville: *University of Tennessee
  Press*, 1985.
Eipper, Laura. "Miller's 'First' Not His Best." *Nashville Tennessean*,
  April 5, 1978.
Elder, Rob. "Miller, Reeves Share Top *Billboard* Honors."
  Nashville Tennessean, October 15, 1965.

Bibliography

Escott, Colin. "Inside Starday Records: A Conversation with Don Pierce."
    Journal of Country Music, Vol 17, No. 1. 1994.
"Examining Motel Plans." *Nashville Banner*, September 21, 1968
"Flag For The King." *Nashville Banner*, February 24, 1970.
    (picture and cutline)
Fong-Torres, Ben. *The Hits Just Keep On Coming: The History of Top 40
    Radio.* San Francisco: *Miller Freeman Books*, 1998.
"For Americans It's Music, Music And More Music, Says BMI Report,"
    Billboard, January 1, 1966.
Fourth Circuit and Probate Courts: Davidson County, TN:
    Barbara Miller filed against Roger Miller. BILL FOR SEPARATE
    MAINTENANCE, September 27, 1963.
Fourth Circuit Court: Davidson County, TN: BILL FOR SEPARATE
    MAINTENANCE, November 20, 1961.
Fox, William Price, Jr. "Dang Him!: Roger Miller can't roller skate in a
    buffalo herd, but he swings like a pendulum do." *TV Guide*,
    November 12, 1966
Friskics-Warren, Bill. "Kris Kristofferson: To Beat the Devil: Intimation of
    Immortality." *No Depression*. March-April, pp 90-105.
Ghianni, Tim. "Me and Kris: time-traveling with a legend on Music Row."
    Nashville Tennessean. December 12, 2003 pp 1, 7.
Gibson, Nathan D. with Don Pierce. *The Starday Story: The House that
    Country Music Built.* Jackson: *University Press of Mississippi*, 2011.
Goldsmith, Thomas. "Roger Miller rolls on 'Big River' tide."
    Nashville Tennessean, October 29, 1989.
Goldsmith, Thomas. "'Big River' Sessions a Recording."
    Nashville Tennessean June 19, 1985.
Goldsmith, Thomas. 'King of the Road' king of stage in Nashville Symphony
    concert." *Nashville Tennessean*. November 4, 1989.
Gordon, Roxy. "Partly Truth and Partly Fiction: A pilgrim's perspective on
    Kris Kristofferson." *No Depression*, November-December, 1999. pp. 82-93.
"Grammy TV'er Backing Urged," *Billboard*, May 14, 1966.
"Grammy TV-ER on Tuesday," *Billboard*, May 22, 1965.
"Grammy TV-er Wins Show Category; Loses in Format,"
    Billboard, May 29, 1965.
Gray, Michael." "Roger Miller Remembered: Country greats to honor hall-of-
    famer at Grand Ole Opry." *Nashville Banner*, No. D.

Bibliography

Hackett, Vernell. *"Roger Miller"* in Song: The World's Best Songwriters on Creating the Music That Moves Us, edited by J. Douglas Waterman. Cincinnati, Ohio: *Writer's Digest Books*, 2007.

Hall, Claude. "Country Television Programs Enjoying Coast-to-Coast Hayride," *Billboard*, November 13, 1965.

Hall, Claude. "Grammy Awards TVer: Million $ Worth of Talent," *Billboard*, May 28, 1966.

Hance, Bill. "Cooley's Fiddle Loaned To Music Hall of Fame." *Nashville Banner*, January 30, 1973.

Hance, Bill. "Roger Miller: Off Pills, Heads King of the Road." *Nashville Banner*, N.D., 1971

Harris, Frank. "The Many Successes of Roger Miller." *Country Music Life*, November, 1965, pp 10-13, 29.

Havighurst, Craig. *Air Castle of the South: WSM and the Making of Music City.* Urbana and Chicago: *University of Illinois Press*, 2007.

"Help" *Nashville Tennessean*, April 1, 1976. Picture with cutline

Hemphill, Paul. "Kris Kristofferson is the New Nashville Sound." *New York Times*, December 6, 1970.

Hickey, Dave. "Hillbilly Heaven: The Solution According to Ray Price." *Country Music*, Volume Five, Number Six, March, 1976.

Hieronymus, Clara. "Friend awaits witty Roger Miller in 'Big River.'" *Nashville Tennessean*, December 20, 1987.

Hieronymus, Clara. "Roger Miller comes full circle as Pap in 'Big River' at TPAC." *Nashville Tennessean*. October 6, 1987.

Hieronymus, Clara. "Roger Miller Sets Huckleberry Finn's Life to Music." *Nashville Tennessean*, February 6, 1985.

Hieronymus, Clara. "TPAC audience embraces Roger Miller, 'Big River'". *Nashville Tennessean*. January 6, 1988.

Hieronymus, Clara. "'Big River' brings Roger Miller home." *Nashville Tennessean*, January 5, 1988.

"Hootenanny Here Tonight." *Nashville Tennessean*, September 10, 1963.

Hopper, Hedda. Syndicated Column, January 9, 1965.

Jones, George with Tom Carter. *I Lived To Tell It All. New York: Villard*, 1996.

Jones, Loyal. *Country Music Humorists and Comedians.* Urbana and Chicago: *University of Illinois Press*, 2008.

Keel, Pinckney. "Roger Miller Nominated For Nine Grammy Awards." *Nashville Tennessean*, February 14, 1966.

Bibliography

Killen, Buddy with Tom Carter. *By the Seat of My Pants: My Life in Country Music*. New York: *Simon and Schuster*, 1993.

"King of Road Unit Marks First Year." *Nashville Banner*, March 5, 1971.

"King of the Road's' Motel Idea: 1st Unit in National Chain Planned Here." *Nashville Banner*, September 9, 1968.

Kittsinger, Otto. Liner notes on boxed set *King of the Road: The Genius of Roger Miller*, released August 22, 1995 on Mercury Nashville.

Kosser, Michael. *How Nashville Became Music City U.S.A.: 50 Years of Music Row. New York: Hal Leonard*, 2006.

Lago, Don. "King of the Road," *The Ol' Pioneer*, The biannual magazine of the Grand Canyon Historical Society. Fall, 2008; Volume 20; Number 2, pp 4-6.

Landesman, Rocco. "Roger Miller; King of the Rhyme." *New York Times*, "Arts & Leisure," Sunday, July 20, 2003.

"Man At His Best: Kris Kristofferson." *Esquire*: March, 2006, p. 84

Mathews, Jack. "Wanted: Kris Kristofferson," http://www.findarticles.com.

May, Carl. "1st Hootenanny Gets Wild Cheers." *Nashville Tennessean*, September 11, 1963.

Mays, Sammie. "Roger Miller: I've beaten cancer: Love of my wife & kids pulled me through, he says," *National Enquirer*. February 11, 1992.

McCall, Michael. "Freedom's Not Just Another Word," *Nashville Scene*, September 18, 2003.

McCall, Michael. "Miller is a symbol of city, its music." *Nashville Banner*, June 6, 1988

McCall, Michael. "Roger Miller's 'Big River' to be recorded in Nashville." *Nashville Banner*, June 18, 1985.

McCall, Michael. "Roger Miller's style simple, symphonic." *Nashville Banner*, November 2, 1989.

McCall, Michael. "An emotional Carl Perkins honored." *Nashville Banner* October 4, 1985.

McCall, Michael. "Don't Let the Stars Get in Your Eyes: Ray Price's Singular, Six-Decade Journey Forsakes Shine for Substance." *The Journal of Country Music*, Volume 25, No 2.

McGregor, Craig. "I'm Nobody's Best Friend." *The New York Times*, July 26, 1970.

"Miller Accidentally Shot." *Nashville Banner*, April 20, 1968.

"Miller Date Out," *Billboard*, October 2, 1965.

Bibliography

"Miller Set for Grammy Special," *Billboard*, April 9, 1966.

"Miller Sings in Rainstorm," *Billboard*, May 13, 1966.

"Miller Wins MOA Awards," *Billboard*, September 11, 1965.

"Miller, Reeves Sweep Country Music Awards." *Nashville Banner*, October 15, 1965.

Miller, Stephen. *Johnny Cash: The Life of an American Icon.* London: *Omnibus Press*, 2003.

Miller, Stephen. *Kristofferson: The Wild American.* London and New York: *Omnibus*, 2008.

"Miller, Tree Top BMI Awards," *Billboard*, October 22, 1966.

"Minnie Pearl Billboard's Country Man of Year," *Billboard*, October 29, 1966.

Monin, Beth. "'Big River': Miller returns with his big show." *Nashville Banner*, January 4, 1988.

Morse, Steve. "King of the Road Tunes up for the stage," *Boston Globe*, February 12, 1984.

Morthland, John. "Ray Price: Back on the Road." *Country Music*, Volume eight, Number seven, April 1980.

"NARAS' Nashville Unit Gets 200 New Members," *Billboard*, September 17, 1966.

"NARAS Puts Grammy Wheels in Motion With 'Eligibility' Forms." *Billboard*, January 29, 1966.

"NARAS Revamps Grammy Awards Format; Fewer Prizes, Wider Scope." *Variety*, September 21, 1966.

Nelson, Rick. "King of the Road Roger Miller a homebody these days." *Tacoma, WA News-Tribune.* Jan 26, 1989

New Pop LPs: Welcome to the World of Pop, "Roger Miller–an updated Stan Freeberg." *NME*, June 12, 1965, p. 16.

O'Donnell, "Round the Clock: It Was Just Him," *Nashville Banner*, October 21, 1966.

O'Donnell, Red, "Miller Gets 5 Grammy Awards," *Nashville Banner*, April 14, 1965.

O'Donnell, Red. "It Was Just Bus To Him." *Nashville Banner*, October 21, 1966.

O'Donnell, Red. "Miller To Sing On Atkins Special." *Nashville Banner*, May 13, 1980.

Oermann, Robert K. "All Aboard, Nashville, for Broadway's 'Big River.'" *Nashville Tennessean*, October 22, 1985.

Bibliography

Oermann, Robert K. "Broadway's 'Big River' Will Record on Music Row."
Nashville Tennessean, June 8, 1985.

Oermann, Robert K. "Music Row mourns Roger Miller."
Nashville Tennessean, October 27, 1992.

Oermann, Robert K. "Roger Miller Back, Sticks To Favorites."
Nashville Tennessean, April 9, 1983.

Oermann, Robert K. "Roger Miller Returns 'Home' On Crest of 'Big River'
Wave." *Nashville Tennessean*, June 23, 1985.

Oermann, Robert K. "Roger Miller special could be a series."
Nashville Tennessean, October 4, 1988.

Oermann, Robert K. and Clara Hieronymus, "Music Row Elite's Party
Applauds Roger Miller's 'Big River' Triumph" *Nashville Tennessean*,
September 5, 1985.

O'Neil, Thomas. *The Grammys: For the Record.* New York: Penguin, 1993.

"Owens, Miller Top Calif. Honors," *Billboard*, March 12, 1966

Piro, Nick. "CMA to Stage Country Show in Chicago," *Billboard*,
May 15, 1965.

Piro, Nick. "CMA's Show Draws Plaudits," *Billboard*, June 19, 1965.

Pop Single Review: King of the Road," *Billboard*, January 23, 1965.

Pop Singles: "Breakout Singles": Dang Me" (Seattle, Houston),
Billboard, June 6, 1964.

"Popsters Swamped the WSM Scene," *Billboard*, November 5, 1966.

Portis, Charles, "That New Sound From Nashville" *Saturday Evening Post*,
February 12, 1965.

Pugh, Ronnie. *Ernest Tubb: The Texas Troubadour.* Durham: *Duke University
Press*, 1996. P. 230-231

"Ray Price Signs Up 'Cherokee Cowboys' Of Houston, Texas." *Pickin' and
Singin' News*, August 14, 1954, p. 1

Redshaw, David. "Roger Miller" in *New Music Express*, June 16, 1973.

"Reserve Tuesday For Hootenanny." *Nashville Tennessean*,
September 5, 1963.

Review: "Hits Most Likely," May 27, 1965, *Record Retailer* p. 3.

Rhodes, Don. "Ramblin' Rhodes," October 8, 1989.

"Roger Miller Bares 7-Year Binge With Amphetamines."
Nashville Banner, February 9, 1972.

"Roger Miller Cancels Show." *AP/ Nashville Tennessean*,
September 20, 1965.

Bibliography

"Roger Miller Coming for BMI Awards Fete." *Nashville Banner*,
  October 20, 1966.
"Roger Miller Fired at Dallas Hotel." *AP. N.D.*
"Roger Miller hits the deck with TV show." *Nashville Tennessean*,
  July 9, 1988.
"Roger Miller Nominated For 9 Grammy Awards. *Nashville Tennessean*,
  February 15, 1966.
"Roger Miller rolls along Mississippi." *Nashville Tennessean*,
  October 2, 1988.
"Roger Miller Tells Why He Quit Drugs." N.D. *Nashville Tennessean*,
  November 18, 1970.
Roland, Tom. "Kristofferson finds 'A Moment of Forever.'" "Weekend" in
  Nashville Tennessean, January 12, 1996.
Roland, Tom. "Roger Miller, Jo Walker-Meador tapped for Hall of Fame."
  Nashville Tennessean, N. D.
Ruppli, Michel. *The Decca Labels: A Discography*: Volume 5:
  Country Recordings, Classical Recordings & Reissues. Westport, CT:
  Greenwood Press, 1996.
Ruppli, Michel and Ed Novitsky. *The Mercury Labels: A Discography:
  Volume II: The 1956-1964 Era*. Westport, CT: *Greenwood Press*, 1993.
Ruppli, Michel and Ed Novitsky. *The Mercury Labels: A Discography:
  Volume III: The 1964-1969 Era*. Westport, CT: *Greenwood Press*, 1993.
Ruppli, Michel and Ed Novitsky. *The Mercury Labels: A Discography:
  Volume IV: The 1969-1991 Era*. Westport, CT: *Greenwood Press*, 1993.
Schipper, Henry. *Broken Record: The Inside Story of the Grammy Awards*.
  New York: *Birch Lane*, 1992
Scott, Vernon. "Scholar Cowboy." *UPI*, January 13, 1998.
"Sessions in progress for Skeeter Davis, Roger Miller and the Avons,"
  Music Reporter, November 16, 1963.
Shelton, Robert. "Nashville's Modern Folk," *New York Times*,
  March 21, 1965.
"Shows Mark Country Fete on W. Coast," *Billboard*, February 26, 1966
"Singer Suffers Stomach Spasms." *UPI. Nashville Banner*, May, 1974.
Singles Reviews: Hit! "Kansas City Star/One Dyin' and a-Buryin'",
  Record Retailer, September 30, 1965.
"Smash Giving Smash Push to Miller TV-er," *Billboard*, January 15, 1966.
Smith, Stacy Jenel. "Roger Miler 'Burned' In 'Quincy' Episode."

Bibliography

Nashville Tennessean, Feb 6, 1983.

Smith, Tracy. "Kris Kristofferson: A Sex Symbol at 70," *http://www.cbsnews.com*. February 5, 2006.

Sobel, Robert. "Miller Is Off and Singing In New Weekly TV Show," *Billboard*, September 24, 1966, p. 26.

"Songwriters awards show to honor Roger Miller." *Nashville Banner*, December 28, 1985.

"Stapp All-Out for Tree Music," *Billboard*, March 27 1965.

"Stapp Signs Miller, Tubb, Tex; Plans Other Expansion Moves," *Billboard*, April 3, 1965.

Stearns, David Patrick, "Dang me! Roger Miller is on Broadway" *USA Today*, March, 1985.

Sternfield, Aaron, "The Vietnam Conflict Spawning Heavy Barrage of Disk Tunes," *Billboard*, June 4, 1966.

Stewart, Elmer. "King of Road Group Acquires 2 Big Properties." *Nashville Banner*, January 13, 1972.

Stewart, Elmer. "Miller, Kerr Singers, Statlers Win Grammys." *Nashville Banner*, March 16, 1966.

Streissguth, Michael. *Like a Moth to the Flame: The Jim Reeves Story*. *Nashville: Rutledge Hill Press*, 1998.

Style, Lyle. *Ain't Got No Cigarettes: Memories of Music Legend Roger Miller*. Winnipeg, MB: *Great Plains Publications*, 2005.

"Tahoe Meeting." *Nashville Banner*, May 10, 1969.

"Tenants Move Into New Long Addition," *Billboard*, December 25, 1965.

"The 'Jimmy Dean Show' Back--In (Country) Style." *Billboard*, September 26, 1964, p. 3.

"The Millers' Daughter." *Nashville Tennessean*, November 29, 1970. Picture and cutline

Top Singles of the Week: "My Uncle Used To Love Me," *Variety*, September 7, 1966.

"Tree Signs Miller." *Music Reporter*, May 19, 1958, p. 11.

Turner, Steve. *The Man Called Cash: The Life, Love, and faith of an American Legend*. Nashville: *W Publishing Group*, 2004.

"TV's New Top 40," *Variety*, October 12, 1966.

"United in Cause." *Nashville Tennessean*, March 3, 1970. Picture with cutline

Warwick, Neil, Jon Kutner & Tony Brown. *The Complete Book of the British Charts: Singles & Albums*. London: *Omnibus Press*, 2004.

Bibliography

"WCMS Files a Suit Against Roger Miller," *Billboard*, July 10, 1965.

Weintraub, Jerry with Rich Cohen. *When I Stop Talking, You'll Know I'm Dead: Useful Stories From a Persuasive Man*. New York: *Twelve*, 2010.

Welch, Pat. "Grammy King Keeps Throne," *Nashville Tennessean*, March 16, 1966.

Whisenhunt, Elton, "Nash. NARAS Starts Campaign," *Billboard*, October 9, 1965.

Whisenhunt, Elton. "Miller & Reeves Country Kings; Craig Man of Year," *Billboard*, October 23, 1965.

Whitburn, Joel. *Top Country Songs: 1944-2005: Billboard*. Menomonee Falls, Wisconsin: *Record Research, Inc.*, 2005.

Whitburn, Joel. *Top Pop Singles: 12th Edition Country Songs: 1944-2005*: *Billboard*. Menomonee Falls, Wisconsin: *Record Research, Inc.*, 2009.

"Who's On First?" *Nashville Banner* Dec 7, 1962 (Picture and cutline)

Willard, Bill. "'Country card' Roger Miller is at Riviera," *N.P.*, December 2, 1983.

Williams, Andy. *Moon River and Me: A Memoir*. New York: *Viking*, 2009.

Wood, Herb. "4,500 Are Pouring Into WSM's Giant Spread," *Billboard*, October 22, 1966.

"Wright Agency Signs RCA Victor's Miller," *Music Reporter*, October 5, 1963.

Wyatt, Eugene. 'King of Road' Does Well in the Air, Too." *Nashville Tennessean*, N.D. 1966

Zabriskie, Mark. "Musical 'Big River' may soon become major motion picture." *Nashville Banner* September 5, 1985.

Zibart, Eve. "Tammy Reroutes Honeymoon Train Via White House." *Nashville Tennessean*, N. D. 1976

Discography

ALBUMS:

Roger Miller: Dang Me/Chug-A-Lug
(originally released as Roger and Out) Smash/Mercury (1964)

Side One:
Chug-A-Lug (Roger Miller)
Private John Q (Roger Miller)
Squares Make the World Go Round (Roger Miller)
It Takes All Kinds to Make a World (Roger Miller)
I Ain't Comin' Home Tonight (Roger Miller)
If You Want Me To (Roger Miller)

Side Two:
The Moon Is High (Roger Miller)
Feel of Me (Roger Miller)
Lou's Got the Flu (Roger Miller)
Got 2 Again (Roger Miller)
Dang Me (Roger Miller)
That's Why I Love You Like I Do (Roger Miller)

The Country Side
Starday (1964) (also released as Wild Child)

Side 1:
Poor Little John (Roger Miller)
Under Your Spell Again (Buck Owens-Rhodes)
Jimmy Brown, The Newsboy (A.P. Carter
I Wish I Could Fall in Love Today (Harlan Howard)
Pillow (Roger Miller)
Can't Stop Loving You (Roger Miller)

Side 2:
I Ain't Never (Mel Tillis-Webb Pierce)
The Tips of My Fingers (Bill Anderson)
Country Girl (Roy Drusky)
Playboy (Roger Miller)
You're Forgetting Me (Roger Miller)
Who Shot Sam (Edwards-Jackson-Jones)

Discography

ALBUMS:

The One and Only
RCA/Camden (1964)

Side 1:
It Happened Just That Way (Roger Miller)
But I Love You More (Roger Miller)
Burma Shave (Roger Miller)
I Catch Myself Crying (Roger Miller)
I Get Up Early in the Morning (Harlan Howard)

Side 2:
I Know Who It Is (Roger Miller)
A Part of Me (Ray Pressley-Speedy Price)
You Can't Do Me This Way (Roger Miller)
I'll Be Somewhere (Roger Miller)
If You Want Me To (Roger Miller)

Roger Miller
RCA/Camden (1964)

Side 1:
Footprints in the Snow(Arr by Roger Miller)
Every Which-A-Way (Roger Miller)
Sorry Willie (Roger Miller)
Hey Little Star (Roger Miller)
Lock Stock and Teardrops (Roger Miller)

Side 2:
When Two World's Collide (Roger Miller-Bill Anderson)
Fair Swiss Maiden (Roger Miller)
Hitch-Hiker (Roger Miller)
Trouble on the Turnpike (Roger Miller)
You Don't Want My Love (In the Summertime) (Roger Miller)

Discography

ALBUMS:

The Return of Roger Miller
Smash/Mercury (1965)

Side 1:
Do-Wacka-Do (Roger Miller)
Atta Boy Girl (Roger Miller)
Reincarnation (Roger Miller)
That's The Way It's Always Been (Roger Miller)
As Long As There's a Shadow (Roger Miller)
Hard Headed Me (Roger Miller)

Side 2:
King of the Road (Roger Miller)
You Can't Roller Skate in a Buffalo Herd (Roger Miller)
Our Hearts Will Play the Music (Roger Miller)
Love Is Not for Me (Roger Miller)
In the Summertime (Roger Miller)
There I Go Dreamin' (Roger Miller)
Ain't That Fine (Dorsey Burnett)

The 3rd Time Around
Smash/Mercury (1965)

Side 1:
Engine Engine No. 9 (Roger Miller)
This Town (Roger Miller)
The Last Word in Lonesome Is Me (Roger Miller)
Water Dog (Roger Miller)
I'll Pick Up My Heart and Go home (Roger Miller)
Swiss Maid (Roger Miller)

Side 2:
It Happened Just That Way (Roger Miller)
The Good Old Days (Roger Miller)
One Dyin' And A Buryin' (Roger Miller)
Kansas City Star (Roger Miller)
Big Harlan Taylor (Roger Miller)
Swing Low, Swingin' Chariot (Roger Miller)

Discography

ALBUMS:

Golden Hits
Smash/Mercury (1965)

Side 1:
King of the Road (Roger Miller)
Dang Me (Roger Miller)
Engine Engine No. 9 (Roger Miller)
In the Summertime (Roger Miller)
Buffalo Herd (Roger Miller)
Do-Wacka Do (Roger Miller)

Side 2:
England Swings (Roger Miller)
Chug-A-Lug (Roger Miller)
One Dyin' And A Buryin' (Roger Miller)
Kansas City Star (Roger Miller)
Atta Boy Girl (Roger Miller)
It Happened Just That Way (Roger Miller)

Words and Music
Smash/Mercury (1966)

Side 1:
Husbands and Wives (Roger Miller)
Train of Life (Roger Miller)
Billy Bayou (Roger Miller)
Dad Blame Anything A Man Can't Quit (Roger Miller-Curly Putman)
You're My Kingdom (Roger Miller)
I've Been a Long Time Leavin' (Roger Miller)

Side 2:
Every Which-A-Way (Roger Miller)
Less and Less (Roger Miller)
Home (Roger Miller)
Workin' Girl (Roger Miller)
Heartbreak Hotel (Mae Boren Axton-Thomas Durden-Elvis Presley)
My Uncle Used to Love Me But She Died (Roger Miller)

Discography

ALBUMS:

Walkin' In the Sunshine
Smash/Mercury (1967)

Side 1:
Walkin' In The Sunshine (Roger Miller)
You Didn't Have To Be So Nice (Roger Miller)
Green Green Grass of Home (Curly Putman)
Absence (Roger Miller)
Pardon This Coffin (Roger Miller)
Hey Good Lookin' (Hank Williams)

Side 2:
A Million Years Or So (Roger Miller)
Ruby (Don't Take Your Love to Town) (Mel Tillis)
I'd Come Back To Me (Roger Miller)
Our Little Love (Roger Miller)
The Riddle (Roger Miller)

A Tender Look At Love
Smash/Mercury (1968)

Side 1:
Toliver (Roger Miller)
By The Time I Get to Phoenix (Jimmy Webb)
What I'd Give (Roger Miller)
Gentle On My Mind (John Hartford)
With Pen in Hand (Bobby Goldsboro)
The Twelfth of Never (Jerry Livingston-Paul Webster)

Side 2:
Less of Me (Roger Miller)
My Elusive Dreams (Curly Putman-Billy Sherrill)
Little Green Apples (Bobby Russell)
Honey (Bobby Russell)
Dear Heart (Raymond Evans-Jay Livingston-Henry Mancini)

Discography

ALBUMS:

Roger Miller
Smash/Mercury (1969)

Side 1:
Me and Bobby McGee (Kris Kristofferson--Fred Foster)
Colonel Maggie (Dennis Linde)
Swiss Cottage Place (Mickey Newbury)
The Best of All Possible Worlds (Kris Kristofferson)
Where Have All the Average People Gone (Dennis Linde)
I'm Gonna Teach My Heart to Bend (Instead of Break) (Roger Miller)

Side 2:
Darby's Castle (Kris Kristofferson)
Boeing Boeing 707 (Roger Miller)
Meanwhile Back in Abilene (Dennis Linde)
Shame Bird (Roger Miller)
Vance (Bobby Russell)

Roger Miller
1970 Smash/Mercury (1970)

Side 1:
The Tom Green County Fair (Dennis Linde)
Precious Baby (Bobby Russell)
The Man Who Stayed in Monterey (Dennis Linde)
Jody and the Kid (Kris Kristofferson)
Mystery Train (Junior Parker-Sam Phillips)
I Know Who It Is (Roger Miller)

Side 2:
All Fall Down (Dennis Linde)
Everybody's Talkin' (Fred Neil)
The Fool (N. Ford)
T.J.'s Last Ride (Dennis Linde)
Crystal Day (Dennis Linde)

Discography

ALBUMS:

A Trip In the Country
Smash/Mercury (1970)

Side 1:
Tall Tall Trees (Roger Miller-George Jones)
A World I Can't Live In (Roger Miller)
My Ears Should Burn (Roger Miller)
Don't We All Have Right (Roger Miller)
Half a Mind (Roger Miller)
When a House Is Not a Home (Roger Miller)

Side 2:
Nothing Can Stop My Love (Roger Miller)
When Two Worlds Collide (Roger Miller-Bill Anderson)
A World So Full of Love (Roger Miller)
That's The Way I Feel (Roger Miller)
Invitation to the Blues (Roger Miller)

Best of Roger Miller
Smash/Mercury (1972)

Side 1:
Little Green Apples (Bobby Russell)
Ruby (Don't Take Your Love to Town) (Mel Tillis)
Husbands and Wives (Roger Miller)
I've Been a Long Time Leavin' (Roger Miller)
The Tom Green County Fair (Dennis Linde)
Tomorrow Night in Baltimore (Kenny Price)

Side 2:
Loving Her Was Easier (Kris Kristofferson)
Walking in the Sunshine (Roger Miller)
Me and Bobby McGee (Kris Kristofferson-Fred Foster)
My Uncle Used to Love Me But She Died (Roger Miller)
South (Bobby Russell)

Discography

ALBUMS:

Dear Folks Sorry I Haven't Written Lately
CBS (1973)

Side 1:
Open Up Your Heart (Roger Miller-Buddy Killen)
Whistle Stop (Roger Miller)
Mama Used To Love Me But She Died (Roger Miller)
Qua La Linta (Roger Miller)
I Believe in the Sunshine (Roger Miller)

Side 2:
The Animal of Man (Roger Miller)
What Would My Mama Say (Roger Miller)
The Day I Jumped From Uncle Harvey's Plane (Red Lane)
Shannon's Song (Roger Miller)
The 4th of July (Roger Miller)

Supersongs
CBS (1975)

Side 1:
Lady America (Roger Miller)
Won'tcha Come Be My Friend
Lovin' You Is Always On My Mind (Roger Miller)
Our Love (Roger Miller)
Husbands and Wives (Roger Miller)

Side 2:
I Love a Rodeo (Roger Miller)
The Yester Waltz (Roger Miller)
Wanda Iguana (Roger Miller)
Somewhere There's a Lady (Roger Miller)
All I Love Is You (Roger Miller)

Discography

ALBUMS:

Off The Wall
RCA (Windsong) (1977)

Side 1:
Oklahoma Woman (Roger Miller)
Baby Me Baby (Roger Miller)
Stephen Foster (Roger Miller)
I've Gotten Used to the Cryin' (Roger Miller)
Ain't Gonna Work No More (Roger Miller)

Side 2:
There's Nobody Like You (Roger Miller)
Dark Side of the Moon (Roger Miller)
Some People Make It (Roger Miller)
Roll Away (Roger Miller-Micheal Smotherman)
Na-Nominee (Roger Miller)

Making a Name For Myself
20th Century Fox (1979)

Side 1:
The Hat (Roger Miller)
If I Ever Fall In Love (Roger Miller)
Ringing Up Rosie (Roger Miller)
Freedom (Roger Miller-Chuck Blore)
Hey Would You Hold It Down (Roger Miller)

Side 2:
It's a Miracle That You're Mine (Roger Miller)
Pleasing the Crowd (Roger Miller)
Disco Man (Roger Miller)
Old Friends (Roger Miller)
The Opera Ain't Over Till the Fat Lady Sings (Hal Stanley-Erving Taylor)

Discography

ALBUMS:

Roger Miller
MCA (1986)

Side 1:
River In the Rain (Roger Miller)
Some Hearts Get All the Breaks (Roger Miller-Grant Boatwright)
Leavin's Not the Only Way to Go (Roger Miller)
Guv'ment (Roger Miller)
You Oughta Be Here With Me (Roger Miller)

Side 2:
Hand for the Hog (Roger Miller)
Arkansas (Roger Miller)
Indian Giver (Roger Miller)
Days of Our Wives (Roger Miller)
Muddy Water (Roger Miller)

Discography

SINGLES:

1957: My Pillow/Poor Little John Starday
1958: Under Your Spell Again/I Ain't Never Starday
1958: You're Forgetting Me/Can't Stop Loving You: Starday
1958: On This Mountain Top (w/ Donny Young): Decca
1958 Mine Is a Lonely Life (w/ Justin Tubb): Decca
1959: A Man Like Me/The Wrong Kind of Girl: Decca
1959: Sweet Ramona/Jason Fleming: Decca
1960: Yu Don't Want My Love/Footprints In The Snow: RCA
1961: When Two Worlds Collide/Every Which-A-Way: RCA
1961: Fair Swiss Maiden/Burma Shave: RCA
1962: Hitch Hiker/Sorry Willy: RCA
1962: Hey Little Star/TroubleOn the Turnpike: RCA
1963: Lock Stock and Teardrops/I Know Who It Is: RCA
1964: Dang Me/Got 2 Again: Smash
1964: Chuck-A-Lug: Reincarnation: Smash
1964: Do Wacka Do/Love Is NOt For Me: Smash
1965: Poor Little John/Playboy: Starday
1965: Under Your Spell Again/I Ain't Never: Starday
1965: The Tips Of my FIngers/I Wish I Could Fall In Love Today: Starday
1965: You're Forgetting Me/Can't Stop Loving Me: Musicor
1965: Country Girl/Jimmie Brown The Newsboy: Starday
1965: If You Want Me to/Hey Little Star: RCA
1965: King of the Road/Atta Boy Girl: Smash
1965: Engine Engine No. 9/The Last World In Lonesome Is Me: Smash
1965: One Dyin' And A-Buryin'/It Happened Just That Way: Smash
1965: Kansas City Star/Guess I'll Pick Up My Heart and Go Home: Smash
1965: England Swings/Good Old Days: Smash
1966: Husbands and Wives/I've Been a Long Time Leavin': Smash
1966: You Can't Roller Skate In a Buffalo Herd/Train of Life: Smash
1966: My Uncle Used to Love Me But She Died/You're My Kingdom: Smash
1966: Heartbreak Hotel/Less and Less: Smash
1967: Walkin' In The Sunshine/Home: Smash
1967: Ballad of Waterhole No. 3/Rainbow Valley: Smash
1967: Old Toy Trains/Silent Night: Smash
1968: Little Green Apples/Our Little Love: Smash
1968: What I'd Give (To Be The Wind)/Tolivar: Smash
1968: Vance/Little Children Run: Smash

Discography

SINGLES:

1969: Me and Bobby McGee/I'm Gonna Teach My Heart To Bend: Smash
1969: Where Have All the Average People Gone/Boeing Boeing 707: Smash
1970: The Tom Green County Fair/I Know Who It Is: Smash
1970: South/Don't We All Have the Right: Mercury
1971: Tomorrow Night in Baltimore/A Million Years Or So: Mercury
1971: Loving Her Was Easier/Qua La Linta: Mercury
1972: We Found It In Each Others Arms/Sunny Side of My Life: Mercury
1972: Rings For Sale/Conversation: Mercury
1973: Hoppy's Gone/The Day I Jumped Form Uncle Harvey's Plane: Mercury
1973: Qua La Linta/Open Up Your Heart: CBS
1973: I Believe In the Sunshine/Shannon's Song: CBS
1974: Whistle Stop/The 4th of July: CBS
1974: Our Love/The Yester Waltz: CBS
1975: I Love a Rodeo/Loving You Is Always On My Mind: CBS
1977: Baby Me Baby/Dark Side of the Moon: RCA
1979: The Hat/Pleasing The Crowd: 20th Century
1981: Old Friends/When a House Is Not a Home: CBS
1981: Everyone Gets Crazy Now and Then/Aladambama: Elektra
1985: River In The Rain/Hand For the Hog: MCA
1985: Some Hearts Get All The Breaks/Arkansas: MCA

SOUNDTRACK ALBUMS:

Waterhole #3:
(Soundtrack) Smash/Mercury 1968
Ballad of Waterhole #3 (Code of the West)
Rainbow Valley

Robin Hood
(Soundtrack) Disney 1973
Whistle Stop
Not in Nottingham
Oo-De-Lally

Superman III
(Soundtrack) Warner Bros. 1983
They Won't Get Me

Discography

SOUNDTRACK ALBUMS:

Big River
Original Cast Album: MCA

Do Ya Wanna Go To Heaven
The Boys
Waitin' For the Light To Shine
Guv'ment
Hand for the Hog
I, Huckleberry, Me
Muddy Water
The Crossing
River In The Rain
When the Sun Goes Down In the South
The Royal Nonesuch
Worlds Apart
Arkansas/How Blest We Are
You Oughta Be Here With Me
Leavin's Not the Only Way to Go
Waitin' For the Light To Shine (Reprise)
Free at Last
Muddy Water (Reprise)

DUET ALBUM

Old Friends
(With Willie Nelson) CBS 1982

When a House Is Not A Home (Roger Miller)
When Two Worlds Collide (Roger Miller)
Half a Heart (Roger Miller)
The Best I Can Give Her (Roger Miller)
I'll Pick Up My Heart and Go Home (Roger Miller)
Old Friends (with Willie Nelson & Ray Price) (Roger Miller)
Aladambama (Roger Miller)
Husbands and Wives (Roger Miller)
Sorry Willie (Roger Miller)
Invitation to the Blues (Roger Miller)

Songs Written by Roger Miller

4th of July, The
A World So Full of Love
  (with Faron Young)
Absence
Ain't Gonna Work No More
Aladambama
All I Love Is You
All Together
Animal of Man, The
Are You Forgetting
Arkansas
Arkansas
As Long as There's a Shadow
Atta Boy, Girl
Australian Sheepherder (stage joke)
Baby Me Baby
Best I Can Give Her, The
Better Forget Her
Big Harlan Taylor
Big River Overture
Billy Bayou
Boeing Boeing 707
Boomerang
Boys, The
Bring Back My Baby To Me
Burma Shave
But I Love You More
Can't Stop My Loving You
Chicken Thief
  (with Robert Lee Schudalla)
Chinese Dang Me
  (parody of "Dang Me")
Chug-A-Lug
Come Her to Me
Crossing, The
Dad Blame Anything A Man Can't
Quit (with Curly Putman)
Dang Me
Dark Side of the Moon
Days of Our Wives

Dear Lonesome
Della Jo
Dern Ya
  (Parody of with Justin Tubb)
Disco Man
Do Ya Wanna Go To Heaven
Do You Care (If I Care Just a Little)
Do You Love Me
Don't Do This To Me
Don't You Worry
Don't Jump From the Bridge (w/
Justin Tubb)
Don't We All Have the Right
Don't Write Letters To My Dog
Don't You Know My Nature By Now
Do-Wacka-Do
Empty Heart
Every Tom Dick and Harry S Nam
Engine Engine #9
Engine, Engine #10
  (parody of "Engine Engine #
  (with Stovall and Stewart)
England Swings
Entracte
Every-Which-A-Way
Father Adam (with Morris Levy)
Feel of Me
Footprints in the Snow
  (arr by R. Miller with Jerry Elliott)
Free At Last
Freedom (with Chuck Blore)
Freedom to Say What You Feel (with
Chuck Blore)
Ghost Story
Golden Tear
Good Old Days, The
Got Two Again

Songs Written by Roger Miller

Guess I'll Pick Up My Heart
and Go Home
Guitar Strums
Guv'ment
Half a Mind
Hand For the Hog
Happy Child
Hard-Headed Me
Hat, The
Heartache For a Keepsake, A
Hearts in My Dreams
Heaven Help Me
Here's Bud in Your Eye
Hey Little Star
Hey Would You Hold It Down
Hey Would You Hold It FDown
Hitch-Hiker
Home
How Blessed We Are
How To Tell It To a Child
Husbands and Wives
I Ain't Comin' Home Tonight
I Believe In the Sunshine
I Catch Myself Crying
I Had to Leave Her
(with Larry Allan)
I Just Don't Love You, That's All
I Know Who It Is and I'm Gonna
Tell On 'Em
I Love a Rodeo
I Need Lovin'
I Pawned My Past Today
I Should Know Better
I Want to Know Why
(With Robert Lee Schudalla)
I Wouldn't (with Curtis Gordon)
I, Huckleberry, Me

I'm Getting Used to the Crying
I'm Gonna Teach My Heart to Be
I've Got to Know (with Ray Price)
I'd Come Back to Me
If Heartache is the Fashion
(with Jim Reeves)
If I Could Live That Way
If I Ever Fall in Love
If You Ever See Utah Again
(with Larry Gatlin)
If You Think You Feel Lonesome
If You Want Me To
If You Won't Be My Number One
I'll Be Somewhere
I'll Pick Up My Heart
(and Go Home)
I'm a Fool About Somebody
I'm Just Killing Time
'Till This Heartache Kills Me
In Love With Love
(w/ Lane, Killen, Kirby, Martin
& Cochran)
In the Summertime
(You Don't Want My Love)
Indian Giver
Into My Arms Again
Invitation to the Blues
It Happened Just That Way
It Only Hurts When I Cry
(with Dwight Yoakam)
It Takes All Kinds to Make a World
It's a Miracle That You're Mine
It's Not Right
I've Been a Long Time Leaving (But
I'll Be a Long Time Gone)
I've Gotta Know
(with Ray Price)

Songs Written by Roger Miller

Jason Fleming
Just a Waitin'
Just Down at the Corner
Kansas City Star
King of the Camp
   (Parody of "King of the Road with
   Kenneth Burns and Henry Haynes)
King of the Cops
King of the Road
Knock Knock Rattle Rattle
Lady America
Last Night at a Party
   (with Faron Young)
Last Word in Lonesome Is Me, The
Leavin's Not the Only Way to Go
Less and Less
Let's Stay Young Forever
Light of Love
Lille, I Do
Lock, Stock and Teardrops
London Sun
Loneliness All Around Me
Lonely Girl
Lonesome Is My Middle Name
Look in the Mirror (with Jimmy
Copeland and D. James
Lou's Got the Flu
Love Is Not For Me
Love Love Love
Lover Boy
Lovin' You Is Always On My Mind
Lucky Luke
Man Like Me, A
Meadow Green
Million Years or So, A
Moon Is High, The
Much Too Well

Muddy Water
Muddy Water (Reprise)
My Ears Should Burn
   (When Fools Are Talked About)
My Pillow
My Uncle Used to Love Me
   But She Died
My Used to Be Baby
Na Nominee
No Use to Cry
No Wonder I Sing
Not in Nottingham
Nothing Can Stop My Loving You
Number Two on You
Oklahoma Woman
Old Friends
Old Man and the River, The
Old Toy Trains
One Dyin' and a Buryin'
Oo De Lally
Open Up Your Heart
   (with Buddy Killen)
Our Hearts Will Play the Music
Our Little Love
Our Love
Out of Your Heart
Out of Your Heart
   (I'd Go Out of My Mind)
Pardon This Coffin
Part of Me
Pee Wee Herman
Pleasing the Crowd
Poison Is Coming Out, The
   (with March Levy)
Poor Little John
Poor Man's Troubles
Preserve the Wildlife

Songs Written by Roger Miller

(with Mary Miller, Dean Miller
   and Marty Stuart)
Private John Q
Qua La Linta
Queen of the House
   (Answer song to "King of the
   Road" w/ Mary Taylor)
Reincarnation
Riddle, The
Ringing Up Rosie
River in the Rain
Robin Hood
Rolled Away
   (with Micheal Smotherman)
Royal Nonesuch, The
Save Me the Moonlight
Second Fiddle
Shame Bird
Shannon's Song
She's Gone
Shores of Massachusetts
   (with Morris Levy)
Shotgun Miller (with Robert Lee
Schudalla)
Silly Babe
So Saith He The Lord
Soldier's Plea
Some Hearts Get All the Breaks
   (with Grant Boatwright)
Some People Make It
Somewhere There's a Lady
Sorry Willie
Squares Make the World Go Round
Stephen Foster
Sweet Ramona
Swing Low Swinging Chariot
Swiss Fair Maiden, The

Tall Tall Trees (with George Jones)
Tarnished Angel
That's How It Is
   (when You're Lonesome)
That's The Way I Feel
   (with George Jones)
That's the Way It's Always Been
That's Why I Love You Like I Do
That's Why I'm Drinking
   (with Mel Tillis)
There I Go Dreamin' Again
There's Nobody Like You
They're Playing My Song
This Town
Three Brave Men
Tolivar
Train of Life
Treat Me Like a Human
Trouble on the Turnpike
Uncle John (with Ken Marvin)
Waitin' For the Light to Shine
Walkin' in the Sunshine
Walkin' Talkin' Cryin' Barely Beatin'
   Broken Heart (with Justin Tubb)
Wallflower
Wanda Iguana
Water Dog
Way She Puts Me Down, The
We Are the Boys
What She Don't Hurt Don't Know Her
What Would My Mama Say
What's a Heartache Made Out Of
When a House is Not a Home
When the Sun Goes Down in the South
When Two Worlds
   Collide (with Bill Anderson)
When Your Love's Gone

Songs Written by Roger Miller

Where Your Arms Used to Be
Whistle Stop (Instrumental)
Wild Hearts (with Dean Miller)
Willow Weeps, The (Instrumental)
Wind-Up Doll (with Justin Tubb)
Wish I Hadn't Called Home
Won'tcha Come Be My Friend
Workin' Girl
World I Can't Live In, A
Worlds Apart
Wrong Kind of Girl, The
Yester Waltz, The
You
You Can't Do Me This Way

(And Get By With It)
You Can't Roller Skate in a
    Buffalo Herd
You Didn't Have To Be So Nice
You Don't Want My Love
You Know How It Is
    (When You're Lonesome)
You Know Me Much Too Well
You Make Every Day
You Oughta Be Here With Me
You Used To Be My Baby
You're Forgetting Me
You're My Kingdom

Roger Miller Photos

The Family of Elisha (Elijah)Baker Miller & Sarah Cordelia Bales
Omer, Emmett, Elisha, Rowe, Margie and Jean Miller circa 1916

Miller Brothers 1938

Omer

Luther

Rowe

Jean

Elmer

Margie May

Emmett

Jean and Laudean Miller - shortly after their marriage on October 5, 1929.

Wendell Jean, Harold Duane and Roger Dean Miller 1938 in Fort Worth, TX.

Jean Miller, Roger Dean, Wendell Jean, Laudene Holt Miller and Harold Duane Miller 1936

*Early
School
Pictures*

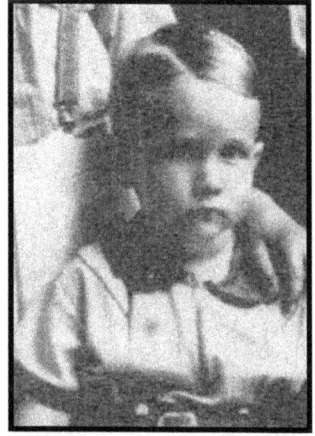

Roger on his Uncle's Farm.

SCHOOL DAYS 1952-53
DELHI

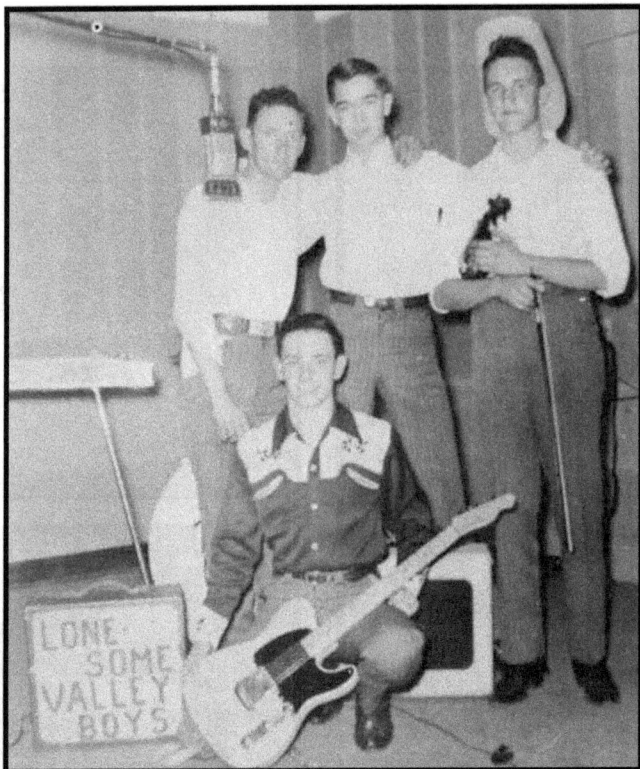

Roger's first Band, The Lonesome Valley Boys. That's Roger with the Fiddle.

Roger's Band, Grand Canyon. Roger is standing on the left.

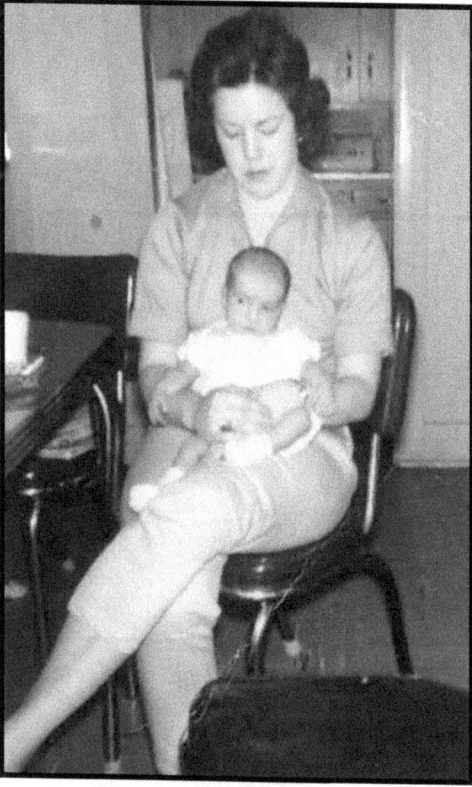

Barbara with baby Alan Miller.

Barbara Crow

James and Barbara Crow.

The Crow Family. Roger sits happily on the right.

Roger in Korea.

The Miller Family 1965. Leah is holding Dean Miller.

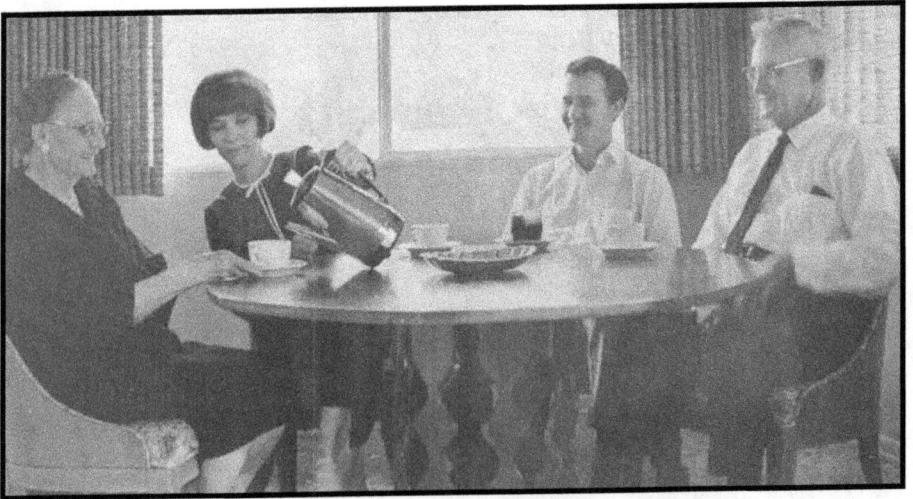

Roger and Leah Miller at home in Los Angeles with Roger's Mom and dad, Elmer and Armelia Miller.

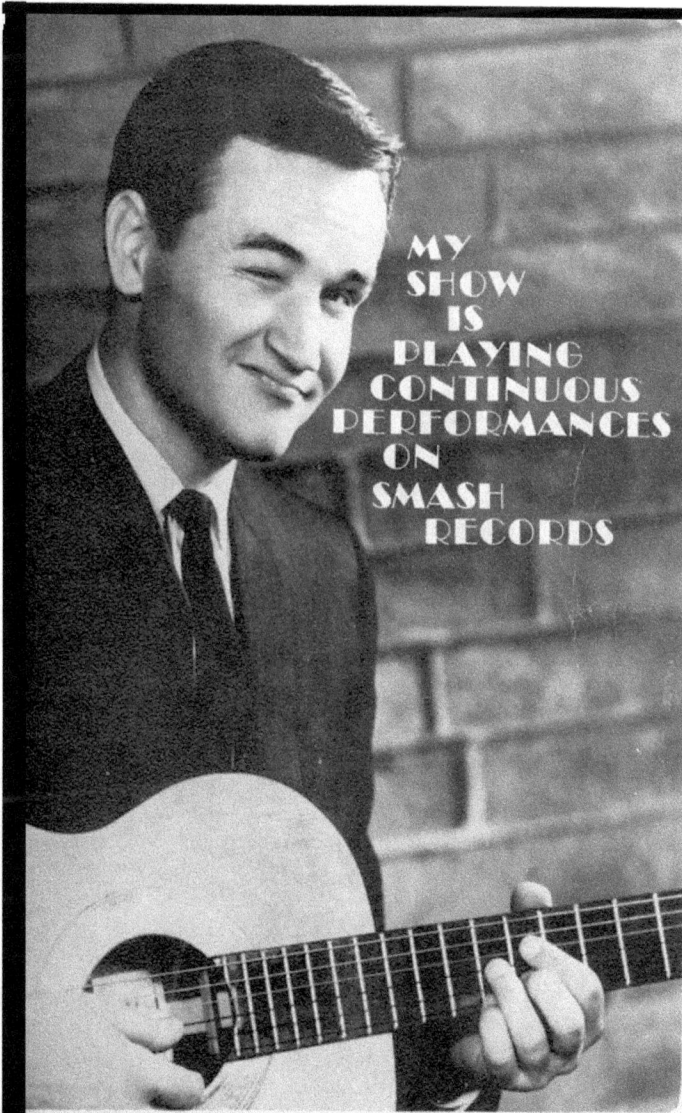

MY
SHOW
IS
PLAYING
CONTINUOUS
PERFORMANCES
ON
SMASH
RECORDS

**ROGER MILLER
HIT ALBUMS ON
SMASH RECORDS**

DANG ME
MGS 27049   SRS 67049
Dang Me, Chug-A-Lug and
10 other Miller favorites.

THE RETURN OF
ROGER MILLER
MGS 27061   SRS 67061
Such hits as King Of The
Road, Do-Wacka-Do and
10 others.

THE 3rd TIME AROUND
MGS 27068   SRS 67068
Kansas City Star, One
Dyin' and A Buryin' and
10 more.

ROGER MILLER
GOLDEN HITS
MGS 27073   SRS 67073
Including England Swings,
In The Summertime and
10 other great hits.

WORDS AND MUSIC BY
ROGER MILLER
MGS 27075   SRS 67075
12 brand new Miller origi-
nals.

Roger on the set of The Roger Miller Show.

Roger Miller with five Grammys. From the left; Jack Stapp of Tree Publishing, Roger's music publisher; Jerry Kennedy of Smash Records, Roger's A & R man; Miller and Buddy Killen of Tree Publishing.

ROGER MILLER

Roger with Tree Publishing Executive Buddy Killen.

Roger and RCA Records Executive Chet Atkins.

Roger and his son Dean on the Mike Douglas Show.

Roger in Santa Fe, New Mexico.

Big River Show Poster.

Roger Miller on stage.

Mary and Roger Miller.

Dean, Mary and Roger Miller at Roger and Mary's wedding.

Roger and Mary Miller.

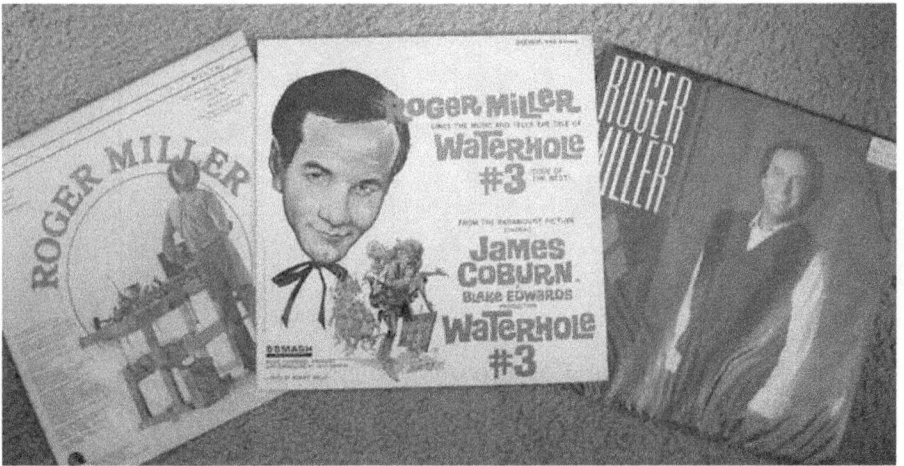

Index

194, 195, 199, 200, 203, 205,
207, 208, 209, 210, 211, 213,
214, 216, 217, 221, 222, 226,
227, 229, 231, 239, 242, 246,
248, 249, 250, 251, 254
Miller, Melva 17, 19, 22
Miller, Michael Dean 49, 213
Miller, Omer 16, 17
Miller, Rhonda 11, 59, 62, 72,
155, 254
Miller, Roger: "The Roger Miller
Show" 128-130, 132-134, 135;
Band members: first bands 25,
26, 32-34; professionals 88,
168-169, 176-177, 178-179,
182, 202-203; Cancer: 240,
242-243, 244-245, 247, 248,
249-251; Cocaine 163-164,
168, 176, 177, 227; Death of
251; Drugs 201; England 98-
99, 112-114, 159; Erick, Oklahoma: growing up 17, 18-23,
25-32; 153, 168-169, 185-186,
252; Erick High School 21-22,
27; Family background, 17-18;
Faron Young, 54-56; Induction
into Country Music Hall of
Fame, 9-11; Korea, 35; Management: Don Williams 88-89,
96; Stan Moress 194-196, 198,
248-249; and booking agent
Hal Smith 5960; and book
agent Tony Conway 195-196,
199, 200, 247-248, Musicianship 182-183; "On The Ralph

Emery Show" 119-120, 152-
155; 227-229; interviewed by
Ralph Emery 152-155, 227-
229; On "The Tonight Show"
66-67, 67-68, 69, 160, 170,
220, 229; Performing: 33, in
Las Vegas 86, 105-106, 132,
202, 177-189, 203-204, 206, in
Reno 137-138, reviews 71-72,
191, review 206; 214, 239-
240; at Smithsonian Institute
193, for President Gerald Ford
170-171, 199-200, 203-204,
and touring 247-248, 230-231,
appearances 53, One man show
230-231, in Big River in Nashville 232; last performance
246; end of performing career
247; Pills 65-66, 108, 133, 141,
150-151, 201; Recorded: for
Starday 54, Sound-a-Likes 54,
for Decca 51, 52, for RCA 57,
58-59, 61, 66, 67, 69, 72-73,
78, for Smash 72-73, 79-82,
91-92, 94, 102, for Columbia
158-159, live album 193; Off
the Way album 192-192, Old
Friends album 193-194, Big
River soundtrack 223-224, for
MCA Records 226; Record-
ings: first songs 42, Hoffman
Candy Bars commercial 83-84,
"You Don't Want My Love"
57, "Dang Me" 86-88, "King
of the Road" 91, "Husbands

www.ingramcontent.com/pod-product-compliance
Lightning Source LLC
Chambersburg PA
CBHW060747100426
42813CB00032B/3424/J